Instructor's Manual
to accompany

SIXTH EDITION

Dos mundos

Comunicación y comunidad

Tracy D. Terrell
Late, University of California, San Diego

Magdalena Andrade
Irvine Valley College

Jeanne Egasse
Irvine Valley College

Elías Miguel Muñoz

Boston   Burr Ridge, IL   Dubuque, IA   New York
San Francisco   St. Louis   Bangkok   Bogotá   Caracas   Kuala Lumpur
Lisbon   London   Madrid   Mexico City   Milan   Montreal   New Delhi
Santiago   Seoul   Singapore   Sydney   Taipei   Toronto

The McGraw-Hill Companies

 **Higher Education**

This is an $\boxed{EBI}$ book.

1 2 3 4 5 6 7 8 9 0 BKM BKM 9 8 7 6 5

ISBN 0-07-303092-9

Editor-in-chief: *Emily G. Barrosse*
Publisher: *William R. Glass*
Director of development: *Scott Tinetti*
Development editor: *Max Ehrsam*
Project manager: *Stacy Shearer*
Production supervisor: *Louis Swaim*
Composition: *11/12.5 TimesNewRomanPS by Eisner/Martin Typographics*
Printing: *BookMart Press*

www.mhhe.com

CONTENTS

HOW TO TEACH WITH *DOS MUNDOS:* AN INTRODUCTORY GUIDED TOUR

Dos mundos is designed for a course in which students, by listening to and interacting with their instructor and classmates, develop the ability to understand spoken and written language and communicate their thoughts and ideas in Spanish. It is based on a philosophy of communicative foreign language teaching known as the Natural Approach (NA). In addition to acquiring Spanish, we feel it is important for students to understand the acquisition process itself and enjoy it. We hope to lay a good foundation for continued acquisition so that students will want to continue with Spanish or repeat the process with another language later in their lives.

Later in this *Instructor's Manual,* we will review some current theories in Second Language Acquisition, outline some principles of communicative language teaching, suggest instructional goals for the various language skills, and describe how to use the activities provided in ***Dos mundos.*** In this first section, we hope to provide a clear introduction to both communicative teaching techniques and ***Dos mundos*** through a narrative description of the pages found in the early chapters of the book. This introductory walk-through includes a reproduction of the student pages of **Pasos A, B,** and **C** and **Capítulo 1,** together with an annotated discussion of Natural Approach communicative teaching techniques.

It is important that the instructor understand the principles that underline the initial stages of language acquisition, since these stages are the basis of the discussion in the annotations that follow. We believe that, in order to acquire a language, the learner must have ample opportunity to comprehend that language, and that production (speech and writing) will emerge naturally from these comprehension experiences. In other words, comprehension must precede production. ***Dos mundos*** allows for three stages of language development.

- Comprehension
- Early speech
- Speech emergence

The activities in **Paso A** give students the chance to develop initial comprehension skills without being required to speak Spanish. The activities in **Pasos B** and **C** continue to emphasize comprehension but also allow students to respond naturally in single words or short phrases. By the end of **Paso C,** many students are making the transition from short answers to longer utterances. The activities and readings in **Capítulo 1** continue to provide interesting comprehension experiences and introduce reading as an additional source of input. Students will pass through the same three stages of language development with the new material of each chapter. Among other things, the annotations in this introductory section discuss this process through the **Pasos** and **Capítulo 1.**

We find that students in classes where communicative techniques are used understand and communicate significantly more than students in most traditional classes. In addition, they enjoy the experience of acquiring a new language. We hope this introductory walk-through of ***Dos mundos*** will help you understand why.

Comprehension Phase

We believe that to acquire a language, the learner must have ample opportunity to comprehend that language, and that production (speech and writing) will emerge naturally from these comprehension experiences. In other words, comprehension must precede production. **Paso A** is designed so that students can hear and begin to understand basic vocabulary in Spanish.

In this first comprehension stage (Stage 1), language learners concentrate on meaning and on understanding the new language they are hearing. **Paso A** contains a variety of Stage 1 activities that do not require students to produce speech, but rather provide them with opportunities to absorb and acquire the meaning of words in context. We have learned from experience that learners comprehend much more quickly when they need only show that they understand what is being said and are free of the pressure engendered by forced production and error correction. The Stage 1 activities are nonthreatening and help students remain open to acquisition.

Pasos

Pasos A, B, and **C** are short introductory chapters designed to acquaint students with a wide range of useful vocabulary and to introduce basic grammatical concepts.

Chapter Opener Page

Each eye-catching chapter includes a colorful photo of art from a Spanish-speaking country and a brief synopsis of the artist or art form. You may wish to take a few minutes to read the caption and discuss the art, artist, and country of origin with the students. To the left of the art are the **Metas** (*Goals*), a brief introduction to the chapter

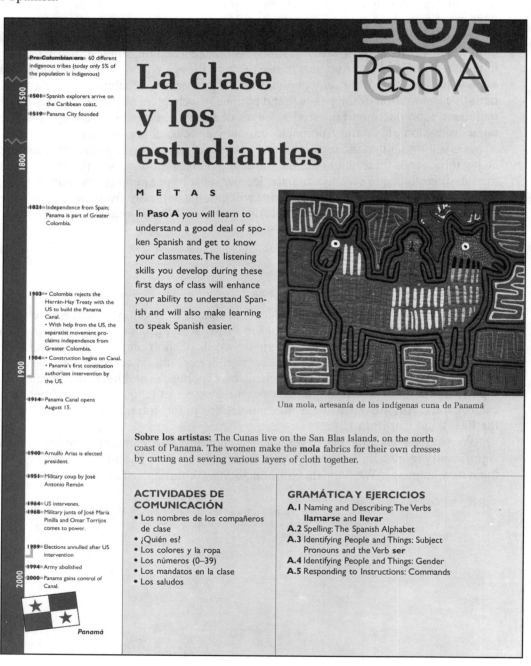

La clase y los estudiantes

Paso A

M E T A S

In **Paso A** you will learn to understand a good deal of spoken Spanish and get to know your classmates. The listening skills you develop during these first days of class will enhance your ability to understand Spanish and will also make learning to speak Spanish easier.

Una mola, artesanía de los indígenas cuna de Panamá

Sobre los artistas: The Cunas live on the San Blas Islands, on the north coast of Panama. The women make the **mola** fabrics for their own dresses by cutting and sewing various layers of cloth together.

Pre-Columbian era 60 different indigenous tribes (today only 5% of the population is indigenous)

1500

1501 Spanish explorers arrive on the Caribbean coast.
1519 Panama City founded

1800

1821 Independence from Spain; Panama is part of Greater Colombia.

1903 • Colombia rejects the Herrán-Hay Treaty with the US to build the Panama Canal.
• With help from the US, the separatist movement proclaims independence from Greater Colombia.
1904 • Construction begins on Canal.
• Panama's first constitution authorizes intervention by the US.

1900

1914 Panama Canal opens August 15.

1940 Arnulfo Arias is elected president.

1951 Military coup by José Antonio Remón

1964 US intervenes.
1968 Military junta of José María Pinilla and Omar Torrijos comes to power.

1989 Elections annulled after US intervention

1994 Army abolished
2000 Panama gains control of Canal.

2000

Panamá

ACTIVIDADES DE COMUNICACIÓN

• Los nombres de los compañeros de clase
• ¿Quién es?
• Los colores y la ropa
• Los números (0–39)
• Los mandatos en la clase
• Los saludos

GRAMÁTICA Y EJERCICIOS

A.1 Naming and Describing: The Verbs **llamarse** and **llevar**
A.2 Spelling: The Spanish Alphabet
A.3 Identifying People and Things: Subject Pronouns and the Verb **ser**
A.4 Identifying People and Things: Gender
A.5 Responding to Instructions: Commands

to familiarize students with the communicative goals of that chapter. Each chapter opener page also includes a timeline of the same country featured in the art. Timelines in **Pasos A, B,** and **C** are in English. Starting in **Cápitulo 1** timelines are in Spanish. A list of the **Actividades de Comunicacíon** and **Gramática** familiarize students with the communicative themes and corresponding grammar points of the chapter.

Pre-Text Oral Activities

Our approach to acquiring Spanish is easy to understand. Students first begin to comprehend new language through oral input ("teacher-talk") that is accompanied by visual aids (photos and realia) and gestures. Their only task is to show that they understand what they hear. Before students open their books, the instructor should use the Pre-Text Oral Activities to begin the acquisition process. These activities ask students to verify their comprehension by saying someone's name, by following commands that require physical movements, or by answering **sí/no** to questions.

Through these activities, students discover that they can understand when the instructor speaks Spanish. They begin to establish a basic vocabulary, and they start to develop listening skills essential to language acquisition. Many instructors find that they do not need to use the book at all in class for the first few days.

Student-Centered Input with Association Activities

A very useful activity for introducing vocabulary items is the Input Association Activity, in which words are associated with members of the class. The *Instructor's Edition* notes provide ideas for various association activities. An input association activity is a great way to help yourself and your students learn and remember everyone's name

by associating a classmate's name with an item of clothing or hair color. **Buenos días, mi nombre es Adela Martínez. ¿Cuál es su nombre? (Rachel.) Mucho gusto, Rachel. Clase, Rachel lleva lentes** (mime and/or point) **y tiene pelo largo y castaño.** Continue in this fashion with other students, and when three or four have been "introduced" ask the whole class: **¿Cómo se llama la estudiante de pelo largo y castaño que lleva lentes? (Rachel.) Sí, se llama Rachel.**

Using a Picture File (PF)

Another Pre-Text Oral Activity that greatly enhances the acquisition process is the use of visuals, particularly ads and photographs from magazines. These feel very "real" and provide an excellent variety of contexts for oral input activities. In **Paso A,** we recommend that the instructor use photographs to teach words for naming and describing people (e.g., **muchacho, hombre, niño, amigo, pelo, castaño, alto, bonita, guapo,** names of clothing, and colors). In addition, pictures of well-known people make it easy to introduce **¿Quién es? Es _____. Él/Ella se llama _____. ¿Qué lleva él/ella?** and **¿Cómo es él/ella?** in input such as **Aquí tenemos la foto de un hombre. Es actor. Es bastante famoso. ¿Quién es? / ¿Cómo se llama? (Will Smith.) Sí, se llama Will Smith.**

Input and the Vocabulary Display

After doing TPR and the other Pre-Text Oral Activities for a day or two before opening their books, students will need only to transfer what they are able to understand to the printed words when they look at the vocabulary display for the first time. As there is no new vocabulary to learn, the instructor can use the displays and activities as vehicles for additional input.

ACTIVIDAD 2   Diálogos: ¿Cómo se escribe?

RECEPCIONISTA: Su nombre y apellido, por favor.
SEÑOR: Me llamo Juan Cruise.

RECEPCIONISTA: ¿Cómo se escribe su apellido? ¿Ce-ere-u-zeta? (Cruz)
SEÑOR: No, mi apellido se escribe ce-ere-u-i-ese-e. (Cruise)

Ahora usted.

RECEPCIONISTA: Su nombre y apellido, por favor.
SEÑOR (SEÑORA): Me llamo _____. (Mi nombre es _____.)

RECEPCIONISTA: ¿Cómo se escribe su apellido?
SEÑOR (SEÑORA): Mi apellido se escribe __ - __ - __ - __ - __ - __ - __...

✳ ¿Quién es?

Lea Gramática A.3.

Pedro Ruiz · don Eduardo Alvar · doña Rosita Silva · Graciela Herrero · Rafael Quesada · Paula Saucedo Muñoz

ACTIVIDAD 3   Asociaciones: Las descripciones de las personas famosas

¿Quién es _____?

1. rubio/a ~ moreno/a
2. alto/a ~ bajo/a
3. guapo/bonita ~ feo/a
4. joven ~ viejo/a
5. delgado/a (flaco/a) ~ gordo/a

Salma Hayek   Antonio Banderas   Brad Pitt   Jack Nicholson
Sammy Sosa   Matt Damon   Barbra Streisand   Danny DeVito
Liza Minelli   Oprah Winfrey   Angelina Jolie   Tiger Woods

Grammar References

Grammar study is separated from the acquisition activities in ***Dos mundos,*** and all components of the grammar are designated as homework. Depending on the instructor's emphasis, students may be asked to read grammar and complete the exercises as a means of complementing language activities introduced and used in the classroom. The instructor may choose to assign grammar before, during, or after a particular section. Each section of communication activities contains references (**Lea Gramática...**) to the explanations and exercises that correspond to that particular section.

Asociaciones (Matching Activities)

This is the first "matching" activity. These **Asociación** activities are designed to be done with the whole class, with ample teacher input. Give students a minute or two to match the items, and then review with the entire class.

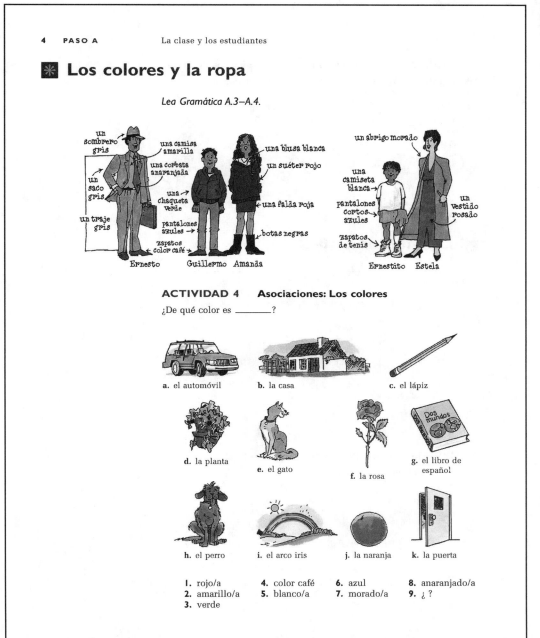

✳ Los colores y la ropa

Lea Gramática A.3–A.4.

ACTIVIDAD 4   Asociaciones: Los colores

¿De qué color es _____?

a. el automóvil   b. la casa   c. el lápiz

d. la planta   e. el gato   f. la rosa   g. el libro de español

h. el perro   i. el arco iris   j. la naranja   k. la puerta

1. rojo/a	4. color café	6. azul	8. anaranjado/a
2. amarillo/a	5. blanco/a	7. morado/a	9. ¿ ?
3. verde			

Identificaciones (Identification Activities)

This type of activity encourages students to match descriptions with an item or fill in blanks with simple information already acquired in class. Use this activity to reinforce the Pre-Text Oral Activities of clothing and colors.

Teaching Numbers

We suggest that the instructor provide input with numbers by counting students in class. At first, have students listen. Then they may respond with **sí/no** as you give them statements with counts of different groups in the classroom: **¿Hay dos hombres de bigote en nuestra clase? ¿Hay cuatro mujeres rubias?** As students grow accustomed to hearing numbers, they will gradually join in as the instructor counts **las mujeres, los hombres, las mujeres de pelo rubio, los hombres de barba, los estudiantes que llevan pantalones vaqueros,** and so on.

ACTIVIDAD 5   Identificaciones: Mis compañeros de clase

Mire a cuatro compañeros de clase. Diga el nombre de cada estudiante, la ropa y el color de la ropa que lleva.

	NOMBRE		ROPA	COLOR
1.	*Carmen*	lleva	*una blusa*	*amarilla.*
2.	_____	lleva	_____	_____
3.	_____	lleva	_____	_____
4.	_____	lleva	_____	_____
5.	_____	lleva	_____	_____

✳ Los números (0–39)

0 cero	10 diez	20 veinte
1 uno	11 once	21 veintiuno
2 dos	12 doce	22 veintidós
3 tres	13 trece	23 veintitrés
4 cuatro	14 catorce	24 veinticuatro...
5 cinco	15 quince	30 treinta
6 seis	16 dieciséis	31 treinta y uno
7 siete	17 diecisiete	32 treinta y dos
8 ocho	18 dieciocho	33 treinta y tres...
9 nueve	19 diecinueve	39 treinta y nueve

ACTIVIDAD 6   Identificaciones: ¿Cuántos hay?

Cuente los estudiantes en la clase que...

LLEVAN		TIENEN	
_____	pantalones	_____	barba
_____	lentes	_____	bigote
_____	reloj	_____	el pelo largo
_____	blusa	_____	el pelo castaño
_____	falda	_____	el pelo rubio
_____	botas	_____	los ojos azules
_____	aretes	_____	los ojos castaños

Early TPR (Total Physical Response)

We suggest that the instructor begin teaching classroom commands using the TPR Pre-Text Oral Activity outlined in the *Instructor's Edition* on page 21. Through the commands, students come to understand the imperative forms of a large number of verbs of all types. The focus is on the meaning of the verbs, so there is no need to make grammatical distinctions as to infinitive types or imperative forms. TPR also allows the instructor to introduce the many instructions necessary for class routine: **Abran los libros a la página 2, Cierren los libros, Saquen un bolígrafo,** and so on. The *Instructor's Manual* and the *Instructor's Edition* notes outline how to begin and develop TPR activities. Each activity should be repeated over a period of several days, gradually expanding the vocabulary it includes. (See the *Instructor's Resource Kit* for these TPR sequences in easy-to-read print suitable for carrying with you around the room or for putting on your desk while doing a TPR activity.)

Teaching Commands

Formal instruction in command forms is in **Capítulo 11,** but through TPR students can come to comprehend a variety of common commands and class-room instructions.

6 PASO A   La clase y los estudiantes

✳ Los mandatos en la clase

Lea Gramática A. 5.

saque un bolígrafo · cuente uno, dos, tres, ... · escuche · la profesora Martínez · escriba · póngase de pie · siéntese · lea · muéstreme el texto

Ian   Pablo   Nora   Esteban   Alberto   Carmen   Luis   Mónica

ACTIVIDAD 7   Identificaciones: Los mandatos

a. Dé una vuelta.
b. Abra el libro.
c. Cierre el libro.
d. Camine.
e. Saque un bolígrafo.
f. Salte.
g. Corra.
h. Mire hacia arriba.
i. Muéstreme el reloj.

¡Ojo! (Pay Attention!)

This feature in the **Actividades de comunicación** helps students to understand similarities and differences between Hispanic and Anglo cultures. You may want to read these aloud as your students read along silently. Cognates and your use of gestures and examples will help students to understand these brief segments.

Diálogos (Dialogues)

There are two types of dialogues in *Dos mundos,* model and open dialogues. The model dialogues in **Paso A** are very short and are intended to be models for conversation. They are not intended to be memorized. We suggest that the instructor read the dialogues aloud once or twice, with as natural an intonation as possible, while the class follows along in the book. Students should be allowed to identify any words or phrases they do not understand so that the instructor can explain them. After the meaning is clear, the instructor should put students in pairs for practice. (The "read, look up, and say" technique may be helpful here: Students read a line silently to themselves, then look at their partner and say the line as meaningfully as possible without looking at the text.) Instruct students to exchange roles, so that each one plays each role. At this stage of language acquisition, the main function of a

dialogue is to let students feel like real participants with Spanish. Naturally, we do not expect students to produce utterances of this length spontaneously.

Open dialogues require students to complete short conversations with information of their own selection. Open dialogues will begin in **Paso B,** as students make the transition to early speech (Stage 2).

✳ Los saludos

> ¡OJO!
>
> En el mundo hispano los saludos son muy importantes. También es importante preguntar por la familia.

ACTIVIDAD 8   **Diálogos: Los saludos**

1. Nacho Padilla saluda a Ernesto Saucedo.
NACHO: Buenos días. ¿Cómo está usted?
SR. SAUCEDO: Muy bien, gracias. ¿Y usted?
NACHO: Muy bien.

2. La señora Silva habla por teléfono con el señor Alvar.
SRA. SILVA: Señor Alvar, ¿cómo está usted?
SR. ALVAR: Estoy un poco cansado. ¿Y usted?
SRA. SILVA: Regular.

3. Amanda habla con doña Lola Batini.
DOÑA LOLA: Buenas tardes, Amanda.
AMANDA: Buenas tardes, doña Lola.
¿Cómo está la familia?
DOÑA LOLA: Bien, gracias.

4. Rogelio Varela presenta a Carla.
ROGELIO: Marta, ésta es mi amiga Carla.
CARLA: Mucho gusto.
MARTA: Igualmente.

5. Un nuevo amigo / Una nueva amiga en la clase de español.
USTED: _____, éste/ésta es mi amigo/a _____.
AMIGO/A 1: _____.
AMIGO/A 2: _____.

Estudiantes en la Universidad Nacional de San Marcos en Lima, Perú

Photographs

Dos mundos has many captioned color photos that illustrate aspects of the geography, culture, and daily life of the Hispanic world. These captioned photos may be used to provide additional comprehensive input. You may want to take a few minutes to read and discuss the captions for each photograph.

Vocabulario (Vocabulary)

The **Vocabulario** section contains the most important new words from the **Actividades de comunicación** of each chapter. Communicative language classes foster the acquisition of language by exposing students to a wide and "real" vocabulary that recurs often in many different contexts. This results in a larger and more varied vocabulary than that presented in textbooks based on a mastery approach. Insofar as possible, all new vocabulary items are grouped by topic in the **Vocabulario** to facilitate acquisition through association with themes and ideas.

While we hope that many of these lexical items will eventually become part of students' productive vocabulary, we do not expect students to memorize them, nor produce all of them while still working through the chapter. A realistic goal is for students to recognize most of the vocabulary in context.

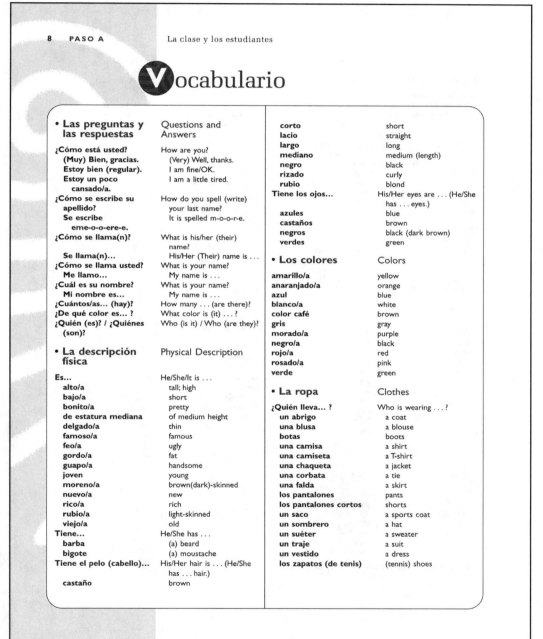

8   PASO A   La clase y los estudiantes

Vocabulario

• **Las preguntas y las respuestas**	Questions and Answers
¿Cómo está usted?	How are you?
(Muy) Bien, gracias.	(Very) Well, thanks.
Estoy bien (regular).	I am fine/OK.
Estoy un poco cansado/a.	I am a little tired.
¿Cómo se escribe su apellido?	How do you spell (write) your last name?
Se escribe eme-o-o-ere-e.	It is spelled m-o-o-r-e.
¿Cómo se llama(n)?	What is his/her (their) name?
Se llama(n)...	His/Her (Their) name is ...
¿Cómo se llama usted?	What is your name?
Me llamo...	My name is ...
¿Cuál es su nombre?	What is your name?
Mi nombre es...	My name is ...
¿Cuántos/as... (hay)?	How many ... (are there)?
¿De qué color es... ?	What color is (it) ...?
¿Quién (es)? / ¿Quiénes (son)?	Who (is it) / Who (are they)?

• **La descripción física**	Physical Description
Es...	He/She/It is ...
alto/a	tall; high
bajo/a	short
bonito/a	pretty
de estatura mediana	of medium height
delgado/a	thin
famoso/a	famous
feo/a	ugly
gordo/a	fat
guapo/a	handsome
joven	young
moreno/a	brown(dark)-skinned
nuevo/a	new
rico/a	rich
rubio/a	light-skinned
viejo/a	old
Tiene...	He/She has ...
barba	(a) beard
bigote	(a) moustache
Tiene el pelo (cabello)...	His/Her hair is ... (He/She has ... hair.)
castaño	brown

corto	short
lacio	straight
largo	long
mediano	medium (length)
negro	black
rizado	curly
rubio	blond
Tiene los ojos...	His/Her eyes are ... (He/She has ... eyes.)
azules	blue
castaños	brown
negros	black (dark brown)
verdes	green

• **Los colores**	Colors
amarillo/a	yellow
anaranjado/a	orange
azul	blue
blanco/a	white
color café	brown
gris	gray
morado/a	purple
negro/a	black
rojo/a	red
rosado/a	pink
verde	green

• **La ropa**	Clothes
¿Quién lleva... ?	Who is wearing ...?
un abrigo	a coat
una blusa	a blouse
botas	boots
una camisa	a shirt
una camiseta	a T-shirt
una chaqueta	a jacket
una corbata	a tie
una falda	a skirt
los pantalones	pants
los pantalones cortos	shorts
un saco	a sports coat
un sombrero	a hat
un suéter	a sweater
un traje	a suit
un vestido	a dress
los zapatos (de tenis)	(tennis) shoes

Usually students begin to use words in speech long after they are introduced in a particular chapter. In fact, words that are only recognized in a particular chapter frequently are produced spontaneously during an activity in a subsequent or much later chapter, when the vocabulary finally has been acquired. Some students may find it helpful to skim through the **Vocabulario** section before coming to class. Remember that fluent use of lexical items takes many hours of comprehensible input.

Teaching Vocabulary

An important goal of *Dos mundos* is to help students acquire enough vocabulary to become proficient listeners, readers, and speakers who can function in a wide variety of contexts. We believe that students are capable of acquiring a very large vocabulary if they are given frequent opportunities to hear and see the words in meaningful contexts. This is particularly true for students of

Vocabulario   9

• Las personas	People
el amigo / la amiga	friend
el compañero / la compañera de clase	classmate
don	*title of respect used with a man's first name*
doña	*title of respect used with a woman's first name*
el / la estudiante	student
la familia	family
el hombre	man
el muchacho / la muchacha	boy, young man / girl, young woman
la mujer	woman
el niño / la niña	boy / girl
el profesor / la profesora	professor
el/la recepcionista	receptionist
el señor / la señora	man; Mr. / woman; Mrs.
la señorita	young lady; Miss
yo, usted, él/ella	I, you (*pol.*), he/she
nosotros/as, ustedes, ellos/ellas	we, you (*pl.*), they

• Los verbos	Verbs
es	is
habla (por teléfono)	speaks (on the telephone)
hay	there is / there are
llevo	I am wearing
lleva(n)	is (are) wearing
presenta	introduces
saluda	greets
somos	we are
son	are
soy	I am
tiene	he/she has / you have
tienen	they have

• Las cosas	Things
el arco iris	rainbow
la casa	house
el gato	cat
el lápiz	pencil
los lentes	glasses
el libro (de español)	(Spanish) book
la naranja	orange
el perro	dog
la puerta	door
el reloj	watch, clock

PALABRAS SEMEJANTES (*Cognates*): el automóvil, la planta, la rosa, la foto(grafía)

• Los saludos y las despedidas	Greetings and Good-byes
Buenos días.	Good morning.
Buenas tardes.	Good afternoon.
Buenas noches.	Good evening. / Good night.
Hasta luego.	See you later.
Hola.	Hi.
Adiós.	Good-bye.

• Las presentaciones	Introductions
Ésta es mi amiga... / Éste es mi amigo...	This is my friend . . .
Mucho gusto.	Pleased to meet you.
Igualmente.	Same here.

• Los mandatos	Commands
abra(n) (el libro)	open (the book)
baile(n)	dance
camine(n)	walk
cante(n)	sing
cierre(n)	close
corra(n)	run
cuente(n)	count
dé/den una vuelta	turn around
diga(n)	say
escriba(n)	write
escuche(n)	listen
estudie(n)	study
hable(n)	talk
lea(n)	read
levánte(n)se	stand (get) up
mire(n) (hacia arriba/abajo)	look (up/down)
muéstre(n)me	show me
pónga(n)se de pie	stand up
salte(n)	jump
saque(n) (un bolígrafo)	take out (a pen)
siénte(n)se	sit down

• Palabras del texto	Words from the Text
¿Comprende(n)?	Do you (all) understand?
el español	Spanish
la gramática	grammar
no	no, not
¡Ojo!	Attention!
la página	page
el paso	step
por favor	please

Spanish, due to the rich vocabulary of cognate words that exist between English and Spanish.

Our approach to vocabulary derives from our belief that speech emerges in stages. We expect students to show they understand words used frequently in communicative situations, but we do not believe they should be required to memorize and correctly produce lists of words, nor be responsible for words as soon as they are presented in the book. These end-of-chapter lists are intended as reference only. After more communicative experiences with Spanish, students will have acquired more language and will be able to produce and write more words.

¿Qué?	What?
¿Quién(es)?	Who?
sí	yes

PALABRAS SEMEJANTES: la actividad, las asociaciones, la comunicación, la descripción, el diálogo, la identificación

• Los números	Numbers
cero	0
uno	1
dos	2
tres	3
cuatro	4
cinco	5
seis	6
siete	7
ocho	8
nueve	9
diez	10
once	11
doce	12
trece	13
catorce	14
quince	15
dieciséis	16
diecisiete	17
dieciocho	18
diecinueve	19
veinte	20

veintiuno	21
veintidós	22
veintitrés	23
veinticuatro	24
veinticinco	25
veintiséis	26
veintisiete	27
veintiocho	28
veintinueve	29
treinta	30
treinta y uno	31
treinta y dos	32
treinta y nueve	39

• Palabras útiles	Useful Words
ahora	now
cada	each, every
con	with
de	of, from
el, la, los, las	the
en	in, on
este/esta	this
grande	big
mi(s)	my
pequeño/a	small
su(s)	your
un (una)	a
¿Verdad?	(Is that) true? Really?
y	and

Gramática y ejercicios

The organization of **Dos mundos** derives from our belief that a large vocabulary is necessary for both listening and speaking, but that grammar is useful primarily for editing written work. Students begin Stage 3 (speech emergence) activities with a very reduced and simplified speech, but during the course, their speech gradually improves and becomes more "grammatical." We believe that this improvement occurs because of their exposure to meaningful written and spoken Spanish and, consequently, their increased ability to understand that input. We have included a grammar reference section because many students report that the study of grammar is helpful in improving their writing and because some students enjoy the formal study of grammar they are acquiring through input.

Some Useful Grammatical Terms

This new section reacquaints students with the basic grammatical terms that most college students should know. Students will see these terms throughout the grammar explanations of **Dos mundos.**

Gramática y ejercicios

Introduction

The **Gramática y ejercicios** sections of this book are written for your use outside of class. They contain grammar explanations and exercises that are presented in nontechnical language, so it should not be necessary to go over all of them in class.

The **Lea Gramática...** notes that begin most new topics in the **Actividades de comunicación y lecturas** sections give the grammar point(s) you should read at that time. Study them carefully, then do the exercises in writing and check your answers in the back of the book. If you have little or no trouble with the exercises, you have probably understood the explanation. Remember: It is not necessary to memorize these grammar rules.

Keep in mind that successful completion of a grammar exercise means only that you have understood the explanation. It does not mean that you have *acquired* the rule. True acquisition comes not from study of grammar but from hearing and reading a great deal of meaningful Spanish. Learning the rules of grammar through study will allow you to use those rules when you have time to stop and think about correctness, as during careful writing.

If you have trouble with an exercise or do not understand the explanation, ask your instructor for assistance. In difficult cases, your instructor will go over the material in class to be sure everyone has understood but probably won't spend too much time on the explanations, in order to save class time for real communication experiences.

The grammar explanations in **Paso A** contain basic information about Spanish grammar.

Some Useful Grammatical Terms

You may recall from your study of grammar in your native language that sentences can be broken down into parts. All sentences have at least a subject (a noun or pronoun) and a verb.

Mónica   runs.
  | |
 noun, subject   *verb*

In addition, sentences may have objects (nouns and pronouns), modifiers (adjectives and adverbs), prepositions, conjunctions, and/or articles.

Mónica is tall.
       |
      adjective

Mónica runs quickly.
          |
        adverb

Functional Grammar Explanations

All grammar explanations are written as simply as possible and are in English for students to use during home study. The grammar points are presented in numerical order in each chapter for ease of reference and are listed at the beginning of each chapter along with the chapter themes.

Whenever possible, grammar is approached from a *functional* rather than a *formal* point of view. That is, the starting point is what the structure is used for in everyday natural use. Since the grammar points are supplementary in nature, exhaustive presentations are rarely given. For example, in **A.1** two verbs are presented: **llamarse** and **llevar.** The purpose of the explanation of **llamarse** is to focus attention on the association between ¿**Cómo se llama?** and **Me llamo / Se llama** _____. The section on **llevar** includes a very brief discussion of verb endings, but, at this point, we do not expect students to do more than recognize the forms of the verb **llevar** when used in context.

Margin Notes

Call your students' attention to the short boxed notes next to the grammar explanations. These marginal grammar notes are intended to give students a succinct version of the grammar point or to be available for review at a later date. Also, they often serve to reassure students that, given enough comprehensible exposure to Spanish, many of the grammar rules will be acquired later.

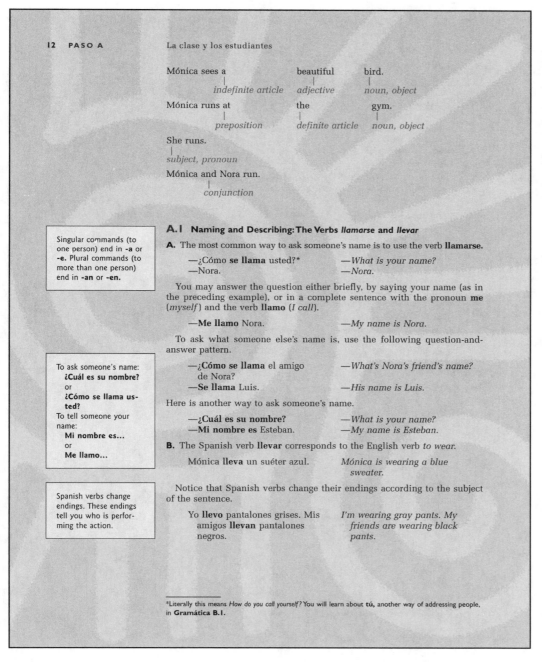

12   PASO A   La clase y los estudiantes

Mónica sees a   beautiful   bird.
        | | |
    indefinite article   *adjective*   *noun, object*

Mónica runs at   the   gym.
        | | |
     preposition   *definite article* *noun, object*

She runs.
   |
subject, pronoun

Mónica and Nora run.
            |
        conjunction

> **Singular commands (to one person) end in -a or -e. Plural commands (to more than one person) end in -an or -en.**

A.1   Naming and Describing: The Verbs *llamarse* and *llevar*

A. The most common way to ask someone's name is to use the verb **llamarse.**

—¿**Cómo se llama** usted?*   —*What is your name?*
—Nora.   —*Nora.*

You may answer the question either briefly, by saying your name (as in the preceding example), or in a complete sentence with the pronoun **me** (*myself*) and the verb **llamo** (*I call*).

—**Me llamo** Nora.   —*My name is Nora.*

To ask what someone else's name is, use the following question-and-answer pattern.

—¿**Cómo se llama** el amigo   —*What's Nora's friend's name?*
 de Nora?
—**Se llama** Luis.   —*His name is Luis.*

Here is another way to ask someone's name.

—¿**Cuál es su nombre?**   —*What is your name?*
—**Mi nombre es** Esteban.   —*My name is Esteban.*

> **To ask someone's name:**
> **¿Cuál es su nombre?**
> or
> **¿Cómo se llama usted?**
> **To tell someone your name:**
> **Mi nombre es...**
> or
> **Me llamo...**

B. The Spanish verb **llevar** corresponds to the English verb *to wear.*

Mónica **lleva** un suéter azul.   *Mónica is wearing a blue sweater.*

Notice that Spanish verbs change their endings according to the subject of the sentence.

> **Spanish verbs change endings. These endings tell you who is performing the action.**

Yo **llevo** pantalones grises. Mis   *I'm wearing gray pants. My*
 amigos **llevan** pantalones   *friends are wearing black*
 negros.   *pants.*

---

*Literally this means *How do you call yourself?* You will learn about **tú**, another way of addressing people, in **Gramática B.1.**

13

Spiraling of Grammar

Since the grammar points are a supplement to the acquisition activities of the **Actividades de comunicacíon,** grammar is spiraled. This means that a particular point is first presented in an initial section and then reintroduced and expanded in later sections as the need arises. Through spiraling, complex or difficult topics are treated in a number of smaller chunks that are introduced progressively throughout the course. In **A.1,** students learn about **-ar** verbs using two verbs that they have already heard in your input from the Pre-Text Oral Activities. A more in-depth introduction to **-ar** verbs follows in **Paso C.**

Here are some of the common endings for Spanish verbs.*

llevar (to wear)		
(yo)	llev**o**	I wear
(usted, él/ella)	llev**a**	you (sing.) wear; he/she wears
(nosotros/as)	llev**amos**	we wear
(ustedes, ellos/as)	llev**an**	you (pl.) wear; they wear

llevar = to wear

The subject pronouns (**yo, usted, nosotros, ellas,** etc.) are in parenthesis because it is not always necessary to use them. The verb itself or the context usually tells you who the subject is.

—¿Qué ropa llev**a** (usted) hoy? — What are you wearing today?
—Llev**o** una falda verde y una blusa blanca. — I am wearing a green skirt and a white blouse.
—¿Y ellos? — And what about them?
—Llev**an** traje y corbata. — They are wearing a suit and tie.

These endings are used on most Spanish verbs, and you will soon become accustomed to hearing and using them.

In **Paso C** you will see the forms of the verb **tener** (to have), which you have also heard in class.

La profesora Martínez **tiene** el pelo negro.   Professor Martínez has black hair.
Yo **tengo** los ojos azules.   I have blue eyes.

tengo = I have
tiene = he/she has

EJERCICIO I

Complete los diálogos con estos verbos: **me llamo, se llama, llevo, lleva, llevan.**

—¿Cómo _____¹ usted?
—_____² Esteban Brown.
—Esteban, ¿cómo _____³ la amiga de Mónica?
—_____⁴ Carmen.
—Y, ¿cómo se llama la profesora?
—¿La profesora de español? _____⁵ Adela Martínez.
—¿Qué ropa _____⁶ la profesora Martínez hoy?
—_____⁷ un vestido rojo muy bonito.
—Y Luis y Alberto, ¿qué ropa _____⁸ ellos?
—_____⁹ camiseta y pantalones vaqueros.
—Y yo _____¹⁰ pantalones vaqueros y un suéter.

---

*You will learn more about verb endings in **Gramática C.5, I.2,** and **3.2.**

A.2 presents the Spanish alphabet in the context of asking and giving information about names.

A.2 Spelling: The Spanish Alphabet

LETTER	NAME	EXAMPLE	LETTER	NAME	EXAMPLE
a	a	Ana	ñ	eñe	Íñigo
b	be, be grande	Bárbara	o	o	Olga
c	ce	Celia	p	pe	Pedro
d	de	David	q	cu	Quintín
e	e	Ernesto	r	ere	Mario
f	efe	Franco	s	ese	Sara
g	ge	Gerardo	t	te	Tomás
h	hache	Hortensia	u	u	Úrsula
i	i	Isabel	v	uve, ve chica	Vicente
j	jota	Juan	w	doble ve, uve doble	Walter
k	ca	Kati	x	equis	Ximena
l	ele	Laura	y	i griega	Yolanda
m	eme	Miguel	z	zeta	Zulema
n	ene	Nora			

Learn how to spell your first and last names in Spanish; that is what you will be expected to spell most frequently.

A. Letters are feminine: **la «ele», la «i», la «equis».** The letter combinations **ll** (often referred to as **elle** or **doble ele**) is pronounced like a *y*. The letter combinations **ch, ll,** and **rr** cannot be divided when splitting a word into syllables. Until recently, the letter combinations **ch** and **ll** were considered single units, had separate names (**che** and **elle** or **doble ele**), and affected alphabetization (for example, **chico** after **cumpleaños, llamar** after **luna**). You will still see this pattern of alphabetization in many dictionaries and textbooks. The grouping **rr** is not considered a separate letter by the **Real Academia.**

B. B and **v** are pronounced identically, so speakers use different devices to differentiate them; the most common is to call one **la be grande** and the other **la ve chica** (or **la be larga** and **la ve corta**). Many people say **la be de burro, la ve de vaca** (b as in **burro,** v as in **vaca**). The letters **k** and **w** are used mostly in words of foreign origin: **kilo, whisky.**

C. Spanish speakers do not normally spell out entire words but rather tend to refer only to the letters that might cause confusion. For example, if the name is **Rodríguez,** one might ask: **¿Se escribe con *zeta* o con *ese*?** (*Is it written with a z or with an s?*) Common spelling questions asked by most Latin Americans are the following.

s, z	¿Con **ese** o con **zeta**?	y, ll	¿Con **i griega** o con **doble ele**?
c, s	¿Con **ce** o con **ese**?	g, j	¿Con **ge** o con **jota**?
c, z	¿Con **ce** o con **zeta**?	v, b	¿Con **ve chica** o con **be grande**?

Spiraling

The grammar explanations of *Dos mundos*
supply only as much grammatical information as
students need at a particular point in the syllabus.
In **Gramática A.3** the forms of **ser** and personal
pronouns that students have already heard in the
instructor's input are presented for the first time.
The **tú** and **vosotros** forms will be presented in
B.1 when **ser** is reintroduced.

Because the letter **h** is never pronounced in Spanish, a common question
is: ¿**Con o sin hache**? (*With or without h?*)

Only with foreign words (or perhaps very unfamiliar Spanish words) do
Spanish speakers spell out the entire word.

—¿Cómo se escribe *Dorwick*, por favor?
—Se escribe: **de, o, ere, doble ve, i, ce, ca.**
—Gracias.

EJERCICIO 2

Escoja la respuesta correcta.

MODELO: ¿Cómo se escribe _____apato?
     ⓐ con zeta
     b. con ese

1. ¿Cómo se escribe tre_____e?
   a. con ce
   b. con zeta
2. ¿Cómo se escribe mu_____er?
   a. con ge
   b. con jota
3. ¿Cómo se escribe nue_____o?
   a. con ve chica
   b. con be grande
4. ¿Cómo se escribe a_____ul?
   a. con zeta
   b. con ese
5. ¿Cómo se escribe pá_____ina?
   a. con ge
   b. con jota
6. ¿Cómo se escribe _____abla?
   a. con hache
   b. sin hache
7. ¿Cómo se escribe amari_____o?
   a. con doble ele
   b. con i griega
8. ¿Cómo se escribe _____ombre?
   a. con hache
   b. sin hache
9. ¿Cómo se escribe cie_____e?
   a. con ere
   b. con erre
10. ¿Cómo se escribe lle_____an?
    a. con ve chica
    b. con be grande

A.3 Identifying People and Things: Subject Pronouns and the Verb *ser*

A. Spanish uses the verb **ser** (*to be*) to identify things or people.

—¿Qué **es** eso?	—*What is that?*
—**Es** un bolígrafo.	—*It's a pen.*
—¿Quién **es**?	—*Who is it?*
—**Es** Luis.	—*It's Luis.*

> **ser** = *to be* (identification)
> **Soy estudiante.** (*I am a student.*)

B. Personal pronouns are used to refer to a person without mentioning
the person's name. Here are some of the most common personal pronouns
that can serve as the subject of a sentence, with the corresponding
present-tense forms of **ser.** It is not necessary to memorize these
pronouns. You will see and hear them again and again.

ser (to be)			
(yo)	soy	I	am
(tú)	eres*	you (inf. sing.)	are
(usted)	es	you (pol. sing.)	are
(él†/ella)	es	he/she	is
(nosotros/nosotras)	somos	we	are
(vosotros/vosotras)‡	sois	you (inf. pl.)	are
(ustedes)	son	you (pol. pl.)	are
(ellos/ellas)	son	they	are

> Remember that most subject pronouns are optional in Spanish:
> **(Yo) Soy estudiante.** (*I'm a student.*)
> **(Nosotros) Somos amigos.** (*We're friends.*)

yo = *I*
tú = *you* (informal singular)
usted = *you* (polite singular)
él = *he*
ella = *she*

nosotros = *we* (masculine)
nosotras = *we* (feminine)
vosotros = *you* (masculine informal plural)
vosotras = *you* (feminine informal plural)
ustedes = *you* (plural)
ellos = *they* (masculine)
ellas = *they* (feminine)

—¿Usted es profesor?   —*Are you a professor?*
—Sí, soy profesor de historia.   —*Yes, I'm a history professor.*

C. Spanish does not have a subject pronoun for *it* or for *they*, referring to things. When subject pronouns *are* used in Spanish, they often express emphasis.

¿Mi automóvil? Es pequeño.   *My car? It's small.*
¿Las faldas? Son caras.   *The skirts? They're expensive.*
Yo soy de Atlanta.   *I am from Atlanta.*

D. Subject pronouns may be used by themselves without verbs, either for emphasis or to point someone out.

¿Quién, **yo**? Yo no soy de Texas;   *Who, me? I'm not from Texas;*
soy de Nueva York.   *I'm from New York.*

—¿Cómo está usted?   —*How are you?*
—Estoy bien. ¿Y **usted**?   —*I'm fine. And you?*

E. The pronouns **ellos** (*they*), **nosotros** (*we*), and **vosotros** (*you, inf. pl.*) can refer to groups of people that consist of males only or of males and females. On the other hand, **ellas** (*they, fem.*), **nosotras** (*we, fem.*), and **vosotras** (*you, inf. pl. fem.*) can refer only to two or more females.

—¿Y **ellos**? ¿Quiénes son?   —*And those guys (they)?*
                                   Who are they?

---

*Tú is an informal singular form of *you*, whereas **usted** is a polite singular form of *you*. See **Gramática B.I** for more information.
†The pronoun **él** (*he*) has an accent to distinguish it in writing from the definite article **el** (*the*).
‡The pronouns **vosotros/vosotras** are used only in Spain. Latin America uses **ustedes** for both polite and informal plural *you*.

Spiraling

The topic of grammatical gender and noun-adjetive agreement in **A.4** is another example of the spiraling technique used in *Dos mundos.* This section simply introduces the concept of grammatical gender and gender distinction in articles. A more detailed discussion of gender agreement, including placement of adjectives is in **B.5**.

—¿Esteban y Raúl? Son amigos.	—*Esteban and Raúl? They're friends.*
—¿Y **ellas**? ¿Son amigas?	—*What about them? Are they friends?*
—Sí, Nora y Carmen son compañeras de mi clase de español.	—*Yes, Nora and Carmen are classmates from my Spanish class.*
—¿Y Esteban y Alicia? ¿Son amigos?	—*And what about Esteban and Alicia?*
—Sí, son muy buenos amigos.	—*Yes, they are very good friends.*

EJERCICIO 3

Escoja el pronombre lógico.

MODELO: —Y *ella,* ¿lleva pantalones? →
       —¿Quién, Mónica? Lleva una falda azul.

1. —¿_____ es profesor aquí?
  —¿Quién, Raúl? No, es estudiante.
2. —¿_____ son mexicanos?
  —Sí, Silvia y Nacho son mexicanos.
3. —¡Viejos, _____! No, doña María Eulalia y yo somos muy jóvenes.
4. —Señor Ruiz, _____ tiene bigote, ¿verdad?
5. —¿Y _____? ¿Son estudiantes aquí?
  —No, Pilar y Clara son estudiantes en Madrid.

a. ellos
b. usted
c. ellas
d. él
e. nosotros

EJERCICIO 4

Complete los diálogos con la forma correcta del verbo **ser: soy, es, somos, son.**

—¿Cómo se llama usted?
—_____[1] Raúl Saucedo.

—¿Quién _____[2] ella?
—¿La chica de la blusa roja? Se llama Mónica. Ella y Carmen (ellas) _____[3] amigas.

—¿_____[4] estudiantes ustedes?
—¡No! El profesor López y yo (nosotros) _____[5] profesores de la universidad.

A.4 Identifying People and Things: Gender

A. Nouns (words that represent people or things) in Spanish are classified as either masculine or feminine. Masculine nouns often end in **-o** (**sombrero**); feminine nouns often end in **-a** (**falda**). In addition, words ending in **-ción, -sión,** or **-dad** are also feminine.

> Masculine nouns usually end in **-o.**
> Feminine nouns usually end in **-a.**

18

Margin Notes

Remind students to read the margin notes as a
way of reviewing the Grammar.

La clase y los estudiantes

> You will acquire these endings later. For now, don't worry about them as you speak. You can refer to your text if you have any doubts when you are editing your writing.

Madrid es una ciu**dad** bonit**a**.	*Madrid is a pretty city.*
La civiliza**ción** maya fue muy avanza**da**.	*The Mayan civilization was very advanced.*

But the terms *masculine* and *feminine* are grammatical classifications only; Spanish speakers do not perceive things such as notebooks or doors as being "male" or "female." On the other hand, words that refer to males are usually masculine (**amigo**), and words that refer to females are usually feminine (**amiga**).

Esteban es mi **amigo** y Carmen es una **amiga** de él.	*Esteban is my friend, and Carmen is a friend of his.*

> **El** and **la** both mean *the.* **El** is used with masculine nouns, and **la** is used with feminine nouns.

B. Because Spanish nouns have gender, adjectives (words that describe nouns) *agree* with nouns: They change their endings from **-o** to **-a** according to the gender of the nouns they modify. Notice the two words for *black* in the following examples.

Lan tiene el pelo **negro**.	*Lan has black hair.*
Luis lleva una chaqueta **negra**.	*Luis is wearing a black jacket.*

> **Un** and **una** both mean *a/an.* **Un** is used with masculine nouns, and **una** is used with feminine nouns.

C. Like English, Spanish has definite articles (*the*) and indefinite articles (*a, an*). Articles in Spanish also change form according to the gender of the nouns they accompany.

	DEFINITE (*the*)	INDEFINITE (*a, an*)
Masculine	**el** suéter	**un** sombrero
Feminine	**la** blusa	**una** chaqueta

Hoy Mónica lleva **un** vestido nuevo.	*Today Mónica is wearing a new dress.*
La chaqueta de Alberto es azul.	*Alberto's jacket is blue.*

> Spanish nouns are classified grammatically as either masculine or feminine. The articles change according to grammatical gender and agree with the nouns they modify.
> **un abrigo** = *a coat*
> **una blusa** = *a blouse*
> **una universidad** = *a university*
> **el libro** = *the book*
> **la casa** = *the house*

D. How can you determine the gender of a noun? The gender of the article and/or adjective that modifies the noun will tell you whether it is masculine or feminine. In addition, the following two simple rules will help you determine the gender of a noun most of the time.

Rule 1: A noun that refers to a male is masculine; a noun that refers to a female is feminine. Sometimes they are a pair distinguished by the endings **-o/-a**; other times they are completely different words.

un muchacho	una muchacha	*boy/girl*
un niño	una niña	*(male) child / (female) child*
un amigo	una amiga	*(male) friend / (female) friend*
un hombre	una mujer	*man/woman*

Acquisition of Grammar

Gender of nouns is acquired fairly late. These explanations introduce the concept of gender and the exercises are intended to verify student comprehension. At this point students will not be able to produce correct gender agreement with articles in either speech or writing.

For some nouns referring to people, the masculine form ends in a consonant and the feminine form adds **-a** to the masculine noun.*

un profesor	una profesora	(*male*) *professor* / (*female*) *professor*
un señor	una señora	*a man* (*Mr.*) / *a woman* (*Mrs.*)

Other nouns do not change at all; only the accompanying article changes.

un elefante	(*male*) *elephant*
una elefante	(*female*) *elephant*
un estudiante	(*male*) *student*
una estudiante	(*female*) *student*
un joven	*young man*
una joven	*young woman*
un recepcionista	(*male*) *receptionist*
una recepcionista	(*female*) *receptionist*

Rule 2: For most nouns that refer to things (rather than to people or animals), the gender is reflected in the last letter of the word. Nouns that end in **-o** are usually grammatically masculine (**un/el vestido**), and nouns that end in **-a** are usually grammatically feminine (**una/la puerta**).†
   Words that end in **-d** (**una/la universidad**) or in the letter combinations **-ción** or **-sión** (**una/la nación; una/la diversión**) are also usually feminine.

> Nouns that end in **-o** are usually masculine; nouns that end in **-a** are usually feminine.

MASCULINE: -o	FEMININE: -a
un/el bolígrafo	una/la descripción
un/el sombrero	una/la casa
un/el libro	una/la puerta
un/el vestido	una/la universidad

Words that refer to things may also end in **-e** or in consonants other than **-d** and **-ión.** Most of these words that you have heard so far are masculine, but some are feminine.

un/el borrador	*eraser*	una/la clase	*class*
un/el automóvil	*automobile*	una/la luz	*light*
un/el lápiz	*pencil*	una/la mujer	*woman*
un/el traje	*suit*		
un/el reloj	*clock*		

> Don't worry if you can't remember all these rules! Note where they are in this book so you can refer to them when you are editing your writing and when you are unsure of what gender a noun is.

---

*This rule includes a few common animals. Some pairs end in **-o/-a**; others end in consonant / consonant + **-a.**

un gato	una gata	(*male*) *cat* / (*female*) *cat*
un perro	una perra	(*male*) *dog* / (*female*) *dog*
un león	una leona	*lion/lioness*

†Three common exceptions are **la mano** (*hand*), **el día** (*day*), and **el mapa** (*map*).

Spiraling

Command forms are explained in detail in
Gramática 11.1. The commands in **A.5** are
intended to acquaint students with common
commands that they may hear in the classroom.

La clase y los estudiantes

| You will develop a *feel* for gender as you listen and read more in Spanish. |

EJERCICIO 5

Conteste según el modelo.

MODELO: ¿Es un bolígrafo? (lápiz) →
No, no es un bolígrafo. Es *un* lápiz.

1. ¿Es una chaqueta? (camisa)
2. ¿Es una mujer? (hombre)
3. ¿Es una falda? (vestido)
4. ¿Es un sombrero? (blusa)
5. ¿Es una naranja? (reloj)

EJERCICIO 6

Complete las oraciones con **el** o **la.**

1. _____ estudiante es rubia.
2. _____ profesor de matemáticas es guapo.
3. _____ clase es buena.
4. _____ reloj es negro.
5. _____ lápiz es amarillo.
6. _____ puerta es blanca.
7. _____ motocicleta es negra.
8. _____ automóvil es nuevo.
9. _____ casa es grande.
10. _____ sombrero es rojo.

A.5 Responding to Instructions: Commands*

| Singular commands (to one person) end in **-a** or **-e.** Plural commands (to more than one person) end in **-an** or **-en.** |

In English the same form of the verb is used for giving commands, whether to one person (singular) or to more than one person (plural).

Steve, please stand up.
Mr. and Mrs. Martínez, please stand up.

In Spanish, however, singular commands end in **-a** or **-e**, and plural commands add an **-n.**

Alberto, **saque** el libro por favor.	*Alberto, please take out your book.*
Alberto y Nora, **saquen** el libro, por favor.	*Alberto and Nora, please take out your books.*
Mónica, **abra** la puerta.	*Mónica, open the door.*
Mónica y Luis, **abran** la puerta.	*Mónica y Luis, open the door.*

*Your instructor will give you commands during the Total Physical Response activities. Other classroom instructions will also use command forms. You will learn more about how to give commands in **Gramática 11.1** and **14.3.**

EJERCICIO 7

Escriba la forma correcta del mandato con verbos de la lista.

abra(n)	corra(n)	escuche(n)	saque(n)
camine(n)	cuente(n)	estudie(n)	siénte(n)se
cante(n)	diga(n)	lea(n)	
cierre(n)	escriba(n)	salte(n)	

1. —Lan y Mónica, _____ «Buenas tardes».
2. —Alberto, _____ su nombre con lápiz.
3. —Nora y Luis, _____ de cero a quince por favor.
4. —Pablo y Esteban, _____ el libro.
5. —Carmen, _____ la Actividad 2 en la página 6.
6. —Nora, _____ un bolígrafo.
7. —Lan y Esteban, _____ el diálogo.
8. —Luis, _____ la puerta, por favor.

Early Speech

As students begin **Paso B,** they have learned to understand a basic amount of Spanish and often start to make the transition from comprehension only (Stage 1) to early speech (Stage 2). This usually takes the form of short answers and lists of words. The instructor continues to introduce new material using Stage 1 comprehension techniques that require only **sí/no** or names as responses. Material from **Paso A,** however (and from **Paso B** as students begin to comprehend it), is discussed in such a way that students spontaneously reply with words and short phrases. The instructor begins to elicit answers with either/or (choice) questions: **¿Es alto o bajo el hombre en esta foto? (Bajo.)** Note that students do not have to come up with the words but simply choose and say them. Another useful Stage 2 technique, the unfinished sentence, requires slightly more production and elicits a list of words: **En esta foto, hay una mujer que lleva sombrero, botas, ... (falda, blusa, abrigo, lentes),** and so on. This technique is useful after students have had an opportunity to acquire vocabulary. It is done with the whole group rather than putting any one individual on the spot.

Pre-Text Oral Activities

The Pre-Text Oral Activities that were introduced in **Paso A** are expanded or modified to include the vocabulary in **Paso B.** TPR activities now include names for parts of the body and classroom objects: **Pónganse de pie. Tóquense los pies. Levanten los brazos. Bájenlos. Muéstrenme el reloj. Saquen un bolígrafo.** See Pre-Text Oral Activities on p. 37 of the *Instructor's Edition.*

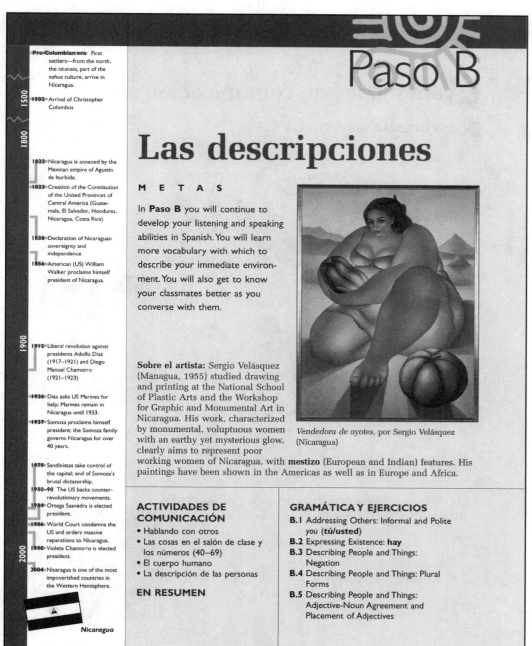

Pre-Columbian era First settlers—from the north, the *nicaraos,* part of the *nahua* culture, arrive in Nicaragua.

1502 Arrival of Christopher Columbus

1822 Nicaragua is annexed by the Mexican empire of Agustín de Iturbide.

1823 Creation of the Constitution of the United Provinces of Central America (Guatemala, El Salvador, Honduras, Nicaragua, Costa Rica)

1838 Declaration of Nicaraguan sovereignty and independence

1856 American (US) William Walker proclaims himself president of Nicaragua.

1912 Liberal revolution against presidents Adolfo Díaz (1917–1921) and Diego Manuel Chamorro (1921–1923)

1926 Díaz asks US Marines for help; Marines remain in Nicaragua until 1933.

1937 Somoza proclaims himself president; the Somoza family governs Nicaragua for over 40 years.

1979 Sandinistas take control of the capital; end of Somoza's brutal dictatorship.

1980–90 The US backs counter-revolutionary movements.

1984 Ortega Saavedra is elected president.

1986 World Court condemns the US and orders massive reparations to Nicaragua.

1990 Violeta Chamorro is elected president.

2004 Nicaragua is one of the most impoverished countries in the Western Hemisphere.

Nicaragua

Paso B

Las descripciones

M E T A S

In **Paso B** you will continue to develop your listening and speaking abilities in Spanish. You will learn more vocabulary with which to describe your immediate environment. You will also get to know your classmates better as you converse with them.

Sobre el artista: Sergio Velásquez (Managua, 1955) studied drawing and printing at the National School of Plastic Arts and the Workshop for Graphic and Monumental Art in Nicaragua. His work, characterized by monumental, voluptuous women with an earthy yet mysterious glow, clearly aims to represent poor working women of Nicaragua, with **mestizo** (European and Indian) features. His paintings have been shown in the Americas as well as in Europe and Africa.

Vendedora de ayotes, por Sergio Velásquez (Nicaragua)

ACTIVIDADES DE COMUNICACIÓN

• Hablando con otros
• Las cosas en el salón de clase y los números (40–69)
• El cuerpo humano
• La descripción de las personas

EN RESUMEN

GRAMÁTICA Y EJERCICIOS

B.1 Addressing Others: Informal and Polite *you* (**tú/usted**)
B.2 Expressing Existence: **hay**
B.3 Describing People and Things: Negation
B.4 Describing People and Things: Plural Forms
B.5 Describing People and Things: Adjective-Noun Agreement and Placement of Adjectives

Diálogos (Model Dialogues)

Model dialogues are short, realistic language situations that provide input composed of standard chunks of language (see **Actividad 2**). They give students an opportunity to practice using the language without having to produce it spontaneously. The instructor reads both parts and makes sure that students understand the new vocabulary before pairing them up to practice. We do not recommend asking students to memorize these dialogues or calling on them to read them aloud in class, since this generally raises the affective filter and is not a productive source of input. Some instructors ask if there are volunteers who would like to perform. The success of this technique, however, depends on both the composition of the class and the instructor's approach to classroom management.

Actividades de comunicación

❋ Hablando con otros

Lea Gramática B.1.

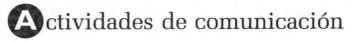

> **¡OJO!**
>
> El uso de *tú* varía mucho en los países hispanos. En Colombia, por ejemplo, los miembros de la familia se hablan de *usted*, mientras que en España y en muchas ciudades grandes del mundo hispano prefieren usar *tú*.

ACTIVIDAD 1   Identificaciones: ¿Tú o usted?

Usted habla con estas personas. ¿Usa **tú** o **usted**?

1. un amigo de la universidad	**5.** una señora de treinta y nueve años
2. el profesor de matemáticas	**6.** una recepcionista
3. una niña de diez años	**7.** su doctor
4. un amigo de su papá	**8.** su hermano/a

ACTIVIDAD 2   Diálogos: ¿Cómo está usted? ¿Cómo estás tú?

El señor Olivera saluda a su joven vecina Amanda.

DON ANSELMO: Hola, Amanda.
AMANDA: Buenos días, señor Olivera. ¿Cómo está usted?
DON ANSELMO: Muy bien, gracias. ¿Cómo está tu mamá?
AMANDA: Ella está bien, gracias.

Amanda saluda a su amiga Graciela.

AMANDA: ¿Qué tal, Graciela? ¿Cómo estás?
GRACIELA: Regular. ¿Y tú?
AMANDA: Un poco cansada.

Diálogos abiertos (Open Dialogues)

Open dialogues are short samples of basic functional languages that students complete with information of their own selection (see **Actividad 3**). The instructor should model the dialogue, pausing at the blank spaces for the whole class to fill in appropriate words. Some vocabulary useful for completing the dialogues may be included. It may be helpful to write on the board a list of additional appropriate words for each blank as a reference for students. Then pair students up. Remind them that each partner should have the opportunity to play both roles.

TPR: Beginning the Transition to Early Speech

By the end of **Paso B,** students should be able to understand a large vocabulary of commands. One good way of introducing a few salutations is to include a few commands such as **Saquen un lápiz, escriban su nombre,** and **escuchen a la profesora.** One can also include commands such as **Digan «Buenos días» («Buenas tardes/noches»), Digan «¿Cómo está?»** and then **Miren a un compañero o una compañera de clase y díganle «Buenos días» («Buenas tardes/noches»). Ahora pregúntenle, «¿Cómo está?» Y ahora díganle, «Muy bien, gracias.»**

Errors

As students begin to speak, we expect them to make errors. We believe that this is a normal part of the acquisition process when students are concentrating on the meaning of what they are saying and do not have time to monitor (edit) their speech. Errors will diminish with more exposure to input. In fact, encouraging students to monitor carefully what they say at this

---

24 PASO B   Las descripciones

ACTIVIDAD 3   Diálogos abiertos: Más saludos
▶ **PALABRAS ÚTILES**

el chico, el señor, la señora
la recepcionista, la estudiante, el profesor, la profesora
regular, muy bien, un poco cansado/a
rubio, lacio

LA NUEVA ESTUDIANTE

E1: Hola, *Mónica.* ¿Cómo estás?
E2: *Bien.* ¿Y tú?
E1: *Regular.*
E2: ¿Quién es *la chica* de pelo *negro rizado?*
E1: Es la nueva *estudiante.* Se llama _____.

EN LA OFICINA

E1: Buenos días, profesora Martínez. ¿Cómo está usted?
E2: Estoy *muy bien.* ¿Y usted?
E1: *Un poco cansado.* ¿Cómo está la familia?
E2: *Bien,* gracias. Profesora, ¿quién es *el señor* de *traje gris?*
E1: Es _____. Se llama _____.

✳ Las cosas en el salón de clase y los números (40–69)
Lea Gramática B.2–B.4.

---

point may even be counterproductive, impeding acquisition. For this reason we recommend a form of expanded response. If a student makes a mistake, rather than correcting overtly, the instructor restates or rephrases the reply correctly, maintaining the focus on the message: **¿Qué hay en el salón de clase? (Una mesa largo.) Sí, la mesa en este salón de clase es larga, y es muy vieja también. ¿Qué más hay en nuestro salón de clase?** In this way, no one is put in an embarrassing situation, and the entire class hears more input. The focus remains on the message, and students' concentration on what is being said is not interrupted.

Intercambios (Interactions)

Intercambios activities provide students with a chance to interact in a guided way

(see **Actividad 5** and **Actividad 6**). Students are given a model question and answer and some information (sketches, realia, charts) from which to ask and answer questions. We recommend that the Instructor model the **Intercambios** one or two times for the whole class before dividing students into pairs. As students attain Stage 3, they are encouraged to expand on the topics in Spanish as they are able.

ACTIVIDAD 4   Identificaciones: ¿Qué hay en el salón de clase?

MODELOS: En mi clase hay... → *un lápiz amarillo.*
En mi clase hay... → *una pizarra grande.*

1. una computadora	a. azul ~ color café
2. una ventana	b. moderno/a ~ antiguo/a
3. una pizarra	c. interesante ~ aburrido/a
4. un reloj	d. fácil ~ difícil
5. un bolígrafo	e. blanco/a ~ negro/a ~ gris
6. una mesa	f. largo/a
7. un libro	g. viejo/a ~ nuevo/a
8. una puerta	h. pequeño/a ~ grande
9. un mapa	i. ¿ ?
10. un cartel	

ACTIVIDAD 5   Intercambios: El salón de clase

MODELO: E1: ¿Cuántos/as _____ hay en el salón de clase?
E2: Hay _____.

1. estudiantes	5. ventanas
2. mesas	6. paredes
3. borradores	7. puertas
4. pizarras	8. luces

ACTIVIDAD 6   Intercambios: ¿Cuánto cuesta?

MODELO: E1: ¿Cuánto cuesta *la mochila*?
E2: Cuesta *$39.50 (treinta y nueve dólares y cincuenta centavos).*

40 cuarenta	50 cincuenta	60 sesenta
41 cuarenta y uno	52 cincuenta y dos	63 sesenta y tres
45 cuarenta y cinco	58 cincuenta y ocho	69 sesenta y nueve

$39.50 la mochila

el cuaderno $1.69
la calculadora $15.49
el diccionario
la silla
el reloj $40.55
la mesa $57.75
el cartel
la patineta $69.59

Descripción de dibujos (Description of Drawings)

These activities focus around a series of small drawings and may be either instructor- or student-centered. Give students time to look at the drawing before you bring your descriptions. Later activities of this sort often involve pair work.

Effective Instructor Input

Good instructor input allows for spontaneous and innovative student responses without being threatening. It is simplified speech, which is essential to learners, and should be interesting to students, varied and natural, never artificial or over-controlled. If the instructor reacts naturally to students' responses (for example, **¿Usted es reservado y trabajador, Pablo? ¡Pero usted habla mucho en esta clase! Clase, ¿es reservado Pablo?**), new situations arise that provide additional information for discussion, thus allowing re-entry of past vocabulary and structures many times without a plan for specific review. It is also essential that the principle of comprehensible input be kept in mind. This means that as the instructor talks with the class at a level students can understand, some new language that has not been introduced before is also included. Such input is just above students' current level of competence, but it contains enough of the previous key words and structures so that they can interpret new vocabulary and structures by using what they do understand and by using context (knowing what the topic is about, looking at visuals, playing attention to gestures, and so on).

Successful instructor input also contributes to a positive classroom environment. Each instructor is different, so there is no one way to ensure that the atmosphere remains interesting and nonthreatening. We find that students acquire

✳ El cuerpo humano

Lea Gramática B.5.

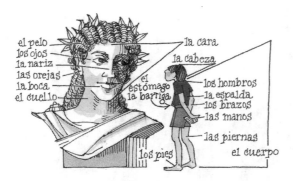

el pelo
los ojos
la nariz
las orejas
la boca
el cuello

el estómago
la barriga

la cara
la cabeza

los hombros
la espalda
los brazos
las manos

las piernas

el cuerpo

los pies

ACTIVIDAD 7   Descripción de dibujos: ¿Quién es?

Mire a estas personas. Escuche la descripción que da su profesor(a) y diga cómo se llama la persona.

1. Rosa   2. el robot   3. Lupe   4. Reinaldo   5. Víctor   6. María

most rapidly when they believe that the instructor is taking a personal interest in their progress, seems confident about their eventual success, encourages all efforts at communication, and sets realistic, useful, and attainable goals. Spanish class should be fun and should appeal to students' desire to learn. We suggest that instructors bring cultural information into as many activities as possible, relate personal experiences, show PowerPoint™ presentations or DVDs, provide games, and bring magazines and newspapers to class. The course can easily be a cultural as well as a linguistic experience.

✳ La descripción de las personas

Lea Gramática B.5.

ACTIVIDAD 8   **Diálogo: La nueva amiga**

ESTEBAN: ¿Cómo es tu nueva amiga, Luis?
LUIS: Es alta, delgada y de pelo castaño. ¡Y muy talentosa!
ESTEBAN: ¿Cómo se llama?
LUIS: Cecilia Teresa.
ESTEBAN: Es un nombre muy bonito.
LUIS: ¡Es una chica muy bonita también!

ACTIVIDAD 9   **Diálogo abierto: Los nuevos amigos**

E1: ¿Tienes nuevos amigos?
E2: Sí, tengo dos.
E1: ¿Cómo se llaman?
E2: Se llaman _____ y _____ y son muy _____.
E1: ¿Y son _____ también?
E2: ¡Claro que sí! (¡Claro que no!)

¡Ojo!

The ¡Ojo! cultural margin notes are written in Spanish. You may want to read these aloud as your students read along silently. Cognates and your use of gestures and examples will help students to understand these brief segments. You may wish to give a brief explanation or expand on the information.

Entrevista (Interview)

In this first **Entrevista** activity, Student 1 is given a question and Student 2 is given a guided answer. In this and in subsequent interviews we recommend that the instructor first ask and answer all questions personally and write possible answers on the board for reference.

En resumen

This is the culminating section of the **Actividades de comunicación.** The activity or activities in **De todo un poco** incorporate one or more of the chapters themes in a creative pair or group activity. In **Capítulo 1,** two other features—**¡Dígalo por escrito!** and **Cuéntenos usted**—also are included in this section.

---

28 **PASO B**   Las descripciones

ACTIVIDAD 10   Intercambios: Mis compañeros y yo

Diga cómo es usted. Dé tres descripciones afirmativas y dos negativas.

MODELO: E1: Soy *talentoso/a, idealista* y *trabajador*(a). No soy *agresivo/a* ni *tonto/a*. ¿Y tú?
           E2: Yo soy *cómico/a, atlético/a* y *generoso/a*. No soy *tímido/a* ni *tacaño/a*.

agresivo/a	entusiasta	mentiroso/a	sincero/a
antipático/a	estudioso/a	nervioso/a	tacaño/a
atlético/a	filosófico/a	optimista	talentoso/a
callado/a	generoso/a	perezoso/a	temperamental
cómico/a	idealista	pesimista	tímido/a
conservador(a)	impulsivo	práctico/a	tonto/a
considerado/a	inteligente	simpático/a	trabajador(a)
egoísta	materialista		

ACTIVIDAD 11   Entrevista: Mi mejor amigo/a

ESTUDIANTE 1

1. ¿Cómo se llama tu mejor amigo/a?
2. ¿De qué color tiene los ojos?
3. ¿Es alto/a, bajo/a o de estatura mediana?
4. ¿De qué color tiene el pelo?
5. ¿Tiene bigote/barba?
6. ¿Cómo es? ¿Es simpático/a? ¿tímido/a? ¿trabajador(a)? ¿Es _____?

ESTUDIANTE 2

Se llama _____.
Tiene los ojos _____.
Es _____.
Tiene el pelo _____.
(No) Tiene _____.
Es _____.

¡OJO!

Para expresar la palabra «tacaño/a», uno se puede tocar el codo con la mano.

En resumen

De todo un poco

A. Un mundo ideal

Use su imaginación y complete estas descripciones.

1. El salón de clase ideal es _____ y _____. En el salón de clase hay _____. No hay _____.
2. El amigo / La amiga ideal es _____ y _____. No es _____.
3. El/La estudiante ideal es _____ y _____. No es _____.
4. El profesor / La profesora ideal es _____ y _____. No es _____.
5. El novio (El esposo) / La novia (La esposa) ideal es _____ y _____. No es _____.

Vocabulario

The words in the **Vocabulario** are intended for reference and review. Since they are grouped thematically, they are useful both for instructors preparing lesson plans and for students as they do the activities. Some instructors prefer to designate certain words or thematic groups as important for study, but students should not be held accountable for producing and spelling all the words in any **Vocabulario** section. The goal should be understanding the meaning of most of the words when used in context.

The instructor can determine which words students have truly acquired, but the rate of vocabulary acquisition will vary from student to student.

Some students often forget words that have not been used recently in your input. A good rule of thumb before doing any activity is to ask the class, **¿Hay palabras que no comprenden?** or **¿Hay preguntas de vocabulario?** Try to explain new words in simple Spanish; this way your students will acquire other vocabulary items and structures while they listen to your definition.

B. Su opinión

Exprese su opinión con su compañero/a.

MODELO: E1: La clase de español *es interesante.*
E2: Estoy de acuerdo. La clase de español *es muy interesante (no es aburrida).*

▶ EXPRESIONES ÚTILES

(No) Estoy de acuerdo.

1. La clase de español es (interesante ~ aburrida).
2. Hay muchos estudiantes (inteligentes ~ tontos) en esta clase.
3. El profesor / La profesora de español es (reservado/a ~ entusiasta).
4. El salón de clase es (bonito ~ feo).
5. Yo soy (tacaño/a ~ generoso/a).

Vocabulario

• Las cosas en el salón de clase	Things in the Classroom	• El cuerpo humano	The Human Body
el borrador	eraser	la barriga	tummy; belly
el cartel	poster	la boca	mouth
el cuaderno	workbook; notebook	el brazo	arm
el diccionario	dictionary	la cabeza	head
el escritorio	desk	la cara	face
la luz / las luces	light / lights	el cuello	neck
la mesa	table	la espalda	back
el papel	paper	el estómago	stomach
la pared	wall	el hombro	shoulder
el piso	floor	la mano	hand
la pizarra	board	la nariz	nose
la pluma	pen (*Mex.*)	el ojo	eye
el pupitre	desk (student)	la oreja	ear
la silla	chair	el pie / los pies	foot
el techo	roof; ceiling	la pierna	leg
la tiza	chalk		
la ventana	window	• Las personas	People

REPASO (*Review*): **el bolígrafo, el lápiz, el libro, la puerta, el reloj, el texto**

el chico / la chica	young man / young woman	
el esposo / la esposa	husband / wife	

el hermano / la hermana	brother / sister
el novio / la novia	boyfriend / girlfriend
tú	you (inf.)
el vecino / la vecina	neighbor

PALABRAS SEMEJANTES: el doctor / la doctora, la mamá, el papá, el robot

• Las descripciones — Descriptions

¿Cómo es él/ella?	What is he/she like?
¿Cómo es usted? / ¿Cómo eres tú?	What are you like?
abierto/a	open
aburrido/a	boring; bored
antiguo/a	antique; ancient
antipático/a	unpleasant
callado/a	quiet
de... años	. . . years old
derecho/a	right
difícil	difficult
divertido/a	fun
egoísta	selfish, self-centered
entusiasta	enthusiastic
fácil	easy
fuerte	strong
izquierdo/a	left
mejor	best; better
mentiroso/a	dishonest, liar
perezoso/a	lazy
simpático/a	nice, pleasant
tacaño/a	stingy
tímido/a	shy
tonto/a	silly, dumb
trabajador(a)	hard-working

PALABRAS SEMEJANTES: afirmativo/a, agresivo/a, atlético/a, cómico/a, conservador(a), considerado/a, estudioso/a, filosófico/a, generoso/a, ideal, idealista, impulsivo/a, inteligente, interesante, materialista, moderno/a, negativo/a, nervioso/a, optimista, pesimista, práctico/a, reservado/a, sincero/a, talentoso/a

• Los verbos — Verbs

busque	look for
complete	complete
conteste(n)	answer
de(le)	give (to him/her)
eres	you (inf. sing.) are
exprese	express
mueva	move
señale	point to
¿Tienes... ?	Do you have . . . ?

Tengo...	I have . . .
usa	uses

• Expresiones útiles — Useful Expressions

Claro que sí/no	Of course (not)
¿Cómo estás tú?	How are you?
¿Cuánto cuesta(n)?	How much is (are) . . . ?
Cuesta(n)...	It costs (They cost) . . .
de nada	You are welcome.
(No) Estoy de acuerdo	I (do not) agree.
¿Qué tal?	How's it going?

• Palabras del texto — Words from the Text

de todo un poco	a bit of everything
el dibujo	drawing
en resumen	to sum up
la entrevista	interview
hablando	talking
intercambios	interactions
el modelo	model

• Palabras útiles — Useful Words

la calculadora	calculator
el centavo	cent
la computadora	computer
esto	this (thing)
la mochila	backpack
mucho/a(s)	a lot, many
el mundo	world
muy	very
o	or
otro/a	other, another
la patineta	skateboard
también	also
tu(s)	your (inf.)

PALABRAS SEMEJANTES: el dólar / los dólares, la imaginación, el mapa, las matemáticas, la oficina, la opinión, la universidad

• Los números — Numbers

cuarenta	forty
cuarenta y uno	forty-one
cuarenta y cinco	forty-five
cincuenta	fifty
cincuenta y uno	fifty-one
cincuenta y dos	fifty-two
cincuenta y ocho	fifty-eight
sesenta	sixty
sesenta y nueve	sixty-nine

Using the *Gramática y ejercicios* Section

An important principle of the Natural Approach is the distinction between form-focused exercises and communicative activities. Most class time will be devoted to teacher-talk and student interaction. We do not consider excessive study and memorization of grammar rules to be very helpful since they cause students to spend their time focusing on discrete forms rather than on acquiring language. Grammar, like vocabulary, is an important part of communicating meaning, but detailed knowledge about grammar is not necessary to function in a language. Only real communicative experiences result in true acquisition of grammatical forms and structures. Thus, the grammar explanations are intended as an introduction and as a reference tool.

Gramática y ejercicios

B.1 Addressing Others: Informal and Polite *you* (*tú/usted*)

A. English speakers use the pronoun *you* to address a person directly, whether or not they know that person well. In older forms of English, speakers used an informal pronoun—*thou*—among friends, but today *you* is used with everyone.

Spanish has two pronouns that mean *you*, singular: **usted** and **tú**. The polite (*pol.*) pronoun **usted** is appropriate for people you do not know well, such as salespeople, receptionists, other professionals, and especially for people older than you. The informal (*inf.*) pronoun **tú** is reserved for friends, peers, children, and other people you know well. In some places in Latin America, including Argentina and Central America, speakers use **vos** instead of **tú** as the informal pronoun for *you*. Everyone who uses **vos**, however, also understands **tú**.

In the activities and exercises, *Dos mundos* addresses you with **usted**. You should use **tú** when speaking to your classmates. Some instructors address their students with **tú**; others use **usted**.

> Both **tú** and **usted** mean *you* (singular). **Tú** is used when speaking to family, friends, and children. **Usted** is used to speak to people you don't know well and people older than you.

Soy puertorriqueño. ¿Y **tú**? ¿De dónde eres?	*I'm Puerto Rican. And you? Where are you from?*
Soy profesora de español. ¿Y **usted**? ¿Es **usted** estudiante?	*I'm a professor of Spanish. And you? Are you a student?*

B. Although both **tú** and **usted** correspond to *you*, the verb forms used with each are different. Present-tense verb forms for **tú** always end with the letter **-s**. Present-tense verb forms for **usted** end in **-a** or **-e** and are always the same as the forms for **él/ella.**

> Use **tú** when speaking to your classmates. Use **usted** when addressing your instructor (unless he/she asks you to use **tú**).

¿Tiene**s** (**tú**) una blusa gris?	*Do you have a gray blouse?*
¿Tiene **usted** un vestido blanco?	*Do you have a white dress?*

We introduced the forms of the verb **ser** (*to be*) in **Gramática A.3.** The **tú** form of **ser** is **eres**; the **usted** form of **ser** is **es** (the same as the form for **él/ella**).

> Present-tense verb forms for **tú** always end in **-s.**

(**Tú**) **Eres** un buen amigo.	*You are a good friend.*
Usted es muy amable, señora Saucedo.	*You are very nice, Mrs. Saucedo.*

C. Spanish distinguishes between singular *you* (**tú** or **usted**) and plural *you* (**ustedes**). Many American speakers of English make this distinction by saying "you guys" or "you all." The verb forms used with **ustedes** end in the letter **-n** and are the same as those used with the pronoun **ellos/as.**

—¿Cómo **están ustedes**?	*—How are you (all)?*
—Bien, gracias.	*—Fine, thanks.*

Most speakers of Spanish do not distinguish between informal and polite address in the plural. **Ustedes** is used with everyone. In Spain, however,

Gramática y ejercicios

The way instructors use the **Gramática y ejercicios** will depend on their own teaching style and on students' learning preferences and background. Many instructors prefer to assign the **Gramática y ejercicios** as a follow-up after they have completed the corresponding section of the **Actividades de comunicación y lecturas.** (The **Lecturas** begin with **Capítulo 1.**)

Others assign parts of the **Gramática y ejercicios** as they are working on a particular section, while still others prefer to assign them before they begin the corresponding section of the **Actividades de comunicación y lecturas.** Some instructors make all grammar study optional. However an instructor chooses to use the grammar, in-class grammar explanations should be kept brief (three to five minutes).

> The plural of both **tú** and **usted** in Latin America is **ustedes.** In Spain, the plural of **tú** is **vosotros/as** and the plural of **usted** is **ustedes.**

most speakers prefer to use **vosotros/as** for the informal plural *you* and reserve **ustedes** for the polite plural *you.*

The regional pronouns **vos** and **vosotros/as** do not appear in the exercises and activities of *Dos mundos.* You will learn them quickly if you travel to areas where they are frequently used. The verb forms corresponding to **vosotros/as** are listed with other verb forms and are given in Appendix 1. The verb forms corresponding to **vos** are footnoted in the grammar explanations. In the listening activities of the *Cuaderno de actividades,* the characters from countries where **vos** and **vosotros/as** are prevalent use those pronouns. This will give you an opportunity to hear **vos** and **vosotros/as** and their accompanying verb forms, even though you will not need to use them yourself.

EJERCICIO I

Usted habla con estas personas: ¿usa **tú** o **usted**?

1. una amiga de su clase de español
   a. ¿Tiene usted dos clases hoy?
   b. ¿Tienes dos clases hoy?
2. la recepcionista
   a. ¿Cómo estás?
   b. ¿Cómo está usted?
3. un niño
   a. Tú tienes una bicicleta nueva.
   b. Usted tiene una bicicleta nueva.
4. una persona de cuarenta y nueve años
   a. ¿Cómo se llama usted?
   b. ¿Cómo te llamas?
5. un vecino de setenta años
   a. Estoy bien. ¿Y tú?
   b. Estoy bien. ¿Y usted?

B.2 Expressing Existence: *hay*

> **hay** = *there is / there are*
> **Hay** is used with singular or plural nouns.

The verb form **hay** expresses the idea of existence. When used with singular nouns it means *there is;* with plural nouns it means *there are.*

—¿Qué **hay** en el salón de clase?   —*What is there in the classroom?*
—**Hay** dos puertas y una ventana.   —*There are two doors and a window.*

Whereas the verb **ser** (*to be*) identifies nouns (see **Gramática A.3**), **hay** simply states their existence.

—¿Qué **es**?   —*What is that?*
—**Es** un bolígrafo.   —*It's a pen.*

—¿Cuántos **hay**?   —*How many are there?*
—**Hay** tres.   —*There are three.*

EJERCICIO 2

> To make a sentence negative, place **no** before the verb.
> **Hay** perros en el salón de clase.
> **No hay** perros en el salón de clase.

Imagínese qué cosas o personas hay o no hay en el salón de clase de la profesora Martínez.

MODELOS: lápices → *Hay* lápices en el salón de clase.
           perros → *No hay* perros en el salón de clase.

Spiraling

Gramática B.3 introduces the concept of negation and shows students how to make a sentence negative by simply putting **no** before the verb. In **Gramática 8.3** negation is reintroduced and expanded with negative words like **nunca, nadie,** and **nada.**

1. libros en la mesa	**6.** papeles en los pupitres
2. un reloj en la pared	**7.** un bolígrafo en el pupitre de Alberto
3. una profesora	**8.** muchos cuadernos
4. un automóvil	**9.** una bicicleta
5. un profesor	**10.** una ventana

B.3 Describing People and Things: Negation

In a negative sentence, the word **no** precedes the verb.

Amanda es una chica muy simpática. (Amanda) **No es** tímida.	*Amanda is a very nice girl. She is not shy.*
Ramón **no es** mi novio. Es el novio de Amanda.	*Ramón isn't my boyfriend. He's Amanda's boyfriend.*

There are no additional words in Spanish that correspond to the English negatives *don't* and *doesn't.*

Guillermo **no tiene** el pelo largo ahora.	*Guillermo doesn't have long hair now.*
Yo soy hombre; **no llevo** vestidos.	*I am a man; I don't wear dresses.*

Spanish, like many other languages in the world, often uses more than one negative in a sentence.*

No hay **nada** en este salón de clase.	*There is nothing in this classroom.*

EJERCICIO 3

Cambie estas oraciones afirmativas a oraciones negativas.

MODELOS: Luis es un chico alto. → Luis **no** es un chico alto.
En el salón de clase hay 68 tizas. → En el salón de clase **no** hay 68 tizas.

1. En el salón de clase hay diez pizarras.
2. Mónica tiene el pelo negro.
3. Carmen lleva una blusa muy fea.
4. Mi carro es morado.
5. La profesora Martínez tiene barba.

B.4 Describing People and Things: Plural Forms

Spanish and English nouns may be singular (**camisa,** *shirt*) or plural (**camisas,** *shirts*). Almost all plural words in Spanish end in **-s** or **-es: blusas** (*blouses*), **pantalones** (*pants*), **suéteres** (*sweaters*), **zapatos** (*shoes*), and so on. In Spanish, unlike English, articles before plural nouns and adjectives that describe plural nouns must also be plural. Here are the basic rules for forming plurals in Spanish.

*You will learn more about negative words and their placement in **Gramática 8.3.** In **Gramática 3.4** you will learn how to answer questions in the negative.

A. Words that end in a vowel (**a, e, i, o, u**) form their plural by adding **-s.**

> To form plurals:
> Words ending in vowels add **s**; words ending in consonants add **-es**; words ending in **-z** change to **-c** and add **-es.** In time, you will acquire a feel for the plural formations.

SINGULAR	PLURAL
el brazo	los brazos
el ojo	los ojos
el pie	los pies
la pierna	las piernas

Words that end in a consonant add **-es.**

SINGULAR	PLURAL
el borrador	los borradores
la pared	las paredes
el profesor	los profesores

If the consonant at the end of a word is **-z,** it changes to **-c** and adds **-es.**

SINGULAR	PLURAL
el lápiz	los lápices
la luz	las luces

B. Adjectives that describe plural words must also be plural.

ojos azules	*blue eyes*	orejas grandes	*big ears*
brazos largos	*long arms*	pies pequeños	*small feet*

En mi salón de clase hay dos **ventanas grandes, varias sillas viejas,** cinco **pizarras verdes** y diez **luces.**

In my classroom there are two large windows, several old chairs, five green chalkboards, and ten lights.

EJERCICIO 4

Marisa y Clarisa tienen muchas cosas. ¡Pero Marisa siempre tiene una y Clarisa dos!

> tienen = *have*
> tiene = *has*

MODELO: Marisa tiene un suéter azul, pero Clarisa tiene dos... → *suéteres azules.*

1. Marisa tiene un par de zapatos, pero Clarisa tiene dos...
2. Marisa tiene un perro nuevo, pero Clarisa tiene dos...
3. Marisa tiene una chaqueta roja, pero Clarisa tiene dos...
4. Marisa tiene un lápiz amarillo, pero Clarisa tiene dos...
5. Marisa tiene una amiga norteamericana, pero Clarisa tiene dos...

Los ejercicios

The grammar exercises are intended to verify students' understanding of the grammar explanations. They check students' ability to recognize or supply correct forms in a controlled, form-focused situation. They are not intended to indicate mastery of a particular grammar point; that will come only after far more exposure to spoken and written Spanish. Answers to exercises are provided in Appendix 4 of the textbook so that students may check their work at home. Some instructors prefer to reserve some class time to answer questions students may have about grammar. It is a good practice to devote no more than five minutes to this portion of the class.

Spiraling

Gramática B.5 introduces noun-adjective agreement rules and expands the discussion of gender that was first presented in **A.4.** Placement of adjectives is also discussed.

EJERCICIO 5

¡Ahora Clarisa tiene una y Marisa tiene dos!

MODELO: Clarisa tiene un sombrero grande, pero Marisa tiene dos... →
sombreros grandes.

1. Clarisa tiene un cuaderno pequeño, pero Marisa tiene dos...
2. Clarisa tiene un gato negro, pero Marisa tiene dos...
3. Clarisa tiene una fotografía bonita, pero Marisa tiene dos...
4. Clarisa tiene un reloj bonito, pero Marisa tiene dos...
5. Clarisa tiene un libro difícil, pero Marisa tiene dos...
6. Clarisa tiene una amiga divertida, pero Marisa tiene dos...

B.5 Describing People and Things: Adjective-Noun Agreement and Placement of Adjectives

A. Adjectives must agree in gender and number with the nouns they describe; that is, if the noun is singular and masculine, the adjective must also be singular and masculine. Adjectives that end in **-o** in the masculine form and **-a** in the feminine form will appear in the vocabulary lists in *Dos mundos* like this: **bonito/a.** Such adjectives have four possible forms.

> A singular adjective is used to describe a singular noun. A plural adjective is used to describe a plural noun.

	SINGULAR	PLURAL
Masculine	viejo	viejos
Feminine	vieja	viejas

Carmen lleva un suéter **bonito** y una falda **nueva.**   *Carmen is wearing a pretty sweater and a new skirt.*
Mis zapatos de tenis son **viejos.**   *My tennis shoes are old.*

B. Adjectives that end in a consonant,* the vowel **-e,** or the ending **-ista** have only two forms because the masculine and feminine forms are the same.

	SINGULAR	PLURAL
Masculine/Feminine	joven	jóvenes
	interesante	interesantes
	pesim**ista**	pesimistas
	azul	azules

---

*Adjectives of nationality that end in a consonant are an exception, since they (like adjectives that end in -o/-a) have four forms: **inglés, inglesa, ingleses, inglesas.** See **Gramática C.4** for more information.

Luis lleva una camisa **azul** y un sombrero **azul**.	*Luis is wearing a blue shirt and a blue hat.*
Mi amigo Nacho es **pesimista**, pero mi amiga Silvia es **optimista**.	*My friend Nacho is pessimistic, but my friend Silvia is optimistic.*

C. In Spanish adjectives generally follow the noun they modify: **zapatos nuevos, camisas blancas, faldas bonitas, sombreros negros.** Adjectives that express inherent characteristics may precede the noun: **la blanca nieve.*** You should not worry too much about placement. For now, you may place descriptive adjectives after the noun.

D. If an adjective modifies two nouns, one masculine and one feminine, the adjective will take the masculine form.

Mónica es simpátic**a** y considerad**a**.
Alberto y Mónica son simpátic**os** y considerad**os**.
Mi blusa y mi falda son blanc**as**.
Mi blusa y mi vestido son roj**os**.

EJERCICIO 6

Seleccione todas las descripciones posibles.

MODELO: Alberto → *chico, guapo, estudiante*

Nora　Alberto　Esteban　Carmen　la profesora Martínez　Luis　Pablo　Mónica

1. Nora	**a.** mujer	**i.** estudiante
2. Alberto	**b.** chico	**j.** profesor
3. Esteban y Carmen	**c.** secretaria	**k.** mexicana
4. la profesora Martínez	**d.** chica	**l.** altas
5. Luis	**e.** guapo	**m.** bajo
6. Mónica y Carmen	**f.** niñas	**n.** morena
7. Pablo	**g.** amigos	**o.** rubio
	h. estudiantes	

---

*Limiting adjectives (numerals, possessives, demonstratives, and indefinite adjectives) also precede the noun: **dos amigos, mis zapatos, esta mesa, otro ejemplo.**

English vs. Spanish

The grammar explanations are written in English, since this component is intended for self-study. The direction lines for each exercise, however, are in Spanish. By now most students have heard enough Spanish in class to be able to understand short directions in Spanish. If you think your students will have trouble with these direction lines, you may want to read them with the whole class before assigning the exercises.

EJERCICIO 7

Escriba frases completas con la información. Use las formas femeninas para las mujeres.

MODELOS: Arnold Schwarzenegger: alto, fuerte → Arnold Schwarzenegger es alto y fuerte.
Oprah Winfrey: simpático, rico → Oprah Winfrey es simpática y rica.

1. Ashley y Mary Kate Olsen: rico, bonito
2. Will Smith: delgado, elegante
3. Hillary Clinton: inteligente, rubio
4. Jennifer López: materialista, talentoso
5. George Clooney: guapo, tímido

EJERCICIO 8

Escriba frases completas con la información. Use la forma correcta: masculina o femenina, singular o plural.

MODELOS: casa: nuevo, pequeño → La casa es nueva y pequeña. / La casa nueva es pequeña.
lápices: amarillo, viejo → Los lápices son amarillos y viejos. / Los lápices amarillos son viejos.

1. libros: difícil, divertido
2. chica: bajo, tímido
3. mujeres: tacaño, trabajador
4. amigo: inteligente, perezoso
5. robots: fuerte, aburrido

Speech Emergence

Stage 3 in the acquisition process is characterized by an increasing ability to comprehend native spoken Spanish and by the emergence of longer utterances. Students will still demonstrate comprehension by giving single words and using short phrases, but they will also begin to develop the ability to produce longer phrases and sentences, to participate in dialogues, and to produce simple, connected narration. Stage 3 activities begin with **Paso C** and continue through **Capítulo 15.**

We do not mean to imply that students begin Stage 3 in **Paso C** and stay there throughout the remainder of the course, however. Students will need to progress through all three stages whenever new vocabulary and structures are introduced. Stage 1 (comprehension) comes into play whenever students encounter new material and begin the acquisition process. At that point, they should be given a lot of interesting, comprehensible input and should only have to demonstrate that they comprehend through **sí/no** answers, gestures, or other simple means. As they show signs of comprehending the new material, the instructor may encourage simple speech via choice questions and other Stage 2 activities. Students should not be asked to use the language more extensively in Stage 3 activities until they have been exposed to considerable input and the acquisition process is at a more advanced stage.

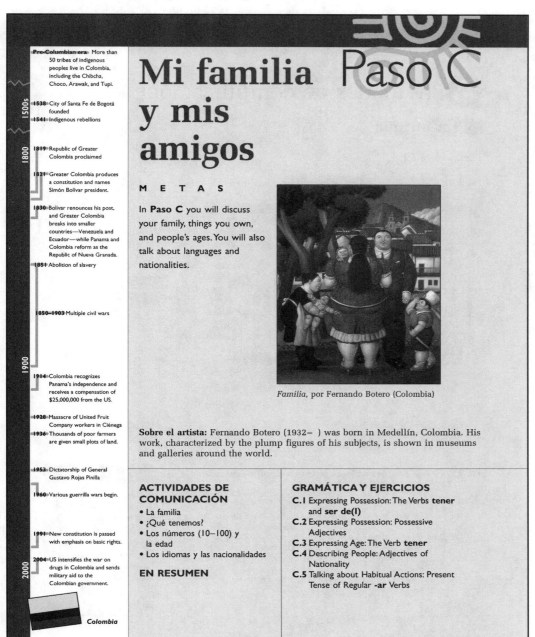

Mi familia y mis amigos — Paso C

Pre-Columbian era More than 50 tribes of indigenous peoples live in Colombia, including the Chibcha, Choco, Arawak, and Tupi.

1500s

1538 City of Santa Fe de Bogotá founded

1541 Indigenous rebellions

1800

1819 Republic of Greater Colombia proclaimed

1821 Greater Colombia produces a constitution and names Simón Bolívar president.

1830 Bolivar renounces his post, and Greater Colombia breaks into smaller countries—Venezuela and Ecuador—while Panama and Colombia reform as the Republic of Nueva Granada.

1851 Abolition of slavery

1850–1903 Multiple civil wars

1900

1914 Colombia recognizes Panama's independence and receives a compensation of $25,000,000 from the US.

1928 Massacre of United Fruit Company workers in Ciénega

1936 Thousands of poor farmers are given small plots of land.

1953 Dictatorship of General Gustavo Rojas Pinilla

1960 Various guerrilla wars begin.

1991 New constitution is passed with emphasis on basic rights.

2000

2004 US intensifies the war on drugs in Colombia and sends military aid to the Colombian government.

Colombia

M E T A S

In **Paso C** you will discuss your family, things you own, and people's ages. You will also talk about languages and nationalities.

Familia, por Fernando Botero (Colombia)

Sobre el artista: Fernando Botero (1932–) was born in Medellín, Colombia. His work, characterized by the plump figures of his subjects, is shown in museums and galleries around the world.

ACTIVIDADES DE COMUNICACIÓN

- La familia
- ¿Qué tenemos?
- Los números (10–100) y la edad
- Los idiomas y las nacionalidades

EN RESUMEN

GRAMÁTICA Y EJERCICIOS

C.1 Expressing Possession: The Verbs **tener** and **ser de(l)**

C.2 Expressing Possession: Possessive Adjectives

C.3 Expressing Age: The Verb **tener**

C.4 Describing People: Adjectives of Nationality

C.5 Talking about Habitual Actions: Present Tense of Regular **-ar** Verbs

Vocabulary Displays

The vocabulary displays in each section of the communication activities contain key words and structures used in that section. Students may have been exposed to all or most of these via daily Pre-Text Oral Activities, so that when they look at a display for the first time, they might see very little language that is unfamiliar to them. The displays often carry cultural messages and always offer a new visual context for familiar language. They are excellent points of departure for further input and review. The *Instructor's Edition* notes provide specific suggestions for each display. We recommend that the instructor do a Pre-Text Oral Activity that includes the language in a particular display before having students look at it. This is an excellent opportunity to recycle past language and, in many cases, to initiate a discussion about cultural matters. Overhead transparencies are available for many displays in *Dos mundos.*

Expansion of Activities

All activities should be used as opportunities to provide additional teacher input. Besides doing an activity in class, the instructor can ask questions about its content, make personal remarks, or create new items of the same type as those in the activity. In **Actividad 1,** for example, the instructor might ask for a show of hands about how many students have two, three, or more siblings. The class will find a discussion about your family or the family members of classmates more interesting than the families we have created in *Dos mundos.* The

Actividades de comunicación

✳ La familia

Lea Gramática C.1.

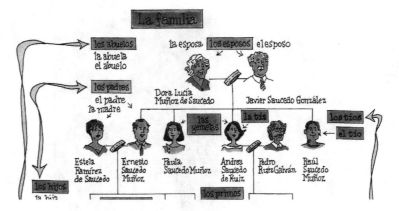

ACTIVIDAD I   Identificaciones: La familia Saucedo (Parte 1)

¿Cierto o falso? Conteste según el dibujo.

1. La esposa de Pedro se llama Paula.
2. Dora y Javier tienen cuatro hijos: tres hijas y un hijo.
3. Estela es soltera.
4. Raúl es casado.
5. Estela, Paula, Andrea y Raúl son hermanos.
6. Paula y Raúl tienen cinco sobrinos.
7. Amanda no tiene primos.
8. Dora tiene cinco nietos: tres nietas y dos nietos.
9. Pedro y Raúl son hermanos.
10. Andrea es la tía de Clarisa y Marisa.

¡OJO!

Las personas solteras llevan el apellido de su padre y el apellido de su madre. Vea la diferencia entre los nombres de Paula Saucedo Muñoz y Andrea Saucedo de Ruiz. En el caso de Andrea, Saucedo es el apellido de su padre y Ruiz el de su esposo.

instructor may also ask individual students for names of siblings and introduce the use of **mayor/menor que: ¿Tiene hermanos? (Sí.) ¿Cuántos? (Tres.) Pablo tiene tres hermanos. ¿Son todos hermanos o tiene una hermana? (Dos hermanas.) ¿Y cómo se llaman sus hermanas? (Kathleen y Kimberly.) ¿Son mayores que usted sus hermanas o son menores?** and so on.

Actividades Adicionales (AA)

The section in this *Instructor's Manual* titled *Expanded Instructor Notes: Chapter Goals, Techniques for Providing Input and Additional Activities* provides many other ideas for activities to complement or expand the activities in the **Actividades de comunicación** section.

ACTIVIDAD 2   Intercambios: La familia Saucedo (Parte 2)

Conteste según el dibujo de la familia Saucedo.

MODELOS: E1: ¿Cómo se llama *el hermano* de *Ernesto, Paula y Andrea?*
E2: Se llama *Raúl.*

E1: ¿Cuántos *hermanos* tiene *Amanda?*
E2: Tiene *dos.*

ACTIVIDAD 3   Diálogo: ¿Quién es?

Don Eduardo Alvar habla con Paula Saucedo.

DON EDUARDO: Perdone, señorita Saucedo. ¿Quién es ese joven (muchacho)?
PAULA SAUCEDO: Su nombre es Jorge Saucedo.
DON EDUARDO: ¿Saucedo? ¿Es su hermano?
PAULA SAUCEDO: No. Su apellido es Saucedo también, pero no es mi hermano. Mis hermanos se llaman Raúl y Ernesto.

ACTIVIDAD 4   Diálogo abierto: Mis hijos

E1: ¿Cómo se llama usted, *señor (señora, señorita)?*
E2: Me llamo _____.
E1: ¿Es usted *casado/a (soltero/a, viudo/a, divorciado/a)?*
E2: Soy _____.
E1: ¿Tiene usted hijos?
E2: Sí, tengo _____ hijo(s) y _____ hija(s). (No, no tengo hijos.)

ACTIVIDAD 5   Entrevista: Mi familia

1. ¿Cómo se llama tu *padre (madre, hermano/a, abuelo/a)?*
Mi *padre* se llama _____.
2. ¿Cuántos *hermanos (primos, abuelos, hijos, nietos)* tienes?
Tengo *dos hermanos.* (Tengo *un primo.* Tengo *una nieta.* No tengo *hijos.*)

¡OJO!

En las familias hispanas, los niños reciben mucha atención de sus padres y abuelos. Frecuentemente, los abuelos viven con la familia.

Instructor's Resource Kit (IRK)

The *Instructor's Edition* notes also include the reference "See IRK for additional activities: **¿Qué tenemos?**" This refers to the supplementary activities in the *Instructor's Resource Kit*. These activities parallel the topics in the **Actividades de comunicación** of *Dos mundos* and include a variety of task-based activities, games, autograph activities, "information gap" activities, surveys, interviews, and others. Beginning with **Paso C,** the IRK also includes two Internet activities for each chapter. These activities ask students to go to specific Web pages and search for cultural information in Spanish. Worksheets are provided for these activities and they are also available on the *Dos mundos* website at **www. mhhe.com/dosmundos6.**

Using Spanish in Class

We believe that conducting class in Spanish and exposing students to a wide vocabulary that recurs frequently in instructor input and communication activities is the best way to help students acquire Spanish and attain true functional proficiency. When the Spanish spoken in class is made comprehensible by the use of visual aids, gestures, cognates, and background knowledge, students not only become comfortable with it but find it satisfying to be able to comprehend and use the language. To aid this progress, we make maximum use of association techniques, cognates,

and art-supported activities so that students can quickly acquire a large vocabulary.

Many instructors conduct their classes almost completely in Spanish, including any brief discussion of grammar, but allow English when students need to ask for a word to express their personal experience or when asking a question about grammar. The important thing is that students become accustomed to hearing Spanish and

✳ ¿Qué tenemos?

Lea Gramática C.1–C.2.

Doña Lola tiene un coche nuevo.

Los discos compactos son de Amanda.

Ernestito y su perro Lobo son amigos.

ACTIVIDAD 6   Diálogo: El coche de don Eduardo

ERNESTITO: ¿Cómo es su coche, señor Alvar?
DON EDUARDO: Mi coche es azul; es un poco viejo.
ERNESTITO: Yo no tengo coche, pero tengo una bicicleta nueva.
DON EDUARDO: Sí, y tu bicicleta también es muy bonita.

ACTIVIDAD 7   Descripción de dibujos: ¿De quién... ?

1. ¿Quién tiene dos camisas nuevas?
2. ¿Quién tiene dos perros?
3. ¿De quién es el vestido nuevo?
4. ¿Quién tiene una computadora?
5. ¿De quién es el carro nuevo?
6. ¿Quiénes tienen helados?

feel comfortable and confident when it is spoken. The confidence and enjoyment that come from being able to comprehend and make oneself understood are at the heart of real proficiency.

Group Work

Students are now entering Stage 3 of the acquisition process, speech emergence; therefore, many activities in **Paso C** are designed for student interaction. The Natural Approach assumes that group work encourages interaction and is essential in a communicative class. Group work refers to pair work as well as small-group work. For some activities, dialogues, interviews, and chart activities, pairs work best. For other activities, realia-based interactions, **Y tú, ¿qué dices?**, situations, and discussions, small groups of three to four students are also appropriate. The *Instructor's Edition* notes provide suggestions for the group size to use in the different activities and for successful facilitation of pair/group work. Group work generally goes more smoothly if the instructor chooses the group makeup; in this way everyone is assured a partner, and students get to know many other classmates. **Actividad 8,** for example, may be done with students working in pairs asking each other questions. Most students enjoy talking with their peers and feel freer to express themselves than they would if called in to speak before the whole class. Group work also frees the instructor to move around the classroom to make sure the activity is going well, to answer questions, and to provide additional input.

ACTIVIDAD 8   Entrevista: Mi perro y mi carro

1. —¿Tienes *perro* (*gato*)?
   —Sí, tengo _____ . / No, no tengo *perro* (*gato*).
2. —¿Cómo es tu *perro* (*gato*)?
   —Mi *perro* (*gato*) es _____ .
3. —¿Tienes *carro* (*motocicleta, bicicleta*)?
   —Sí, tengo _____ . / No, no tengo *carro*. Tengo *motocicleta* (*bicicleta*).
4. —¿Cómo es tu *carro* (*motocicleta, bicicleta*)?
   —Mi *carro* (*motocicleta, bicicleta*) es _____ .

✳ Los números (10–100) y la edad

Lea Gramática C.3.

10	diez	76	setenta y seis
20	veinte	80	ochenta
30	treinta	82	ochenta y dos
40	cuarenta	90	noventa
50	cincuenta	94	noventa y cuatro
60	sesenta	100	cien
70	setenta	110	ciento diez

ACTIVIDAD 9   Diálogos: ¿Cuántos años tienen?

GRACIELA: Amanda, ¿quién es esa niña?
AMANDA: Es mi prima, Clarisa.
GRACIELA: ¿Cuántos años tiene?
AMANDA: Tiene sólo seis años y es muy inteligente.

DON EDUARDO: Señor Ruiz, ¿cuántos hijos tiene usted?
PEDRO RUIZ: Tengo dos hijas.
DON EDUARDO: ¿Y cuántos años tienen?
PEDRO RUIZ: Bueno, Clarisa tiene seis años y Marisa tiene cuatro.
DON EDUARDO: ¡Sólo dos hijas! ¡Cómo cambia el mundo!

ACTIVIDAD 10   Diálogo abierto: ¿Cuántos años tienes?

E1: ¿Cuántos años tienes?
E2: Tengo _____ años.
E1: ¿Tienes hermanos?
E2: Sí, tengo _____ hermanos y _____ hermanas. (No, no tengo hermanos, pero tengo _____ .)
E1: ¿Cuántos años tiene tu hermano/a?
E2: Mi hermano/a tiene _____ años.
E1: ¿Es mayor o menor que tú?
E2: Es _____ .

Vocabulary Displays in Stage 3

Most displays after the first two **Pasos** move from presenting single words to presenting sentences that include key structures and vocabulary from the particular sections. They are useful as a point of departure for expanded teacher input. This display includes adjectives of nationality, the verb **hablar,** and various languages. It can serve as a springboard to discuss languages that students, their parents, or friends speak, as well as other languages of the world. **Masato Hamasaki y Goro Nishimura hablan japonés. ¿Quién en la clase habla japonés? ¿Nadie? Yo tampoco hablo japonés, pero sí hablo francés y hebreo. Hans Schumann habla alemán. ¿Quién en la clase habla alemán? ¿Christina? ¿Hablan alemán sus padres o estudió usted alemán en la universidad?**

✳ Los idiomas y las nacionalidades

Lea Gramática C.4–C.5.

Hans Schumann es alemán y habla alemán.

Gina Sfreddo es italiana y habla italiano.

Iara Gomes y Zidia Oliveira son brasileñas y hablan portugués.

Masato Hamazaki y Goro Nishimura son japoneses y hablan japonés.

Rehana Hezar y Neda Nikraz son iraníes y hablan persa.

PAÍS	NACIONALIDAD	IDIOMA(S)
Afganistán	afgano/a	dari, pashto
Alemania	alemán, alemana	alemán
Argentina	argentino/a	español
Brasil	brasileño/a	portugués
Canadá	canadiense	inglés, francés
China	chino/a	chino
Corea (del Norte / del Sur)	coreano/a	coreano
Cuba	cubano/a	español
Egipto	egipcio/a	árabe
España	español(a)	español
Estados Unidos	estadounidense	inglés
Francia	francés, francesa	francés
Inglaterra	inglés, inglesa	inglés
Irán	iraní	persa
Irak	iraquí	árabe
Israel	israelí	hebreo
Italia	italiano/a	italiano

Errors in Speech

The Natural Approach, like other communicative approaches, assumes that as speech emerges and students start putting sentences together, they will make many grammatical and lexical errors. Since learners are concentrating on expressing meaning they do not have time to monitor their speech. These early errors do not become permanent, nor do they affect students' future language development. Most forms and structures require a large number of communicative experiences before acquisition is complete, and no amount of direct error correction can speed up this process. During communicative activities, the instructor should pay attention primarily to factual errors. Any language correction should be done through rephrasing and expanding students' responses so that the thought processes are not interrupted by overt correction. It is reasonable for the instructor to expect steady improvement throughout the course as students have an opportunity to acquire Spanish, but students will not end the academic year with grammatical accuracy in all the language they have acquired.

PAÍS	NACIONALIDAD	IDIOMA(S)
Japón	japonés, japonesa	japonés
México	mexicano/a	español
República de Sudáfrica	sudafricano/a	inglés, afrikaans, lenguas africanas
Rusia	ruso/a	ruso
Siria	sirio/a	árabe
Vietnam	vietnamita	vietnamita

ACTIVIDAD 11   Asociaciones: ¿Qué nacionalidad? ¿Qué idioma?

Diga cuál es la nacionalidad de estas personas y qué idioma(s) hablan.

MODELO: Salma Hayek... México →
Salma Hayek es mexicana y habla español.

PERSONA	PAÍS
1. Fidel Castro	Cuba
2. Ignacio Lula da Silva	Brasil
3. el príncipe Guillermo	Inglaterra
4. Vladimir Putin	Rusia
5. Jacques Chirac	Francia
6. Hosni Mubarak	Egipto
7. Celine Dion	Canadá
8. el rey Juan Carlos de Borbón	España
9. Luciano Pavarotti	Italia

Salma Hayek, actriz mexicana

Juan Carlos de Borbón, rey de España

En resumen

De todo un poco

This culminating activity in the **En resumen** section is a guided interview. Students have already been introduced to the structures and vocabulary contained in this interview. In later chapters the **De todo un poco** activities become more challenging.

ACTIVIDAD 12   **Diálogo abierto: Amigos internacionales**

E1: ¿Tienes un amigo *japonés* (una amiga *japonesa*)?
E2: Sí, se llama _____.
E1: ¿Hablas *japonés* o *inglés* con él (ella)?
E2: Hablo *inglés*. (Normalmente hablo *inglés*, pero a veces hablo *japonés* con él/ella.)

ACTIVIDAD 13   **Intercambios: Las vacaciones**

MODELO: E1: Quiero viajar *a París* durante las vacaciones.
E2: ¿Hablas *francés*?
E1: Sí, hablo *un poco de francés*. (No, no hablo *nada de francés*. / Sí, hablo *francés muy bien*.)

CIUDADES

Roma	Madrid	Río de Janeiro
Londres	Buenos Aires	Montreal
Toronto	Moscú	Berlín
Los Ángeles	Pekín	Tokio

IDIOMAS

italiano	ruso	francés
inglés	chino	alemán
español	portugués	japonés

▶ FRASES ÚTILES

un poco de	nada de	muy bien

En resumen

De todo un poco

Entrevista: Su familia y sus amigos

Entreviste a su compañero/a.

—¿Son estadounidenses tus padres?
—Sí/No, mis padres son _____.
—¿Cuántos años tienen ellos?
—Mi padre tiene _____ años y mi madre tiene _____ años.
—¿Qué idiomas hablan?
—Mis padres hablan _____. (Mi padre habla _____ y mi madre habla _____.)
—¿Tienes muchos hermanos?
—Sí, tengo _____. (No, tengo sólo _____. / No, soy hijo único / hija única.)
—¿Cómo se llaman tus hermanos?

Vocabulario

As students begin to talk, many will want to use the **Vocabulario** section at the end of the chapter as a reference tool. We suggest that you take a few minutes to explain that the vocabulary is arranged in alphabetical order by topic so that students learn to refer to a particular subject quickly when they forget a word during an activity. Students may also refer to this section when doing writing activities. The list of obvious cognates at the end of many topical sections helps remind them of the importance cognates can have in reading and in enlarging one's functional vocabulary.

—Mis hermanos se llaman _____ y _____. (Mi hermano/a se llama _____.)
—¿Tienes un amigo / una amiga de *España*? (*México, Irán, Rusia, Italia, Francia*, etcétera)
—Sí, tengo un amigo / una amiga de _____.
—¿Cómo se llama tu amigo/a?
—Él/Ella se llama _____.
—¿Qué idiomas habla él/ella?
—Habla _____ y _____. (Habla sólo _____.)

Vocabulario

• **La familia**	The Family
el abuelo / la abuela	grandfather/grandmother
los abuelos	grandparents
el gemelo / la gemela	twin
el hijo / la hija	son / daughter
el hijo único / la hija única	only child (only son / only daughter)
los hijos	sons (sons and daughters; children)
la madre	mother
el nieto / la nieta	grandson / granddaughter
el padre	father
los padres	parents
el primo / la prima	cousin
el sobrino / la sobrina	nephew / niece
el tío / la tía	uncle / aunt

REPASO: el esposo, la esposa, el hermano, la hermana

• **Los países**	Countries
Alemania	Germany
Corea del Norte / del Sur	North / South Korea
España	Spain
(los) Estados Unidos	United States
Inglaterra	England
(la) República de Sudáfrica	South Africa

PALABRAS SEMEJANTES: Afganistán, Argentina, Brasil, Canadá, China, Cuba, Egipto, Francia, Irak, Irán, Israel, Italia, Japón, México, Rusia, Siria, Vietnam

• **Las nacionalidades**	Nationalities
alemán/alemana	German
brasileño/a	Brazilian
chino/a	Chinese
egipcio/a	Egyptian
español(a)	Spanish
estadounidense	American (United States citizen)
francés/francesa	French
inglés/inglesa	English
ruso/a	Russian
sudafricano/a	South African

PALABRAS SEMEJANTES: afgano/a, americano/a, árabe, argentino/a, canadiense, coreano/a, cubano/a, iraní, iraquí, israelí, italiano/a, japonés/japonesa, mexicano/a, portugués/portuguesa, sirio/a, vietnamita

• **Los idiomas**	Languages
el alemán	German
el chino	Chinese
el español	Spanish
el francés	French
el hebreo	Hebrew
el inglés	English
las lenguas africanas	African languages
el ruso	Russian

PALABRAS SEMEJANTES: el afrikaans, el árabe, el coreano, el italiano, el japonés, el pashto, el portugués, el vietnamita

• Las ciudades — Cities

Londres	London
Moscú	Moscow
Pekín	Beijing

PALABRAS SEMEJANTES: Berlín, Buenos Aires, Los Ángeles, Madrid, Montreal, Río de Janeiro, Roma, Tokio, Toronto

• Los adjetivos — Adjectives

casado/a	married
divorciado/a	divorced
mayor (que)	older (than)
menor (que)	younger (than)
soltero/a	single, unmarried
viudo/a	widowed

• Los verbos — Verbs

hablar	to speak
¿Hablas... ?	Do you speak . . . ?
Hablo...	I speak
quiero	I want
tener	to have
viajar	to travel

• Expresiones útiles — Useful Expressions

¡Cómo cambia el mundo!	How the world changes!
¿Cuántos años tiene(s)?	How old are you?
Tengo... años.	I am . . . years old.
¿Cuántos... tiene(s)?	How many . . . do you have?
¿De quién es/son... ?	Whose is/are . . . ?
nada de	nothing, any (at all)
perdone	pardon me; excuse me

un poco de	a little
¿Qué tiene(n)... ?	What do/does . . . have?
¿Quién(es) tiene(n)... ?	Who has . . . ?

REPASO: mi(s), tu(s), su(s)

• Palabras útiles — Useful Words

a veces	sometimes
la bicicleta	bicycle
bueno...	well . . .
el carro / el coche	car
de la	of the
del (de + el)	of the (*required contraction*)
durante	during
la edad	age
el helado	ice cream
el (la) joven	young person
pero	but
según	according to
sólo	only
la videoteca	video library

PALABRAS SEMEJANTES: el disco compacto, la frase, internacional, la motocicleta, la parte, normalmente, vacaciones

• Los números — Numbers

setenta	seventy
ochenta	eighty
ochenta y cuatro	eighty-four
noventa	ninety
noventa y siete	ninety-seven
cien	one hundred
ciento uno	one-hundred one
ciento diez	one-hundred ten

Coordination of Communication Activities and Grammar Exercises

The communication activities and grammar are only loosely coordinated by theme: to talk about one's family one needs the verb **tener** and the possessive adjectives, so grammar points **C.1** and **C.2** are referenced in the communication activities sections **La familia** and **¿Qué tenemos?** We have not attempted to link every grammar point to a particular activity, however. This practice constrains activities and makes them artificial, and in any case, all the grammar students need will be present in the input provided by teacher-talk, communication activities, and readings, and over time will be acquired through input from these sources.

¿Recuerda?

Many grammar sections have a **¿Recuerda?** note in the margin or within the text that recapitulates a previous rule and directs students back to an earlier grammar entry. Call students' attention to these notes; they are intended to help students as they work at home on grammar assignments.

---

ramática y ejercicios

C.1 Expressing Possession: The Verbs *tener* and *ser de(l)*

Just like English, Spanish has several ways of expressing possession. Unlike English, however, Spanish does not use an apostrophe and *s*.

A. Perhaps the simplest way of expressing possession is to use the verb **tener*** (*to have*). Like the verb **ser, tener** is classified as an irregular verb because of changes in its stem.[†] The endings that attach to the stem, however, are regular.

---

tener = *to have*

English: *'s*
  Mike's new car
  Sarah's friends
Spanish: **de** + person
  el carro nuevo **de Miguel**
  los amigos **de Sara**

de + **el** = **del**
de + **la** remains **de la**

---

tener (to have)		
(yo)	tengo	*I have*
(tú)	tienes	*you (inf. sing.) have*
(usted, él/ella)	tiene	*you (pol. sing.) have; he/she has*
(nosotros/as)	tenemos	*we have*
(vosotros/as)	tenéis	*you (inf. pl., Spain) have*
(ustedes, ellos/as)	tienen	*you (pl.) have; they have*

—Profesora Martínez, ¿**tiene** usted un automóvil nuevo?
—Sí, **tengo** un Toyota verde.

—*Professor Martínez, do you have a new automobile?*
—*Yes, I have a green Toyota.*

B. The verb **ser** (*to be*) followed by the preposition **de** (*of*) can also be used to express possession. The equivalent of the English word *whose* is **¿de quién?** (literally, *of whom?* or *to whom?*).

—¿**De quién es** el cuaderno?

—**Es de** Carmen.

—*To whom does the notebook belong?*
—*It's Carmen's.*

C. The preposition **de** (*of*) followed by the masculine article **el** (*the*) contracts to **del** (*of the*).

—¿**De quién es** el bolígrafo?
—**Es del** profesor.

—*Whose pen is this?*
—*It's the professor's.*

The other combinations of **de** + article do not contract: **de la, de los, de las.**

Los zapatos **de la** niña son nuevos.

The girl's shoes are new.

---

*Recognition: **vos tenés**
[†]See **Gramática C.5** for more information on verb stems.

EJERCICIO 1

Diga qué tienen estas personas. Use las formas del verbo **tener.**

MODELO: Luis *tiene* una bicicleta negra.

1. Pablo _____ una chaqueta negra.
2. Esteban y yo _____ un coche viejo.
3. Mónica, tú no _____ el libro de español, ¿verdad?
4. (Yo) _____ dos lápices y un cuaderno sobre mi pupitre.
5. Nora y Alberto no _____ hijos, ¿verdad?

EJERCICIO 2

Diga de quién son estas cosas.

MODELO: Mónica / bolígrafo → El bolígrafo *es de* Mónica.

1. la profesora Martínez / carro

2. Luis / camisa

3. Nora / perro

4. Esteban / lentes

5. Alberto / saco

6. Carmen / bicicleta

C.2 Expressing Possession: Possessive Adjectives

Possession can be indicated by the following possessive adjectives. The particular adjective you choose depends on the owner, but the adjective itself, like other Spanish adjectives, agrees in number and gender with the word it describes: that is, with the *object owned,* not with the owner.

---

su = *his, her, your, their* (one item)
sus = *his, her, your, their* (multiple items)

Remember that you will acquire much of this material in time as you listen to and read Spanish.

SINGULAR OWNER	PLURAL OWNER
mi *my*	nuestro/a *our*
tu* *your (inf. sing.)*	vuestro/a *your (inf. pl., Spain)*
su *your (pol. sing.), his/her*	su *your (pl.); their*

¿**Mi** hermano? Tiene el pelo negro.	*My brother? He has black hair.*
Nuestro carro nuevo es rojo.	*Our new car is red.*
Nuestra profesora es Adela Martínez.	*Our professor is Adela Martínez.*

SINGULAR POSSESSION (PLURAL POSSESSIONS)	SINGULAR POSSESSION (PLURAL POSSESSIONS)
mi(s) *my*	nuestro(s)/a(s) *our*
tu(s) *your (inf. sing.)*	vuestro(s)/a(s) *your (inf. pl., Spain)*
su(s) *your (pol. sing.), his/her*	su(s) *your (pl.); their*

Mi falda es vieja, pero **mis** zapatos son nuevos.	*My skirt is old, but my shoes are new.*
Clarisa y Marisa tienen una casa grande. **Su** casa es grande.	*Clarisa and Marisa have a big house. Their house is big.*
Raúl, ¿**tus** hermanas son gemelas?	*Raúl, are your sisters twins?*
Clarisa y Marisa tienen dos tías y un tío. **Su** tío se llama Raúl.	*Clarisa and Marisa have two aunts and one uncle. Their uncle's name is Raúl.*

Keep in mind that the pronoun **su(s)** can have various meanings: *your, his, her,* or *their.* The context normally clarifies to whom **su(s)** refers.

Luis no tiene **sus** libros.	*Luis doesn't have his books.*
El señor y la señora Ruiz tienen **su** coche aquí.	*Mr. and Mrs. Ruiz have their car here.*

Generally speaking, use **usted** and **su(s)** when addressing a person by his or her last name.

Señor Saucedo, ¿es **usted** mexicano? ¿Y **sus** padres?	*Mr. Saucedo, are you Mexican? And your parents?*

When using a first name to address someone, use **tú** and **tu(s).**

Raúl, **tu** amiga es inglesa, pero **tú** y **tus** padres son mexicanos, ¿no?	*Raúl, your friend is English, but you and your parents are Mexican, aren't you?*

*****Tú** (with an accent mark) corresponds to *you;* **tu** (without an accent mark) corresponds to *your.*

Checking Answers

A number of the grammar exercises use a fill-in-the-blank format. Since students are unable at this point to produce natural discourse beyond the shortest of utterances while also focusing on accuracy, most of the language is supplied for them. In this way, they need only focus on a small set of discrete forms, but they are exposed to input that is relatively natural and native-sounding. Other grammar exercises ask for answers that call for production of one or two sentences. In such cases, most of the

languages is in the exercise, so that students are required only to make a transformation. Any assigned exercises may be written out and checked by the student using Appendix 4.

Side Bar

Small boxed side bars help students to understand language in the **Ejercicios.**

EJERCICIO 3

Complete estas oraciones con la forma apropiada del adjetivo posesivo: **mi(s), tu(s), su(s)** o **nuestro(s)/a(s).**

MODELO: Estela, ¿dónde están *tus* hijos?

1. Mi novia no tiene _____ libro de matemáticas.
2. El profesor no tiene _____ botas.
3. No tienes _____ reloj, ¿verdad?
4. No tengo _____ zapatos de tenis.
5. No tenemos _____ cuadernos.
6. —Señores Ruiz, ¿dónde están _____ hijas?
   — _____ hijas, Clarisa y Marisa, están en casa.
7. Guillermo no tiene _____ chaqueta.
8. Estela y Ernesto no tienen _____ automóvil todavía.
9. Graciela, _____ ojos son muy bonitos.
10. No tengo _____ bicicleta aquí.

> **los señores Ruiz** = Mr. and Mrs. Ruiz

EJERCICIO 4

Complete los diálogos con la forma apropiada del adjetivo posesivo.

MODELO: RAÚL: ¡Qué inteligente es *tu* amiga!
            ALBERTO: Sí, y ella es idealista, también.

1. RAÚL: Silvia, _____ perro, Sultán, es muy inteligente.
   SILVIA: Gracias, Raúl, pero no es _____ perro. Es de Nacho.

2. CLARA: Pilar, ¿tienen carro _____ padres?
   PILAR: Sí, _____ padres tienen un Seat rojo.

3. JOSÉ: ¿Cómo se llama la novia de Andrés?
   PILAR: _____ novia se llama Ana.

4. ABUELA: Marisa y Clarisa, ¡qué bonitas son _____ faldas! ¿Son nuevas?
   MARISA: Sí, abuelita. Y _____ zapatos son nuevos también.

Possession may also be indicated by the use of possessive pronouns. These pronouns agree in gender and number with the noun they describe; that is, with the item possessed.

¿Es ésta tu blusa?	*Is this one your blouse?*
No, no es **mía;** es **tuya.**	*No, it's not mine; it's yours.*
¿Son de Alfredo estos zapatos?	*Are these shoes Alfredo's?*
Sí, son **suyos.**	*Yes, they are his.*
¿Es de Carmen este libro?	*Is this book Carmen's?*
No, no es **suyo;** es mío.	*No, it's not hers; it's mine.*
¿Son de ustedes estos cuadernos?	*Do these notebooks belong to you (all)?*
Sí, son **nuestros.**	*Yes, they are ours.*

Expansión gramatical

Expansión gramatical, located at the end of the *Cuaderno de actividades,* includes ten additional grammar points for student reference. For example, **Gramática C.2** includes a brief explanation of possessive pronouns with a note to students that more detailed information and exercises are available in the **Expansión gramatical.**

A **Gramática y ejercicios** section may refer students to the **Expansión gramatical** for more detailed information and exercises on a grammatical point related to the grammar just presented.

¿Recuerda?

The **¿Recuerda?** notes remind students of previously presented rules. These notes can be particularly helpful for students who need to review a particular area prior to beginning a new grammar point or to completing an exercise successfully.

For more practice with these pronouns see the **Expansión gramatical 1** in the *Cuaderno de actividades.*

SINGULAR OWNER (SINGULAR AND PLURAL POSSESSIONS)		PLURAL OWNER (SINGULAR AND PLURAL POSSESSIONS)	
mío(s)/mía(s)	mine	nuestro(s)/nuestra(s)	ours
tuyo(s)/tuya(s)	yours (inf. sing.)	vuestro(s)/vuestra(s)	yours (inf. pl., Spain)
suyo(s)/suya(s)	his/hers/yours (pol. sing.)	suyo(s)/suya(s)	theirs/yours (pol. pl.)

C.3 Expressing Age: The Verb *tener*

> English: **I am** 24 (years old). Spanish: **Tengo** 24 (años).

In English, the verb *to be* is used for telling age (*I am 21 years old*), but in Spanish the verb **tener** expresses age. To ask about age, use the question **¿Cuántos años... ?** (*How many years . . . ?*)

—Señora Saucedo, ¿cuántos años tiene usted?
—**Tengo** treinta y cinco (años).

—Mrs. Saucedo, how old are you?
—I'm 35 (years old).

EJERCICIO 5

¿RECUERDA?

In **Gramática C.1** you learned the present-tense forms of the verb **tener.** Review them now, if necessary.

Escriba la edad de estos amigos.

MODELO: Rogelio Varela / 21 › Rogelio Varela *tiene 21 años.*

1. Adriana Bolini / 35
2. Carla Espinosa / 22
3. Rubén Hernández Arenas / 38
4. Susana Yamasaki González / 33
5. doña María Eulalia González de Saucedo / 79

EJERCICIO 6

Escriba la edad de estas personas.

¿RECUERDA?

In **Gramática B.5** you learned that adjectives that end in **-o/-a** have four forms:

rojo (masc. sing.)
roja (fem. sing.)
rojos (masc. pl.)
rojas (fem. pl.)

don Eduardo Alvar (n. 1926)   Estela Saucedo (n. 1971)   Ernestito Saucedo (n. 1998)   Amanda Saucedo (n. 1992)   doña Lola Batini (n. 1964)

C.4 Describing People: Adjectives of Nationality

A. Adjectives of nationality that end in **-o/-a,** just like other adjectives that end in **-o/-a,** have four forms.

53

Spiraling

Since the grammar is generated by the topics, similar grammar points occur several times in different semantic areas. In **Gramática C.4,** gender and number are reentered for a third time (**A.4, B.4,** and **B.5**), this time with adjectives of nationality. In addition, regular **-ar** verbs (**hablar**) are reintroduced (**llevar** was introduced in **A.1**) so that the class may discuss languages spoken in various countries. More complete explanations of regular verbs (**-ar, -er, -ir**) are provided in **Gramática 3.2.**

	SINGULAR	PLURAL
Masculine	chino	chinos
Feminine	china	chinas

Victoria no es **china,** pero habla chino muy bien.   *Victoria is not Chinese, but she speaks Chinese very well.*

B. Adjectives of nationality that end in a consonant have four forms also.

	SINGULAR	PLURAL
Masculine	inglés*	ingleses
Feminine	inglesa	inglesas

John es **inglés,** pero su madre es **española.**   *John is English, but his mother is Spanish.*

C. Adjectives of nationality that end in **-e** have only two forms.

	SINGULAR	PLURAL
Masculine/Feminine	canadiense	canadienses

> Do capitalize names of countries in Spanish:
> **Colombia**
> **Panamá**
> **Inglaterra**
> Do not capitalize nationalities or languages in Spanish:
> **colombiano**
> **panameñas**
> **español**
> **inglés**

D. Adjectives of nationality and the names of languages are not capitalized in Spanish. Names of countries, however, are capitalized.

EJERCICIO 7

¿De qué nacionalidad son estas personas?

MODELO: el señor Shaoyi He → *Es chino.*

1. _____ la señorita Fernández	a. iraní
2. _____ los señores Watanabe	b. chino/china
3. _____ el señor Hartenstein	c. español/española
4. _____ las hermanas Lemieux	d. sirio/siria
5. _____ la señorita Cardinale y la señorita Lomeli	e. inglés/inglesa
	f. italiano/italiana
6. _____ la señorita Tang	g. japonés/japonesa
7. _____ el señor Thatcher	h. alemán/alemana
8. _____ la señorita Nikraz	i. francés/francesa
9. _____ los señores Hassan	

*See the *Cuaderno de actividades*—**Capítulos 2, 3, 5, 8,** and Appendix 3 of this text—for details on written accent marks.

Coordination of Communication Activities and Grammar Exercises

Dos mundos is designed with the flexibility to assign the corresponding grammar before, after, or during the **Actividades de comunicación.** For example, **Gramática C.4** and **C.5** are loosely coordinated with the theme of **Los idiomas y las nacionalidades** of the **Actividades de comunicación** of **Paso C.** Depending on time available in class, instructors may want to review the corresponding grammar exercises before or after finishing the thematic activities. In order to maintain the communicative emphasis of the course, some instructors prefer to answer specific grammar questions outside of class.

Gramática ilustrada

This feature occurs once or more per chapter with grammar concepts that may need more in-depth explanation. You may want to read these captioned scenes aloud to the class before assigning the corresponding grammar point.

---

infinitive = verb form ending in **-ar, -er,** or **-ir**

You will not find the conjugated forms of a verb—**hablo, hablas, habla,** and so forth—as main entries in a dictionary. You must know the infinitive in order to look up a verb.

¿RECUERDA?

In Spanish the forms of a verb change to show who is performing the action. You have already seen the forms of **llevar** (Gramática A.1), **ser** (Gramática A.3), and **tener** (Gramática C.1). Now look at the drawings on this page and notice the forms of the verb **hablar** (*to speak*).

C.5   Talking about Habitual Actions: Present Tense of Regular *-ar* Verbs

A. The verb form listed in the dictionary and in most vocabulary lists is the *infinitive.* In Spanish many infinitives end in **-ar** (**llamar, llevar**), but some end in **-er** (**tener**) or in **-ir** (**vivir**). The forms of the verb are called its *conjugation.* Here is the present-tense conjugation of the regular *-ar* verb **hablar.*** Regular verbs are classified as such because their *stem* (the infinitive minus the ending) remains the same in all forms; the only change is in the endings, which are added to the stem.

hablar (*to speak*)		
(yo)	habl**o**	*I speak*
(tú)	habl**as**	*you (inf. sing.) speak*
(usted, él/ella)	habl**a**	*you (pol. sing.) speak; he/she speaks*
(nosotros/as)	habl**amos**	*we speak*
(vosotros/as)	habl**áis**	*you (inf. pl., Spain) speak*
(ustedes, ellos/as)	habl**an**	*you (pl.) speak; they speak*

B. Remember that Spanish verb endings indicate, in many cases, who or what the subject is, so it is not always necessary to mention the subject explicitly. That is why the pronouns are in parentheses in the preceding table.

—¿**Hablas** español?   —*Do you speak Spanish?*
—Sí, y **hablo** inglés también.   —*Yes, and I speak English too.*

These endings take time to acquire. You can understand and communicate with an incomplete knowledge of them, but they are important; make sure you include them when you write.

---

*Recognition: **vos hablás**

55

EJERCICIO 8

Estamos en una fiesta en casa de Esteban. Complete estas oraciones con la forma correcta del verbo **hablar.**

1. Esteban, las dos chicas rubias _____ alemán, ¿verdad?
2. Mónica, ¿_____ francés tu padre?
3. Alberto y Luis no _____ francés.
4. Nora, ¿_____ tú chino?
5. No, yo no _____ chino, pero _____ un poco de japonés.

EJERCICIO 9

¿Qué idiomas hablan estas personas? Complete cada oración con la forma correcta del verbo **hablar** y el idioma apropiado.

1. Adriana Bolini es argentina y _____ italiano y _____.
2. Los señores Saucedo son mexicanos y _____ _____.
3. Li Yuan Tseng y Mei Chang son chinos y _____ _____.
4. Kevin Browne y Stephen Craig son ingleses. _____ _____.
5. Talia Meir y Behira Sefamí son israelíes. _____ _____.
6. ¿Eres rusa? Entonces, tú _____ _____.

Chapter Opener Pages

As seen in the **Pasos,** the chapter opener features art from the Hispanic world and accompanying artist information in Spanish in **Sobre el artista.** Beginning with **Capítulo 1,** each chapter of *Dos mundos* starts with a two-page opener. The historical timelines are in Spanish starting with this chapter. Although some of the vocabulary may be difficult, many of the words are cognates, and we assume that the instructor will review the timelines with the class, perhaps adding in more information.

Speech Emergence

Keep in mind that students will continue to go through all three stages of language development each time they encounter new material. Having completed **Capítulo 1** does not mean that students are at the speech emergence stage for the rest of their course of study with all language that might be "covered"; ongoing comprehensible input will still be the most effective way to get students to Stage 3. This continuous multilayered process will take somewhat less time in subsequent chapters, because students will have developed good listening skills and will be able to build on the language they have acquired during previous chapters. Nonetheless, it is always important to provide sufficient input before students engage in interactive activities or begin to write.

Capítulo 1

Los datos personales y las actividades

M E T A S

In **Capítulo 1** you will learn to tell time and give personal information: your address, your phone number, and your birthday. You and your classmates will talk about sports and other leisure-time activities you enjoy.

Sobre el artista: Casimiro González nació en La Habana, Cuba. Estudió arte en la Escuela Nacional de Bellas Artes y ahora vive en los Estados Unidos. Sus pinturas, de vivos colores, se exhiben en Francia, Italia, España, México, Colombia, Argentina, Puerto Rico, Alemania y Canadá.

CHA, CHA, CHA, por Casimiro González (Cuba)

Cuba

8000 a.C.
La presencia humana en Cuba se inicia con la primera de varias corrientes migratorias de grupos provenientes de otras partes de las Américas.

1821
Movimiento independentista; sus instigadores son apresados y castigados.

29 de enero: Levantamiento revolucionario
1895

1886
Abolición de la esclavitud

1500   1800

1492 a.C.
Comienza la erradicación de la población indígena.

1511
Llegan los primeros esclavos a Cuba.

1868
10 de octubre, primera Guerra de Independencia (1868–1878), encabezada por Carlos Manuel de Céspedes.

Chapter Opener Page

The right-hand opener page includes three columns designed to orient the student to the chapter themes, readings, and grammar. The Multimedia Resources section orients the students to the technological features of **_Dos mundos:_** the newly designed Online Learning Center, the Interactive CD-ROM, the Video on CD. Beginning with **Capítulo 1** there are animated drawings directing the students to the new animated feature in the **Videoteca: Los amigos animados.** The questions that correspond to this animated segment are located in the **Actividades auditivas** of the *Cuaderno de actividades.* Other **Videoteca** segments include **Escenas culturales** and **Escenas en contexto.** Each includes a list of useful vocabulary and postviewing activities, located at the end of each corresponding chapter of the *Cuaderno de actividades.*

Pre-Text Oral Activities in Stage 3

The Pre-Text Oral Activities continue to be necessary for providing comprehensible input for new semantic areas. In the first Pre-Text Oral Activity of **Capítulo 1,** an Input Association Activity is used to talk about favorite activities and introduce **me/le gusta.** The goal in this Association Activity is to talk about as many activities as possible and for students to remember the activities by associating them with others in the

class. It is our experience that this association of information with particular students facilitates acquisition of new vocabulary and structures and helps the instructor and students get to know one another better. It is also a good way for the instructor to show personal interest in students. If the instructor asks one student to be the secretary and write down all the activities from the board with the name of the corresponding student, the

MULTIMEDIA RESOURCES

Check out the following media resources to complement this chapter of *Dos mundos:*

Online Learning Center
www.mhhe.com/dosmundos6

Interactive CD-ROM

Video on CD
• Los amigos animados
• Escenas culturales: Cuba
• Escenas en contexto

Los amigos animados: Para repasar

Antes de comenzar este capítulo, mire los segmentos animados para repasar los tres pasos.

A. La música en KSUN, Radio Sol. Mayín Durán habla de la música en KSUN, Radio Sol de California.

B. En el parque. Doña Lola y don Anselmo Olivera hablan de las personas en el parque.

En este capítulo...

ACTIVIDADES DE COMUNICACIÓN	LECTURAS Y CULTURA	GRAMÁTICA Y EJERCICIOS
• Las fechas y los cumpleaños	• **Ventanas culturales** Nuestra comunidad: La misión personal de Rigoberta Menchú	1.1 Counting: Numbers 100–1000 and Dates
• Datos personales: El teléfono y la dirección		1.2 Talking about Habitual Actions: Present Tense of Regular **-er** and **-ir** Verbs
• La hora	• **Enlace literario** «El interrogatorio», por Virgilio Piñera	1.3 Asking Questions: Question Formation
• Las actividades favoritas y los deportes	• **Ventanas al pasado** Frida y Diego	1.4 Telling Time: Hours and Minutes
EN RESUMEN	• **Lectura** La pasión por los deportes	1.5 Expressing Likes and Dislikes: **gustar** + Infinitive

1898 25 de abril: Los Estados Unidos (EU) le declaran la guerra a España.
1899 1 de enero (hasta el 20 de mayo 1902): Ocupación estadounidense de Cuba.

1952 Golpe militar encabezado por Fulgencio Batista

1989 Desintegración de la Unión Soviética; años difíciles para Cuba
2003 La ONU condena el embargo estadounidense contra Cuba.

1900

2000

1902 EU establece una base naval en Guantánamo.

1959 Cae el régimen de Batista y triunfa la revolución; Fidel Castro controla la isla.

1961 EU rompe relaciones con Cuba y fracasa en su intento de invadir la Bahía de Cochinos.

1992 y 1996 Las leyes Torricelli y Helms Burton causan crisis económica.

instructor can use that sheet to carry over this activity into the next class session.

To do Input Association Activities, the instructor first finds out information from a few students via Stage 1 and Stage 2 techniques: **¿Qué le gusta hacer a Ryan?** (Skate.) **¿Le gusta patinar? A mí también me gusta patinar. ¿Le gusta patinar en el hielo o en ruedas?** (teacher mimes) **(Hielo.) ¿Dónde patina usted? (Chalet.)**

¿En la pista de patinaje Chalet? (Sí.) As more students volunteer and information is obtained, the instructor then asks the whole class: **¿A quién en la clase le gusta patinar? (Ryan.) Sí, y ¿dónde patina él? (Chalet) Sí, en la pista de patinaje Chalet.** When students need to ask for help with vocabulary, this does not have to be an intrusive process: **¿Le gusta jugar al tenis en su tiempo libre, David? (No.) Entonces, ¿qué le gusta hacer? ¿Le gusta ir al lago a nadar?** (No, drive my car.) **¡Ah, le gusta manejar su carro! ¿Qué marca de carro tiene?** As David mentions what he likes to do, the teacher writes **manejar su carro** on the board. Each day more students and activities are added so that the class will hear considerable recycling of previous vocabulary and receive additional input containing new words and structures.

ctividades de comunicación y lecturas

✳ Las fechas y los cumpleaños

Lea Gramática I.I.

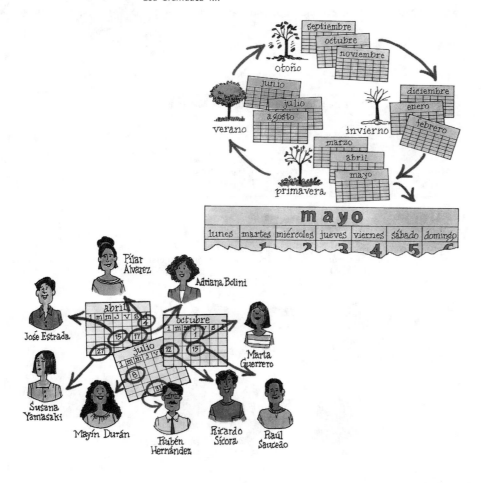

59

Activities for Pair Work

Students should never be restricted to the models that are printed with paired activities, nor to the suggested vocabulary for these activities. If their production ability permits, they should be allowed to ask more questions or supply further information. Each partner should play both roles. Sometimes it is a good idea to have students change partners and do the activity again with a different person; each new partner brings fresh set of tastes and opinions that are interesting to hear. As students get to know more classmates it will be easier to create a sense of community and shared language experiences that enable language acquisition to take place between the four walls of your classroom.

Intercambios (Interactions)

Some **Intercambios** are chart activities; others use art or realia as the basis for input and interaction. Charts (see **Actividad 2**) are an excellent source of material for acquisition activities, since the words for conversational exchanges are already in the chart, and students need to produce very little. Before assigning these activities for partner practice, the instructor should provide language input by talking about the chart, making sure that

students understand all the vocabulary in the chart: **¿Quién es de San Antonio? (Nora.) ¿Quién nació el día 23 de junio de 1987 (Carmen.)** During the follow-up, the instructor expands the activity by including personal information and questions to the class: **¿Dónde nació usted? (Colorado.) ¿En Colorado? ¿En qué cuidad? (Boulder.) Ah, en Boulder, allí hace mucho frío en el invierno, ¿verdad?**

ACTIVIDAD I   Intercambios: El cumpleaños

Hágale preguntas a su compañero/a sobre los dibujos de la página anterior.

MODELOS: E1: ¿Cuándo nació *José Estrada*?
E2: Nació el *15 de abril*.
E1: ¿Quién nació el *15 de octubre*?
E2: *Raúl Saucedo*.

ACTIVIDAD 2   Intercambios: Los estudiantes de la profesora Martínez

MODELO: E1: ¿Quién nació el 19 de agosto de 1988?
E2: Mónica Clark
E1: ¿Dónde nació?
E2: Nació en Ann Arbor, Michigan

Felicidades en tu día
Feliz cumpleaños a mi querido esposo
Virginia

NOMBRE	LUGAR DE NACIMIENTO	FECHA DE NACIMIENTO
Carmen Bradley	Corpus Christi, Texas	23 de junio de 1987
Mónica Clark	Ann Arbor, Michigan	19 de agosto de 1988
Albert Moore	Seattle, Washington	22 de diciembre de 1975
Nora Morales	San Antonio, Texas	4 de julio de 1981
Luis Ventura	Albuquerque, Nuevo México	1 de diciembre de 1985
Lan Vo	Long Beach, California	5 de noviembre de 1986

ACTIVIDAD 3   Intercambios: ¿Qué quieres para tu cumpleaños?

MODELO: E1: ¿Quieres *un reloj* para tu cumpleaños?
E2: Sí, quiero *un reloj*. (No, no quiero *un reloj*, quiero *una mochila*.)

1. un reloj   2. una computadora   3. una bicicleta   4. un reproductor para discos compactos

5. una patineta   6. un suéter   7. unos esquíes   8. entradas para un concierto

In **Actividad 3** the instructor may ask the whole class questions (¿**Cuántos tienen reproductores para discos compactos / un aparato de compact disc?**) to introduce new words from the art. Make sure that students have heard all words pronounced before they are divided up. To expand this interaction the whole class can come up with other items for a "wish list," and the instructor can write these items on the board.

Realia-Based Activities

There are realia-based activities in every chapter of *Dos mundos* starting with **Capítulo 1**. These are based on forms, brochures, advertisements from magazines, and other authentic materials. This first **Del mundo hispano** activity, **Actividad 4**, is a very simple scanning activity with questions for pair work.

9. un coche   10. una mochila   11. una cámara digital

12. un televisor   13. discos compactos   14. un equipo de música

✳ Datos personales: El teléfono y la dirección

Lea Gramática 1.2–1.3.

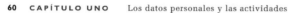

UNIVERSIDAD NACIONAL AUTÓNOMA DE MÉXICO
Nombre: Ignacio Padilla León Dirección: Calle Juárez 528, México, D.F. Teléfono: 5-66-57-42 Fecha de Nacimiento: 26-II-85 Sexo: M   Edo. Civil: soltero Ojos: negros   Pelo: castaño Ciudadanía: mexicana Nº. de Estudiante: 156-87-40-94

UNIVERSIDAD COMPLUTENSE DE MADRID
Nombre: Pilar Álvarez Cárdenas Dirección: Calle Almendras 481, Madrid Teléfono: 4-71-94-55 Fecha de Nacimiento: 4-IV-84 Sexo: F   Edo. Civil: soltera Ojos: castaños Pelo: castaño Ciudadanía: española Nº. de Estudiante: 115-38-95-42

ACTIVIDAD 4   **Del mundo hispano: El pasaporte**

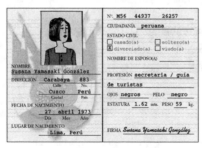

Nº. M56 44937 26257
CIUDADANÍA peruana
ESTADO CIVIL
☐ casado(a)   ☐ soltero(a)
☒ divorciado(a)   ☐ viudo(a)
NOMBRE DE ESPOSO(A)

PROFESIÓN secretaria / guía
de turistas
OJOS negros   PELO negro
ESTATURA 1.62 mts. PESO 59 kg.

NOMBRE
Susana Yamasaki González
DIRECCIÓN Carabaya 883
        Calle   No.
    Cuzco   Perú
    Ciudad   País
FECHA DE NACIMIENTO
    27 abril 1973
    Día   Mes   Año
LUGAR DE NACIMIENTO
    Lima, Perú

FIRMA *Susana Yamasaki González*

1. ¿Cómo se llama la señora?   **2.** ¿Dónde vive?   **3.** ¿En qué mes nació?   **4.** ¿Cuál es su estado civil?   **5.** ¿De qué color tiene los ojos?

61

Readings

The readings in each chapter of *Dos mundos* include author-written texts (**Lecturas** and **Ventanas culturales,** in-depth cultural information about many aspects of the Spanish-speaking world) and **Ventanas al pasado,** cultural information with a historical bent.

Ventanas culturales

These cultural readings are grouped into four categories: **Nuestra comunidad, La vida diaria, Las costumbres,** and **La lengua.** These readings are shorter than most **Lecturas** and are ideal for use as in-class readings. *Instructor's Edition* notes provide background information, and both the **Ventanas culturales** and the **Ventanas al pasado** have a follow-up pair discussion activity, **Ahora... ¡ustedes!** that allows students to explore

personal opinions about the reading selection. **Ventanas culturales: Nuestra comunidad: La misión personal de Rigoberta Menchú** is the first reading in *Dos mundos* and has been selected because of its relatively easy content. Be sure to read aloud slowly while students follow along, stopping frequently to check for comprehension.

VENTANAS CULTURALES   Nuestra comunidad

La misión personal de Rigoberta Menchú

Rigoberta Menchú es de Guatemala, está casada y tiene un hijo. Rigoberta es una mujer maya quiché muy fuerte. Su misión personal es ayudar a la gente indígena de su país y de todo el mundo. Rigoberta viaja mucho. Visita escuelas y universidades para hablar de sus experiencias y para describir la mala situación de los indígenas guatemaltecos.

Esta mujer excepcional recibe el Premio Nóbel de la Paz en 1992. En su libro autobiográfico *Yo, Rigoberta Menchú* (1984), Rigoberta narra una historia muy humana que protesta la violencia militar. La famosa indígena Menchú tiene una meta importante: justicia social para Guatemala y toda la América Latina.

VOCABULARIO ÚTIL

maya	*indigenous*
quiché	*people from western Guatemala*
ayudar	*help*
la gente indígena	*indigenous people*
el Premio Nóbel de la Paz	*the Nobel Peace Prize*
la meta	*goal*

Ahora... ¡ustedes!

¿Qué sabes de tu mejor amigo o amiga? ¿Te gusta su personalidad? ¿Cuáles son sus pasatiempos? ¿Tiene él o ella una misión personal?

ACTIVIDAD 5   Diálogo abierto: Datos personales

E1: ¿Cómo te llamas?
E2: Me llamo _____. ¿Y tú?
E1: _____. ¿Dónde vives?
E2: Vivo en la calle _____, número _____. ¿Y tú?
E1: Vivo en la calle _____, número _____.
E2: ¿Cuál es tu número de teléfono?
E1: Es el _____. ¿Y tú número de teléfono?
E2: Es el _____. ¿Cuál es tu dirección electrónica?
E1: Es _____ @ _____. (No tengo.) ¿Y tu dirección?
E2: Es _____ @ _____. (No tengo.) ¿Tienes (teléfono) celular?
E1: Sí, mi número es el _____. (No, no tengo.) ¿Y tú?
E2: Sí, mi número es el _____. (No, no tengo.)

Reading and Writing

New to this edition is the **Enlace literario** featuring poetry and fiction by well-known Hispanic authors. The **Enlace literario** selection has a creative writing activity, **Actividad creativa,** which may be done in class or assigned as homework. The **Lecturas** have two follow-up activities: **Comprensión** (content questions in various formats) and **Un paso más... ¡a conversar!** (a discussion activity based on the reading or **Un paso más... ¡a escribir!**, a creative writing activity based on the ideas in the reading). **Ahora... ¡usted!** (personal questions to stimulate whole-class discussion), is included for each **Lectura** in the *Expanded Instructor Notes* in this *Instructor's Manual*. The *Instructor's Edition* notes of the main text provide pre-reading suggestions and explain all post-reading activities for the **Lecturas.**

ENLACE LITERARIO[1]

«El interrogatorio», por Virgilio Piñera

Selección de su libro *Un fogonazo* (1987)

Virgilio Piñera (1912–1979) es uno de los escritores más estimados de Cuba. Autor de drama, poesía, cuentos[2] y novelas, Piñera es conocido especialmente por su teatro. Entre sus dramas más populares están *Aire frío* (1959) y *Dos viejos pánicos* (1968). En casi toda la obra[3] de Piñera se nota una preocupación por los aspectos «absurdos» de la vida. El libro *Un fogonazo* incluye once cuentos de varias décadas de la carrera de Piñera (1940–1970). «El interrogatorio» tiene la forma de un diálogo entre dos personajes[4] interesantes: un juez[5] y un hombre acusado de un crimen.

El interrogatorio

¿Cómo se llama?
—Porfirio.
¿Quiénes son sus padres?
—Antonio y Margarita.
¿Dónde nació?
—En América.
¿Qué edad tiene?
—Treinta y tres años.
¿Soltero o casado?
—Soltero.
¿Oficio?[6]
—Albañil.[7]
¿Sabe que se le acusa de haber dado muerte[8] a la hija de su patrona[9]?
—Sí, lo sé.
¿Tiene algo más que declarar?
—Que soy inocente.
El juez mira entonces vagamente al acusado y le dice:
—Usted no se llama Porfirio; usted no tiene padres que se llamen Antonio y Margarita; usted no nació en América; usted no tiene treinta y tres años; usted no es soltero; usted no es albañil; usted no ha dado muerte a la hija de su patrona; usted no es inocente.
—¿Qué soy entonces? —exclama el acusado.
Y el juez, que lo sigue mirando vagamente, le responde:
—Un hombre que cree llamarse[10] Porfirio...

Actividad creativa: Otro interrogatorio

Virgilio Piñera escribe sobre situaciones absurdas y personajes poco comunes. Imagínese esta situación absurda: ¡Usted es el personaje que el juez interroga en el cuento! Si prefiere, puede tener una identidad misteriosa. Use el diálogo de Piñera como modelo y escriba un interrogatorio basado en estas preguntas: ¿Cómo se llama? ¿Quiénes son sus padres? ¿Dónde nació? ¿Qué edad tiene? ¿Es soltero/a o casado/a? ¿Tiene algo que declarar?

[1]*Literary connection or link*   [2]*short stories*   [3]*work*   [4]*characters*   [5]*judge*   [6]*job, profession*   [7]*bricklayer, construction worker*   [8]*haber... having killed*   [9]*boss, employer*   [10]*que... who thinks his name is*

Reading Strategies

For all types of readings, it is important to encourage a global rather than a word-by-word approach concerned with detailed accuracy. We hope students will come to enjoy reading in Spanish for information and for pleasure. This *Instructor's Manual* offers suggestions on teaching strategies that allow students to get the most out of a variety of texts (*Teaching Reading and Writing*). We suggest that the instructor introduce a text by giving a brief summary and then have students skim it in class to get a general idea of what it is about before they read in class or take it home to read. They should be taught that reading a text several times without using a dictionary can enable them to comprehend the main ideas and some supporting detail. When students realize that they can read a great deal of authentic Spanish by making educated guesses based on cognates, similar Spanish words they know, and visuals, they feel successful and often are able to read quite rapidly and with a great deal of pleasure.

Culture and Language

We have included exciting new cultural content in as many areas as possible in *Dos mundos,* including factual information in photo captions, realia-based activities, **¡Ojo!,** brief cultural notes, **Lecturas, Ventanas culturales,** and **Ventanas al pasado.**

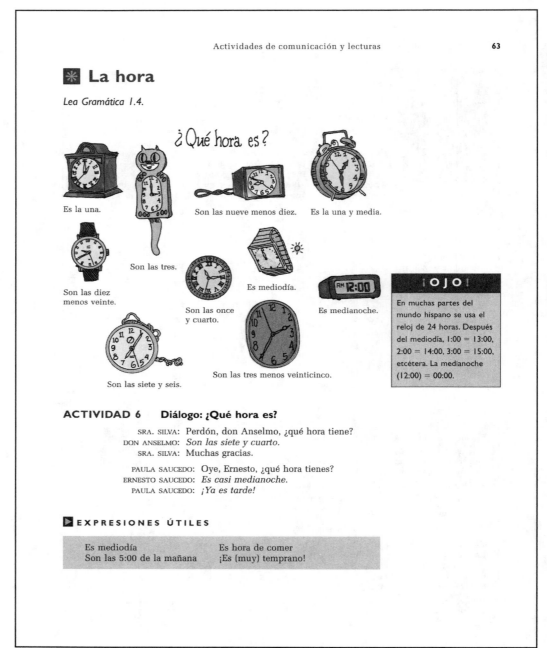

✳ La hora

Lea Gramática 1.4.

¿Qué hora es?

Es la una.

Son las nueve menos diez.

Es la una y media.

Son las tres.

Son las diez menos veinte.

Son las once y cuarto.

Es mediodía.

Es medianoche.

Son las siete y seis.

Son las tres menos veinticinco.

¡OJO!

En muchas partes del mundo hispano se usa el reloj de 24 horas. Después del mediodía, 1:00 = 13:00, 2:00 = 14:00, 3:00 = 15:00, etcétera. La medianoche (12:00) = 00:00.

ACTIVIDAD 6   **Diálogo: ¿Qué hora es?**

SRA. SILVA: Perdón, don Anselmo, ¿qué hora tiene?
DON ANSELMO: *Son las siete y cuarto.*
SRA. SILVA: Muchas gracias.

PAULA SAUCEDO: Oye, Ernesto, ¿qué hora tienes?
ERNESTO SAUCEDO: *Es casi medianoche.*
PAULA SAUCEDO: *¡Ya es tarde!*

▶ **EXPRESIONES ÚTILES**

Es mediodía	Es hora de comer
Son las 5:00 de la mañana	¡Es (muy) temprano!

Del mundo hispano

Realia-based activities contain "real" language, which means that they will almost invariably include unfamiliar structures and vocabulary. Make sure that you allow ample time for scanning realia and for students to ask about unfamiliar vocabulary. Remind students that they do not have to understand every word to participate in the activity. These pieces provide an opportunity to read in class and open the door to cultural discussions. Before introducing **Actividad 8** (textbook pages 64–65), the instructor will want to help students read the **¡Ojo!** on the use of the 24-hour clock in the Hispanic world.

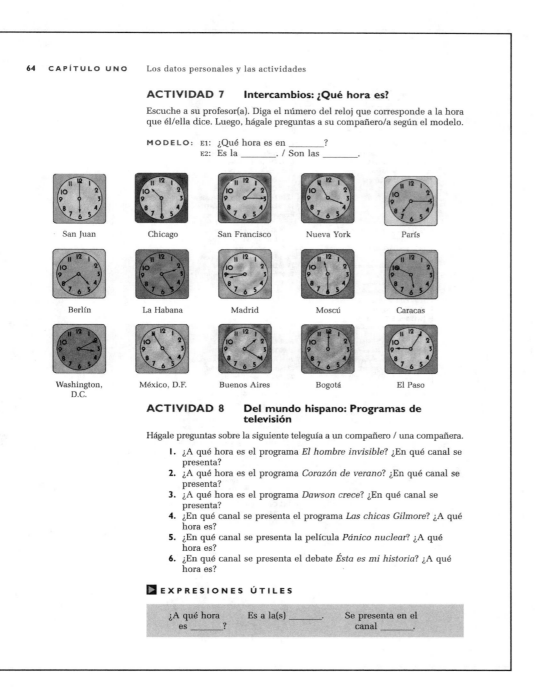

ACTIVIDAD 7   Intercambios: ¿Qué hora es?

Escuche a su profesor(a). Diga el número del reloj que corresponde a la hora que él/ella dice. Luego, hágale preguntas a su compañero/a según el modelo.

MODELO: E1: ¿Qué hora es en _____?
E2: Es la _____. / Son las _____.

San Juan   Chicago   San Francisco   Nueva York   París

Berlín   La Habana   Madrid   Moscú   Caracas

Washington, D.C.   México, D.F.   Buenos Aires   Bogotá   El Paso

ACTIVIDAD 8   Del mundo hispano: Programas de televisión

Hágale preguntas sobre la siguiente teleguía a un compañero / una compañera.

1. ¿A qué hora es el programa *El hombre invisible*? ¿En qué canal se presenta?
2. ¿A qué hora es el programa *Corazón de verano*? ¿En qué canal se presenta?
3. ¿A qué hora es el programa *Dawson crece*? ¿En qué canal se presenta?
4. ¿En qué canal se presenta el programa *Las chicas Gilmore*? ¿A qué hora es?
5. ¿En qué canal se presenta la película *Pánico nuclear*? ¿A qué hora es?
6. ¿En qué canal se presenta el debate *Ésta es mi historia*? ¿A qué hora es?

▶ EXPRESIONES ÚTILES

¿A qué hora es _____?	Es a la(s) _____.	Se presenta en el canal _____.

Jueves, 22 de julio

MAÑANA

06:00 Canal 24 horas Informativo
07:30 Telediario matinal Informativo
10:15 La verdad de Laura Serie
11:00 Por la mañana Magazine.
Con Inés Ballester y Manuel Giménez

07:30 Los Lunnis Infantil. Las aventuras de Emily
y Alexander, Ed, Edd y Eddy, Arthur y Tweenies
09:30 El joven Hércules Serie
10:00 Dawson crece Serie
11:00 Popular Serie
11:00 Ciclismo Tour de Francia
12:00 Los vigilantes de la playa Serie
13:00 Los Lunnis Infantil. Caillou, El patito feo, Los
minimonstruos, Aventuras en pañales y Godzilla

TARDE

13:30 La cocina de Karlos Arguiñano
Gastronomía
14:00 Informativos territoriales
Informativo
14:30 Corazón de verano Magazine.
Con Anne Igartiburu
15:00 Telediario 1 Informativo
15:55 El tiempo Meteorología
16:00 Rebeca Novela
17:15 Ana y los 7 Serie
18:45 Smallville Serie
20:00 Gente Magazine. Con Pepa Bueno

14:15 El rival más débil Concurso
17:30 Los Lunnis Infantil. Las tres mellizas y
Digimon Frontier
19:15 Padres en apuros Divulgativo
19:30 Decogarden Divulgativo
20:00 Informativo territorial Informativo

NOCHE

20:00 Telediario 2 Informativo
21:55 El tiempo Meteorología
22:00 Cuéntame cómo pasó Serie
23:30 Ésta es mi historia Debate.
Con Ana García Lozano
01:30 Telediario 3 Informativo
01:45 Deportes Deportivo
02:00 La economía Informativo
02:15 El hombre invisible Serie
03:00 Canal 24 horas Informativo

20:30 Los Beltrán Serie
21:00 Todo va sobre ruedas Serie
21:30 Academia Eurojunior Concurso
22:00 La 33 Noticias Informativo
22:30 El tiempo Meteorología
22:35 Los campeones de Olimpia Deportivo
23:15 Las chicas Gilmore Serie
00:45 El ala oeste de la Casa Blanca Serie
01:30 Cine Pánico nuclear, con: Morgan Freeman,
Ben Affleck, James Cromwell, Liev Schreiber
(Acción, EU, 2002). Director: Phil Alden
Robinson. Duración: 118 minutos. Tras la muerte
repentina del presidente de Rusia, un hombre
de tendencias políticas prácticamente
desconocidas toma el cargo. El cambio desata
la paranoia entre los oficiales de la CIA y el
director de la CIA recluta a un joven analista.
Entonces sucede lo impensable: un artefacto
nuclear estalla en una ciudad de EU éstos
culpan a los rusos.
03:00 Cultura con Ñ Cultural
03:30 Teledeporte Deportivo
04:30 Euronews Informativo

130 Guía de Ocio

A New Look at Lexical Items

Students have learned to understand a large number of imperative forms as lexical items in TPR activities. Since the focus was on meaning, students were unaware that they were using verbs conjugated in particular patterns. In the last topical section of **Capítulo 1** we present a number of activities (infinitives) following **me gusta.** This permits broader and more sophisticated teacher-student and student-student interactions. In this way students will be able to talk about their own activities and use Spanish to talk about their lives. Since we treat these infinitives as lexical items, it is their categorization as infinitive types that matters.

Characters

Dos mundos has a cast of recurring characters. Most are used in the illustrations from the beginning, but their function begins to become apparent in Stage 3, the speech-emergence stage of language acquisition, as the language becomes richer and more can be said about them. The characters help create a sense of unity for the book and serve as a vehicle for associations. They have physical and personality traits that are useful for expanding discussion at later stages and permit the illustration of many aspects of everyday life in the Hispanic world. A number of the **Actividades** are built around the characters, allowing the instructor to compare their lives and views to those of the members of the class.

Refranes

Beginning with **Capítulo 1,** each chapter includes a **refrán** related to the chapter theme. The instructor may want to read these idiomatic sayings with the entire class and provide for occasional re-entry of all **refranes** introduced.

✳ Las actividades favoritas y los deportes

Lea Gramática 1.5.

Un fin de semana típico de los Saucedo

A Estela le gusta ir de compras.

A Amanda y a Graciela les gusta jugar al tenis.

A Ernesto le gusta leer.

A Guillermo y a sus amigos les gusta jugar al fútbol.

A Ernesto y a Guillermo les gusta ver un partido de béisbol en el estadio.

A Ernestito le gusta andar en bicicleta.

A Amanda le gusta ver su telenovela favorita.

A los Saucedo les gusta cenar en un restaurante italiano.

REFRÁN

No puedes andar y quieres correr.
(*You're biting off more than you can chew. Literally, You can't walk and you want to run.*)

ACTIVIDAD 9   Intercambios: El fin de semana

MODELOS: E1: ¿A quién le gusta *jugar al basquetbol*?
E2: A *Ricardo Sícora.*

E1: ¿Qué le gusta hacer a *Ricardo los sábados*?
E2: Le gusta *ir al cine.*

67

The Organization of the *Actividades*

The communication activities are loosely arranged in order of comprehension and productive difficulty within each thematic section. This permits students to have more exposure to the vocabulary and structures before they truly begin to produce them. **Actividad 9** and **Actividad 10** are typical of activities at the beginning of a section. **Actividad 9** is a chart activity, and students need only supply the information based on a question from their partner.

Preferencias (Affective Activities)

Actividad 10 is a **Preferencias** activity, which means it asks students to make choices. This format is intended mainly for instructor-student interaction. It requires very little production from students and permits the instructor to provide input. The class looks over the activity, and each student decides which choices might be appropriate in his or her case. Then the instructor asks who likes to do the different activities, having students raise their hands, and expands with further input and personalized questions: **¿Le gusta viajar? ¿Adónde? Y a usted, Pilar, ¿le gusta nadar en la piscina? ¿No? Entonces, ¿qué le gusta hacer? Y a mí, ¿qué me gusta hacer? (Cocinar.)**

¿Cocinar? No, no me gusta cocinar, ¡prefiero cenar en un restaurante! Affective Activities produce good information to use in Input Association Activities: **¿Cómo se llama la persona a quien le gusta acampar en las montañas?** These **Preferencias** often have an optional follow-up, **Y tú, ¿qué dices?,** with several comments that students can use as reactions to their partner's statement. Students work in pairs and Student 1

NOMBRE	LOS SÁBADOS LE GUSTA	LOS DOMINGOS LE GUSTA...
Ricardo Sícora, 18 años Caracas, Venezuela	ir al cine	jugar al basquetbol
Adriana Bolini, 35 años Buenos Aires, Argentina	explorar el Internet	jugar al tenis
Raúl Saucedo, 19 años México, D.F., México	salir a bailar	ver un partido de fútbol
Nacho Padilla, 21 años México, D.F., México	ver la televisión	andar en patineta
Carla Espinosa, 22 años San Juan, Puerto Rico	ir de compras	ir a la playa

ACTIVIDAD 10   Preferencias: Los gustos

Exprese su opinión.

1. Durante las vacaciones (no) me gusta...
   a. viajar.
   b. bailar por la noche.
   c. andar en bicicleta.
   d. dormir todo el día.

2. (No) Me gusta...
   a. nadar en una piscina.
   b. acampar.
   c. jugar en la nieve.
   d. patinar en el hielo.

3. Por la noche, a mis padres (no) les gusta...
   a. ver la televisión.
   b. cenar en restaurantes elegantes.
   c. ir a fiestas.
   d. leer el periódico.

4. A mi profesor(a) de español (no) le gusta...
   a. ir a fiestas.
   b. hacer ejercicio.
   c. cocinar.
   d. correr/trotar.

▶ Y TÚ, ¿QUÉ DICES?

¡Qué interesante!	¡No lo creo!
¡Qué divertido!	A mí también.
¡Qué aburrido!	A mí tampoco.

E1: (A mí) No me gusta acampar.
E2: A mí tampoco.

ACTIVIDAD 11   Entrevista: ¿Qué te gusta hacer?

MODELO: E1: ¿Te gusta *viajar*?
E2: Sí, *me gusta mucho* viajar. (No, *no me gusta viajar*.)

1. ver la televisión
2. cenar en restaurantes
3. pescar
4. bailar en discotecas
5. cocinar
6. viajar en carro
7. escuchar música
8. escribir mensajes electrónicos
9. sacar fotos
10. trabajar en el jardín

simply states his or her preference: **Durante las vacaciones me gusta montar en bicicleta.** Student 2 then reacts using one of the comments or one of his or her own choices: **¡Qué divertido! A mí también me gusta.** In later chapters the instructor may want to write comments from previous **Y tú, ¿qué dices?** sections on the board for students to use also. Note that in these and other communication activities, there are no right answers since students talk about their own reality. In Stage 3 activities in subsequent chapters, when students are more advanced, the instructor may ask students why they have particular preferences, how they do things, and so on.

Entrevistas (Interviews)

The interviews, such as the one in **Actividad 11,** are intended for pair work to use **tú** forms, the norm for students talking with one another. This is the first nonguided interview, but it requires only simple **Sí/No me gusta...** answers. Each partner may both ask and answer the questions. This can mean that one student does the complete interview while the partner answers, and then they reverse the process. Some instructors and students feel it is more conversational if the partners do the interview item by item (for example, **Sí, me gusta mucho viajar; y ¿a ti?**). These are completely open-ended questions and should be answered truthfully. Students are invited to explain or expand their answers as they wish. In the early chapters, most interviews can

---

▶ VENTANAS AL PASADO

Frida y Diego

Diego Rivera (1886–1957) es fundador del muralismo mexicano junto con David Alfaro Siqueiros y José Clemente Orozco. Estudia pintura en México y París, donde vive doce años. Muchos de sus murales celebran la victoria sobre los conquistadores españoles y también la Revolución Mexicana. Otros temas frecuentes son las costumbres mexicanas, el obrero, la educación y la historia. Influye en Rivera la escultura de los mayas y los aztecas, pero Rivera combina también el estilo y los colores brillantes del arte popular en sus murales.

Frida Kahlo (1907–1954), esposa de Diego Rivera, es una artista extraordinaria por su persistencia en situaciones difíciles. A la edad de seis años sufre de poliomielitis; a los 18 años sufre un serio accidente en un autobús. Mientras se recupera del accidente, aprende a pintar. En su obra predominan los autorretratos, por razones obvias: las consecuencias de su accidente afectan su movilidad. Los símbolos de Frida son sencillos y revelan sus sufrimientos y su relación con Diego.

VOCABULARIO ÚTIL	
los temas	*themes*
las costumbres	*customs, habits, practices*
el obrero	*worker*
aprende	*learns*
la obra	*work or art*
los autorretratos	*self-portraits*
sencillos	*simple*

Ahora... ¡ustedes!

¿Te gustan las pinturas de Diego Rivera y Frida Kahlo? ¿Qué estilo de arte prefieres? (el primitivista/clásico/neoclásico/realista/surrealista/cubista) ¿Te gusta pintar?

ACTIVIDAD 12   Intercambios: Los Juegos Panamericanos

MODELOS: E1: ¿Qué días hay competición de *baloncesto* (*basquetbol*)?
E2: Del *2 al 6 de agosto y el 8 y el 9 de agosto.*

E1: ¿A qué hora del día son las competiciones de *gimnasia el 2 de agosto?*
E2: *Por la mañana, por la tarde y por la noche.*

(continúa)

be done quite simply. In the later chapters, they begin to include questions that elicit explanation and opinions as answers. The instructor may ask everyone to take notes about his or her partner's answers and, during the follow-up discussion, ask what the partners replied. The instructor should demonstrate interest in the answers and expand on them (for instance, **¿Le gusta cocinar? ¿Qué tipo de comida le gusta preparar?**).

Realia-Based *Intercambios*

Actividad 12 (page 68) and **Actividad 13** (page 69) are typical of activities at the end of a section. Both use realia and will have a fair amount of unfamiliar vocabulary and structures. The two pieces of realia allow the instructor to provide input in the form of a whole-class discussion; the actual interactive task is not difficult, however, and ample guidance for completion is given.

XIII Juegos Deportivos Panamericanos
Agosto 2003
Calendario de competencia
Santo Domingo, República Dominicana

Evento	V 1	S 2	D 3	L 4	M 5	M 6	J 7	V 8	S 9	D 10	L 11	M 12	M 13	J 14	V 15	S 16	D 17
Acto de inauguración	●																
Acuáticos																	
Clavados					●	●	●	●	●								
Natación											●	●	●	●	●	●	●
Polo acuático		●	●	●	●	●	●	●	●	●	●						
Arquería		●	●	●	●	●	●	●	●	●	●						
Atletismo																	
Campo y pista					●	●	●	●	●								
Maratón					●	●		●	●								
Baloncesto		●	●	●	●	●	●		●	●	●						
Béisbol		●	●	●	●	●	●		●	●	●	●					
Boxeo								●	●	●	●	●	●	●	●	●	
Ciclismo										●	●	●	●	●	●		
Fútbol		●	●	●		●	●	●		●		●		●	●	●	
Gimnasia		●	●	●	●	●	●										
Halterofilia											●	●	●	●	●		
Judo										●	●	●	●				
Lucha		●	●	●													
Patinaje											●	●	●				
Pelota vasca			●	●	●	●	●	●	●	●	●	●	●	●			
Tenis				●	●	●	●	●	●	●							
Tenis de mesa						●	●	●	●		●	●	●				
Triatlón										●	●						
Voleibol			●	●	●	●	●	●	●	●		●	●	●	●	●	
Clausura																	●

Leyenda: ● Mañana   ○ Tarde   ● Noche

ACTIVIDAD 13   Del mundo hispano: Escríbanos

Lea la página de la revista *Eres* que aparece en la siguiente página. Hay un grupo de muchachos de México que quieren entablar (tener) correspondencia con otros muchachos. Hágale preguntas a su compañero/a acerca de la información que hay sobre ellos.

MODELOS:
E1: ¿Cuántos años tiene _____?
E2: Tiene _____.
E1: ¿Cuál es el deporte favorito de _____?
E2: Su deporte favorito es el/la _____.
E1: ¿Cuál es el correo electrónico de _____?
E2: Es _____.

E1: ¿Cuál es la dirección de _____?
E2: Su dirección es _____.
E1: ¿Qué le gusta hacer a _____?
E2: Le gusta _____.

Y TÚ ¿QUIÉN ERES?

☸ MIGUEL ÁNGEL OJEDA CEGUEDA
(21 años)
Apdo. Postal 552,
Col. Centro, C.P. 39300, Acapulco, Gro.
correo e.: migan@uol.com.mx
Pasatiempos: ir a la playa, andar en patineta,
jugar al fútbol norteamericano y jugar con la
computadora.

☸ JOSÉ GUADALUPE AYALA
RAMÍREZ (18 años)
Julio V. Plata 74, Héroe de Nacozari, C.P. 07780,
México, D.F.
Pasatiempos: jugar al fútbol, navegar por
Internet y tener amigos por correspondencia.

☸ EFRAÍN MANUEL GALVÁN O.
(20 años)
Motolinía 2317, Centro, Morelia,
C.P. 58000, Mich.
correo e.: emgalvan@correoweb.com.mx
Pasatiempos: ir a los antros, escuchar la música
de Maná, ir al cine, jugar al basquetbol y leer
Eres.

☸ MARÍA CRUZ RODRÍGUEZ P.
(17 años)
Ardilla 341, Col. Benito Juárez, Cd. Neza, C.P.
5700, Edo. De México
Pasatiempos: andar en bici, escuchar la música
de Carlos Vives, ir al cine y leer novelas.

☸ GEMA LETICIA VILLANUEVA R.
(24 años)
Calle Carretera a Tesistán 1051, Col. Arcos de
Zapopán, Zapopán, C.P. 45130, Jal.
correo e.: gemavilla@micorreo.com.mx
Pasatiempos: ir a la piscina, escuchar música,
ver la tele y tener correspondencia con amigos
en inglés o en español.

☸ ANA JAZMÍN PRECIADO
MENDOZA (17 años)
Oriente 176, Col. Moctezuma C.P. 15500,
México, D.F.
correo e.: ajazpreciado@informamex.com.mx
Pasatiempos: escuchar música, en especial
Shakira, bailar en los antros, pasear y tener
amigos.

Abreviaturas:

Apdo. – apartado	C.P. – código postal	Edo. – Estado
Cd. – ciudad	D.F. – Distrito Federal	Gro. – Guerrero
Col. – colonia	e. – electrónico	Jal. – Jalisco
		Mich. – Michoacán

En resumen

De todo un poco

These culminating activities require students to synthesize much of the vocabulary and structures that they have learned in the chapter.

¡Dígalo por escrito!

Starting in **Capítulo 1,** this creative writing feature is part of the **En resumen** section. You will need to help the whole class with unfamiliar vocabulary and make sure that everyone understands the assignment. Students work in pairs or groups for the first part and then complete the writing assignment as homework. **¡Dígalo por escrito!** may be assigned for extra credit.

Cuéntenos usted

This new feature may be prepared at home and done in class. It asks students to tell their own narrative and prompts them with a series of questions. A model is provided and students may either write out their "presentation" or simply make notes. This activity is best done in groups of 3 or 4.

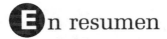n resumen

De todo un poco

La curiosidad
Trabaje con otros estudiantes. Escriban dos o tres preguntas para estas personas famosas o interesantes.

1. el presidente de los Estados Unidos
2. un actor de cine muy guapo
3. una actriz famosa y bonita
4. una mujer muy bonita en una fiesta
5. un hombre muy joven en la clase de español
6. su profesor(a) de español

▶ **PALABRAS ÚTILES**

¿Cuál... ?
¿Cuándo... ?
¿Cuántos... ?
¿Cómo... ?
¿Dónde... ?
¿Por qué... ?
¿Qué... ?
¿Quién... ?

¡Dígalo por escrito!

Descripción de personas

De su revista favorita, seleccione una foto de una o más personas y tráigala a clase. Descríbales la foto a sus compañeros. ¡Use su imaginación!

- ¿Cómo se llama?
- ¿Dónde nació?
- ¿Dónde vive ahora? ¿Con quién(es) vive?
- ¿Cuántos años tiene?
- ¿Cuál es su fecha de nacimiento? ¿su signo del zodíaco?
- ¿Qué idioma(s) habla?
- ¿Cómo es?
- ¿Qué ropa lleva?
- ¿Qué le gusta hacer?
- ¿ ?

Ahora, escriba una descripción de la foto. Incluya la información básica (vea las preguntas de arriba) y otros detalles interesantes/descriptivos.

¡Cuéntenos usted!

Cuéntenos sobre su pariente favorito. ¿Qué relación tiene con usted? (¿es su tío/a, primo/a, abuelo/a... ?) ¿Cómo se llama? ¿Dónde vive? ¿Cuántos años tiene? ¿Cómo es? ¿Qué le gusta hacer en su tiempo libre? ¿Qué les gusta hacer a ustedes juntos?

MODELO: Mi prima es mi pariente favorito. Se llama Isabel y vive en Chicago. Isabel tiene 24 años y es estudiante en la universidad. Es muy inteligente, generosa y optimista. Le gusta mucho montar en bici. Nos gusta ir a museos de arte juntas.

Post-Reading

Many of the post-reading activities of the **Lecturas** can be used for whole-class interaction and teacher input. Some instructors prefer to work through one reading in class and assign others from either *Dos mundos* or the *Cuaderno de actividades.* The **Comprensión** activity can be done individually, in groups, or with the whole class. We suggest you do **Un paso más... (UPM)** on the board with your students first, then assign them to write their own. Students may share their paragraphs in pairs or small groups. Note that some of the **UPM** activities will focus on writing, **¡a escribir!,** and some on conversation, **¡a conversar!** When presented in conversation format, the activity is intended for interaction between you and your class.

PISTAS* PARA LEER

1. Scan title and vocabulary box. What is the main idea of this reading?
2. Now scan text for names of famous Hispanics in sports.
3. Skim the **Lectura** to get the gist of it.
4. As you read, keep these questions in mind: What are the most popular sports in the Hispanic world? Are those sports popular in the United States?

VOCABULARIO ÚTIL

la natación	swimming
el monta-ñismo	mountain climbing
la cancha	court
A propósito	By the way
¡haga el intento!	try!
los extran-jeros	foreign
la Serie Mundial	World Series (baseball)
ayuda	helps
el ciclismo	cycling
el torneo	tournament

LECTURA # La pasión por los deportes

Los hispanos sienten gran pasión por los deportes, ya sea el béisbol, el fútbol o deportes individuales como la natación, el esquí y el montañismo. Esta pasión es una característica esencial de su cultura. Los deportes profesionales son la forma de entretenimiento más popular en España y América Latina y los deportistas famosos tienen muchos admiradores.

El fútbol es el deporte favorito de los argentinos, los uruguayos, los chilenos y los centroamericanos. En muchas ciudades de América Latina es fácil encontrar partidos de fútbol. De hecho, hay lugares públicos que sirven de cancha, como los parques urbanos. Por ejemplo, en el parque La Carolina de Quito, Ecuador, hay partidos de fútbol frecuentemente. A propósito, si usted quiere jugar al fútbol durante sus viajes por América Latina y España, ¡haga el intento! Muchos equipos reciben con entusiasmo a los buenos jugadores extranjeros.

El béisbol también es un deporte muy popular y se juega en los países del Caribe, que son Puerto Rico, Cuba, Venezuela y la República Dominicana. Muchos caribeños miran la Serie Mundial en la televisión o la escuchan en la radio. Es un público muy entusiasta. Hay beisbolistas hispanos de fama internacional, como el dominicano Sammy Sosa y el mexicano Fernando Valenzuela. Sosa es estimado por su talento atlético y su generosidad, pues ayuda mucho a los deportistas jóvenes de su país.

Todas las ciudades grandes de España y América Latina tienen gimnasios donde es posible nadar, levantar pesas y hacer ejercicios aeróbicos. Algunos hispanos prefieren esquiar. En Chile y Argentina hay sitios formidables para practicar el esquí, y los españoles esquían en la Sierra Nevada. Hay además otros deportes que apasionan a los hispanos, como el ciclismo, el baloncesto, el tenis y hasta el rugby. El ciclismo es popular en Colombia, México y España; el baloncesto se asocia con los Estados Unidos, pero también se juega con entusiasmo en México. En Oaxaca, por ejemplo, hay un torneo anual de baloncesto.

Como puede ver, la pasión por las actividades deportivas es un aspecto esencial del carácter hispano y de su cultura.

---

*Pistas means both "clues" and "tracks."

Vocabulario

It is impossible to develop the linguistic flexibility essential for true proficiency at any level without being exposed to a wide vocabulary, and the quantities can overwhelm students. Therefore, we have limited the chapter **Vocabulario** list to the most important new words from only the **Actividades de comunicación.** Remind students that many of these words will recur naturally in conversation and reading in subsequent chapters, and reassure them that you do not expect them to memorize every item for a given chapter.

Comprensión

¿Cierto o falso?

1. El fútbol se practica mucho en Chile y Argentina.
2. Es posible esquiar en los gimnasios.
3. Hay un beisbolista muy famoso en el Caribe.
4. Normalmente, los hispanos no practican deportes individuales.
5. Los mexicanos no tienen interés en el béisbol.
6. El baloncesto es muy popular en Oaxaca, México.
7. Todos los futbolistas hispanos juegan en canchas profesionales.
8. Muchos hispanos esquían en México.

Un paso más... ¡a escribir!

Imagínese que usted es un deportista famoso / una deportista famosa. ¿Cuál es su deporte? ¡Descríbase! Puede incluir una descripción física y también de su personalidad.

MODELO: Me llamo _____ y juego al _____. Soy muy famoso/a. Tengo muchos admiradores. Practico este deporte _____ (frecuencia). Soy _____ (descripción física). ¿Mi personalidad? Soy _____ y _____.

Vocabulario

• **Los meses del año**	Months of the Year	• **Los días de la semana**	Days of the Week
enero	January	**(el) lunes**	Monday
PALABRAS SEMEJANTES: febrero, marzo, abril, mayo, junio, julio, agosto, septiembre, octubre, noviembre, diciembre		**(el) martes**	Tuesday
		(el) miércoles	Wednesday
		(el) jueves	Thursday
		(el) viernes	Friday
• **Las estaciones**	Seasons	**(el) sábado**	Saturday
		(el) domingo	Sunday
la primavera	spring		
el verano	summer	• **¿Cuándo?**	When?
el otoño	fall, autumn	**(ante)ayer**	(day before) yesterday
el invierno	winter	**hoy**	today

Additional Vocabulary

In addition to the chapter vocabulary in the **Vocabulario** sections, the instructor should also point out the Spanish-English glossary at the end of the book, which contains vocabulary from the readings, cultural notes, and authentic materials. Remind students that their vocabulary will increase with continued exposure to spoken and written Spanish. Encourage them to establish friendships with Spanish-speakers at school, at work, or in their neighborhood, and to read Spanish-language newspapers and magazines.

We have also included an English-Spanish glossary of the words from the chapter **Vocabulario** lists. It is available on the *Dos mundos* website; students may access and/or print the files for help when they are doing writing assignments at home.

luego	then, later
(pasado) mañana	(day after) tomorrow
por la mañana/ tarde/noche	in the morning/afternoon (evening)/at night
temprano	early
todo el día	all day (long)

• Los datos personales — Personal Data

la calle	street
la ciudadanía	citizenship
¿Cómo te llamas (tú)?	What is your name?
el correo electrónico	e-mail
¿Cuál es su / tu dirección electrónica?	What is your e-mail (address)?
Es mgomez arroba micorreo puntocom.	It's mgomez@micorreo.com.
¿Cuándo es el día de su / tu cumpleaños?	When is your birthday?
¿Cuándo (Dónde) nació / naciste?	When (Where) were you (was he / she) born?
Nací el (en)...	I was born on (in) . . .
la dirección	address
¿Dónde vive usted (vives tú)?	Where do you live?
Vivo en...	I live in/at . . .
el estado civil	marital status
la fecha (de nacimiento)	date (of birth)
el lugar (de nacimiento)	place (of birth)
el peso	weight

PALABRAS SEMEJANTES: el pasaporte, el sexo
REPASO: el apellido, casado/a, divorciado/a, soltero/a, viudo/a

• La hora — Time; Hour

la medianoche	midnight
el mediodía	noon
¿Qué hora es?	What time is it?
Es la una y media.	It is one-thirty.
Son las nueve menos diez (minutos).	It is ten (minutes) to nine.
¿A qué hora es la película?	What time is the movie?
Es a las 8:30.	It's at 8:30.
Oye, ¿qué hora tienes?	Hey, what time do you have?
Perdón, ¿qué hora tiene?	Excuse me, what time do you have?
y cuarto / menos cuarto	quarter after / quarter till
y media	half past

• Los deportes y los juegos — Sports and Games

el basquetbol (baloncesto)	basketball
el equipo	team
el estadio	stadium
el fútbol (americano)	soccer (football)
jugar (al tenis)	to play (tennis)
nadar (en una piscina)	to swim (in a pool)
el partido	game (in sports), match
patinar (en el hielo)	to skate (on ice)
pescar	to fish
practicar un deporte	to play a sport

PALABRAS SEMEJANTES: el bate, el béisbol, la competición

• Las actividades del tiempo libre — Leisure Time Activities

acampar	to camp (go camping)
andar en bicicleta/ patineta	to ride a bicycle / to skateboard
bailar	to dance
cenar	to dine, have dinner
cocinar	to cook
comer	to eat
correr	to run
dormir	to sleep
escribir mensajes electrónicos	to write e-mail
escuchar (música)	to listen (to music)
explorar el Internet	to surf the Internet
hacer	to do, to make
hacer ejercicio	to exercise
ir	to go
a fiestas	to parties
a la playa	to the beach
al cine	to the movies
de compras	shopping
jugar (en la nieve)	to play (in the snow)
leer el periódico (revistas)	to read the newspaper (magazines)
sacar fotos	to take photos
salir (a bailar)	to go out (dancing)
trabajar en el jardín	to work (in the garden)
ver	to see, to watch
la televisión	television
un partido de...	a game of . . .
una telenovela	a soap opera

Semantic Items

In a few cases, we have chosen to include items in **Gramática y ejercicios** that are not, strictly speaking, grammatical in nature. The sections on Numbers 100–1000 and Dates, **Gramática 1.1,** and the Spanish Alphabet, **A.2,** are examples of such sections. We believe that these particular items are important enough to merit home study and specific practice.

• Palabras y expresiones del texto
Words and Expressions from the Text

Cuéntenos	Tell us (command)
describa(n)	describe (command)
¡Dígalo por escrito!	Say it in writing!
la firma	signature
los gustos	likes
Hágale preguntas a...	Ask . . . questions.
la lectura	reading (n.)
según	according to
seleccione(n)	choose (command)
se presenta	is shown
el refrán	saying
siguiente(s)	next; following
sobre	about
trabaje(n)	work (command)
traiga(n)	bring (command)
vea(n)	see (command)

PALABRAS SEMEJANTES: corresponde, en detalle, incluya(n), la preferencia, use

• Palabras útiles
Useful Words

a, al / a la	to, to the
acerca de	about
aquí	here
casi	almost
las entradas (para un concierto)	tickets (for a concert)
el equipo de música	stereo
los esquíes	skis
el fin de semana	weekend
el/la guía de turistas	tourist guide
navegar (por) el Internet	to surf the Internet
para	for
pero	but

querer	to want
quiero	I want
quieres	you want
el reproductor para discos compactos	CD player
el (teléfono) celular/móvil	cell phone
la teleguía	television guide
el televisor	television set

PALABRAS SEMEJANTES: el actor / la actriz, anterior, asociado/a, básico/a, la cámara digital, el canal, correcto/a, la correspondencia, la curiosidad, el debate, descriptivo/a, la discoteca, elegante, favorito/a, el grupo, hispano/a, la información, panamericano/a, el presidente / la presidenta, la profesión, el programa, la relación, el restaurante, el secretario / la secretaria, típico/a

• Expresiones útiles
Useful Expressions

¿A quién le gusta... ?	Who likes to . . . ?
¡Felicidades!	Congratulations!
¡Feliz cumpleaños!	Happy birthday!
más o menos	more or less
No lo creo.	I don't believe it.
¡Qué aburrido/divertido!	How boring/fun!
¿Qué le/te/les gusta hacer?	What do you (pol. sing. / inf. / pl.) like to do?
Le gusta...	He/She likes (You [pol. sing.] like) (to) . . .
Les gusta...	They / You (pl.) like (to) . . .
Nos gusta...	We like (to) . . .
Te gusta...	You (inf.) like (to) . . .
(No) Me gusta...	I (don't) like (to) . . .
A mí también/tampoco.	I do too . . . / I don't either.
¿Por qué?	Why?
Ya es tarde.	It's late already.
Y tú, ¿qué dices?	And you? What do you say?

Spiraling

Grammar points that are presented in depth in one chapter are often previewed in brief form in an earlier chapter. In **Grámatica 1.2,** for example, we introduce the verbs **leer** and **vivir** as a preview to the more complete present-tense section in **3.2.**

(Recall that a similar brief introduction to **-ar** verbs with **hablar** was made in **C.5.**) Presentation of the verb **vivir** complements the thematic section on **Datos personales,** in which students will often hear the question **¿Dónde vive?**

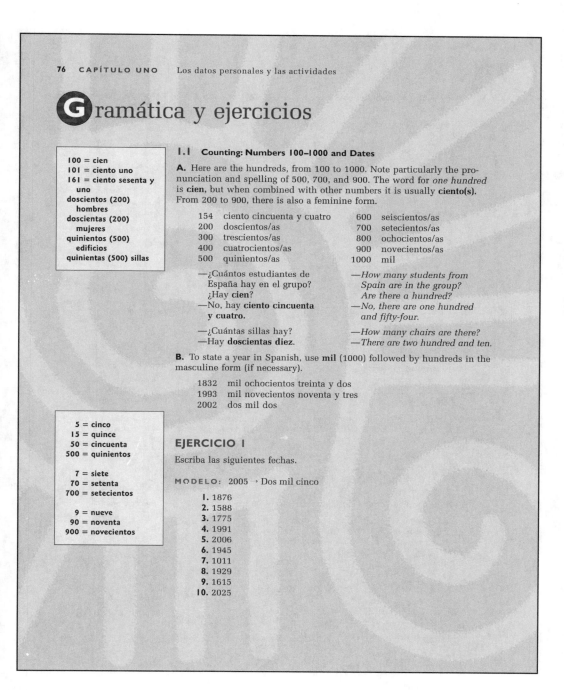

Gramática y ejercicios

100 = cien	
101 = ciento uno	
161 = ciento sesenta y uno	
doscientos (200) hombres	
doscientas (200) mujeres	
quinientos (500) edificios	
quinientas (500) sillas	

1.1 Counting: Numbers 100–1000 and Dates

A. Here are the hundreds, from 100 to 1000. Note particularly the pronunciation and spelling of 500, 700, and 900. The word for *one hundred* is **cien,** but when combined with other numbers it is usually **ciento(s).** From 200 to 900, there is also a feminine form.

154	ciento cincuenta y cuatro	600	seiscientos/as
200	doscientos/as	700	setecientos/as
300	trescientos/as	800	ochocientos/as
400	cuatrocientos/as	900	novecientos/as
500	quinientos/as	1000	mil

—¿Cuántos estudiantes de España hay en el grupo? ¿Hay **cien?**
—No, hay **ciento cincuenta y cuatro.**

—How many students from Spain are in the group? Are there a hundred?
—No, there are one hundred and fifty-four.

—¿Cuántas sillas hay?
—Hay **doscientas diez.**

—How many chairs are there?
—There are two hundred and ten.

B. To state a year in Spanish, use **mil** (1000) followed by hundreds in the masculine form (if necessary).

1832	mil ochocientos treinta y dos
1993	mil novecientos noventa y tres
2002	dos mil dos

5 = cinco	
15 = quince	
50 = cincuenta	
500 = quinientos	
7 = siete	
70 = setenta	
700 = setecientos	
9 = nueve	
90 = noventa	
900 = novecientos	

EJERCICIO 1

Escriba las siguientes fechas.

MODELO: 2005 › Dos mil cinco

1. 1876
2. 1588
3. 1775
4. 1991
5. 2006
6. 1945
7. 1011
8. 1929
9. 1615
10. 2025

¿Recuerda?

Remind students that the **¿Recuerda?** boxes and margin notes are part of the overall presentation of grammar and encourage them to use both of these features as a quick review of the grammar learned to date.

Functional Grammar Titles

Note that all grammar points have a functional title. This lets the student know in which context(s) a particular grammar point would be used.

Gramática y ejercicios   **77**

1.2 Talking about Habitual Actions: Present Tense of Regular -er and -ir Verbs

Following are the present-tense conjugations of the regular **-er** and **-ir** verbs **leer** and **vivir**.*

leer (to read)		
(yo)	**leo**	*I read*
(tú)	**lees**	*you (inf. sing.) read*
(usted, él/ella)	**lee**	*you (pol. sing.) read; he/she reads*
(nosotros/as)	**leemos**	*we read*
(vosotros/as)	**leéis**	*you (inf. pl., Spain) read*
(ustedes, ellos/as)	**leen**	*you (pl.) read; they read*

vivir (to live)		
(yo)	**vivo**	*I live*
(tú)	**vives**	*you (inf. sing.) live*
(usted, él/ella)	**vive**	*you (pol. sing.) live; he/she lives*
(nosotros/as)	**vivimos**	*we live*
(vosotros/as)	**vivís**	*you (inf. pl., Spain) live*
(ustedes, ellos/as)	**viven**	*you (pl.) live; they live*

Remember that, because Spanish verb endings indicate in many cases who or what the subject is, it is not necessary to use subject pronouns in every sentence.

—¿Dónde vives?   —*Where do you live?*
—Vivo en San Juan.   —*I live in San Juan.*

EJERCICIO 2

Complete estas oraciones con la forma correcta del verbo **leer**.

1. Muchos españoles _____ el periódico *El País*.
2. ¿_____ (tú) muchas novelas?
3. Mi amigo _____ la Biblia todos los días.
4. (Yo) _____ libros en español.
5. Profesora, ¿_____ (usted) muchas composiciones?

*For recognition: **vos leés, vivís**

> **¿RECUERDA?**
>
> In **Gramática A.1.** you learned that Spanish verbs change endings, letting you know who is performing the action. You saw these endings for regular **-ar** verbs, like **hablar**, in **Gramática C.5.** The verb form that appears in the dictionary and in most vocabulary lists, however, is the *infinitive*; Spanish infinitives always end in **-ar, -er,** or **-ir.** The endings are added to the *stem* (the infinitive minus **-ar, -er,** or **-ir**).

> It takes time to acquire these endings. As you read, listen, and interact more in Spanish, you will be able to use them with greater accuracy.

> **leer** = *to read*

78

Acquisition of Grammar

Note that by the time **Gramática 1.3** is presented students have heard many questions in your own input and in the **Actividades de comunicación.** Grammar rules often are best learned when the student has already internalized most of the rule through acquisition.

EJERCICIO 3

vivir = to live

Complete estas oraciones con la forma correcta del verbo **vivir.**

1. Pablo _____ en Texas.
2. (Nosotros) No _____ en México.
3. Susana y sus hijos _____ en Perú.
4. ¿_____ (vosotros) en España?
5. (Yo) _____ en los Estados Unidos.
6. ¿_____ (ustedes) en Panamá?

¿RECUERDA?

As you saw in **Gramática C.5** and **1.2,** Spanish verb endings usually indicate who the subject is, so it is generally not necessary to use subject pronouns (**tú, usted, él/ella, nosotros/ as, vosotros/as, ustedes, ellos/as**) in questions.

¿Tienes (tú) teléfono?
¿Dónde vive (ella)?
¿Cómo se llaman (ustedes)?

1.3 Asking Questions: Question Formation

You have already seen and heard many questions in Spanish.

¿Cómo se llama usted?   ¿Es alto Guillermo?
¿Qué hora es?   ¿Habla usted español?
¿Cuándo nació José?   ¿Tienen (ustedes) hijos?
¿Qué tiene Amanda?   ¿Eres (tú) sincera?

A. Statements in Spanish are normally formed by using a subject, then the verb, and then an object and/or description.

Ernestito tiene un perro grande.

subject   verb   object   adjective

Amanda es delgada.

subject   verb   adjective

Negative statements are formed by using a negative immediately before the verb.

Ernestito no tiene un perro grande.
Amanda no es delgada.

¡OJO!

Note that in Spanish no additional words, such as *does* or *do,* are needed to turn a statement into a question.

B. Questions are usually formed by placing the subject after the verb, with the object or any description either following or preceding the subject.*

¿Es joven Esteban?   *Is Esteban young?*
¿Eres trabajadora, Nora?   *Are you (Nora) (a) hard-working (person)?*

¿Tiene hermanos Amanda?   *Does Amanda have brothers and sisters?*

¿Quieres un reloj para el día   *Do you want a watch for your*
de tu cumpleaños?   *birthday?*
¿Nació en abril Pilar?   *Was Pilar born in April?*

---

*Questions with the verb **gustar** are slightly different. The question starts with the verb **gustar** and places the **a** phrase at the end: **¿Le gusta cantar a la profesora Martínez? ¿Les gusta hablar español a los estudiantes? ¿Te gusta bailar a ti?** See **Gramática 8.2** for more information on using these phrases.

To answer a question negatively use **No, no** + verb.

¿Hay gatos en el salón de clase?
No, no hay gatos en el salón de clase.
¿Viven tus padres en Guadalajara?
No, no viven en Guadalajara; viven en Morelia.

C. Another way to ask questions is using interrogative words: **¿Qué?**, **¿Cuándo?**, **¿(De) Quién?**, **¿Dónde?**, **¿Cuántos?**, **¿Cómo?**, **¿Cuál?**, or **¿Por qué?** These words are placed before the verb to create questions.

¿Cuántos hermanos tienes, Guillermo?	*How many brothers (and sisters) do you have, Guillermo?*
¿Dónde vive Susana?	*Where does Susana live?*
¿Cómo está usted hoy?	*How are you today?*
¿Quién es el joven alto?	*Who is the tall young man?*
¿Cuándo nació usted?	*When were you born?*
¿Por qué no hablamos inglés en clase?	*Why don't we speak English in class?*
¿Qué te gusta hacer en tu tiempo libre?	*What do you like to do in your free time?*
¿Cuál es más bonito?	*Which one is prettier?*
¿De quién es este libro?	*Whose book is this?*

> Question words always have a written accent:
> **¿Qué?** = *What?*
> **¿Cuándo?** = *When?*
> **¿Quién(es)?** = *Who?*
> **¿De quién?** = *Whose?*
> **¿Dónde?** = *Where?*
> **¿Cuánto/a/os/as?** = *How much? / How many?*
> **¿Cómo?** = *How?; What?*
> **¿Cuál(es)?** = *Which?; What?*
> **¿Por qué?** = *Why?*

EJERCICIO 4

Cambie las siguientes oraciones por preguntas. Use **¿Cómo?**, **¿Dónde?**, **¿Qué?**, **¿Cuándo?**, **¿Cuantos/as?**

MODELO: Amanda tiene 14 años. →
　　　　　¿Cuántos años tiene Amanda?

1. Rubén Hernández vive en Florida.
2. Susana habla japonés.
3. La clase de español es los lunes y los miércoles.
4. Ernesto y Estela tienen tres hijos.
5. El primer ministro de España se llama José Luis Rodríguez Zapatero.

The Exercises

The grammar exercises are predicated on the expectation that students will already have heard the new forms in teacher-talk, particularly in the Pre-Text Oral Activities, and also in the communicative activities in class. The exercises are generally contextualized in relation to the chapter's theme and, although they require discrete answers, they allow for the processing of meaning. Their purpose is to help students verify that they understood the explanations. Remind students to check their answers with the key in Appendix 4.

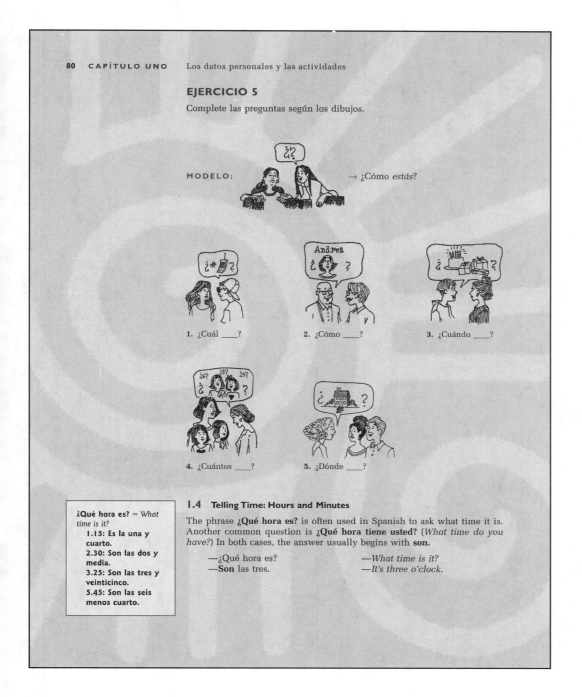

EJERCICIO 5

Complete las preguntas según los dibujos.

MODELO: → ¿Cómo *estás?*

1. ¿Cuál ____?

2. ¿Cómo ____?

3. ¿Cuándo ____?

4. ¿Cuántos ____?

5. ¿Dónde ____?

¿Qué hora es? = *What time is it?*

1.15: Es la una y cuarto.
2.30: Son las dos y media.
3.25: Son las tres y veinticinco.
5.45: Son las seis menos cuarto.

1.4   Telling Time: Hours and Minutes

The phrase **¿Qué hora es?** is often used in Spanish to ask what time it is. Another common question is **¿Qué hora tiene usted?** (*What time do you have?*) In both cases, the answer usually begins with **son.**

—¿Qué hora es?   —What time is it?
—**Son** las tres.   —It's three o'clock.

81

Es (not **son**) is used to tell the time with one o'clock and between one o'clock and two o'clock.

—¿**Es** la una?   —*Is it one o'clock?*
—No, **es** la una y veinte.   —*No, it's one twenty.*

Use **y** (*and*) to express minutes after the hour.

—¿Son las seis **y** diez?   —*Is it ten after six?*
—No, son las seis **y** veinte.   —*No, it's twenty after six.*

Use **menos** (*less*) or **para** (*to, till*) to express minutes before the hour.

Son las siete **menos** veinte.   *It's twenty to seven.* (Literally:
                                                   It's seven less twenty.)

Son veinte **para** las siete.   *It's twenty to (till) seven.*

Use **cuarto** (*quarter*) and **media** (*half*) for fifteen and thirty minutes, respectively.

—¿Qué hora tiene usted?   —*What time do you have?*
—Son las tres y **cuarto** (**media**).   —*It's a quarter after (half past) three.*

Use **a** to express *when* (*at what time*) an event occurs.

a la una   *at one o'clock*
a las cuatro y media   *at four thirty*
Tengo clase **a** las nueve.   *I have class at nine.*
El concierto es **a** las ocho.   *The concert is at eight.*

> **a la una** = *at one o'clock*
> **a las siete menos cuarto** = *at six forty-five / quarter to seven*

EJERCICIO 6

¿Qué hora es?

MODELOS: 2:20 → *Son las dos y veinte.*
           2:40 → *Son las tres menos veinte.*

1. 4:20	**5.** 7:07	**9.** 12:30
2. 6:15	**6.** 5:30	**10.** 5:15
3. 8:13	**7.** 3:00	
4. 1:10	**8.** 1:49	

EJERCICIO 7

¿A qué hora es... ?

MODELO: ¿A qué hora es el concierto? (8:30) → El concierto es a las ocho y media.

1. ¿A qué hora es la clase de español? (11:00)
2. ¿A qué hora es el baile? (9:30)
3. ¿A qué hora es la conferencia? (10:00)
4. ¿A qué hora es la clase de álgebra? (1:00)
5. ¿A qué hora es la fiesta del Club Internacional? (7:30)

Presentation of Grammar

Since we approach grammar in terms of functional usage, we frequently deviate from traditional presentations. Here in **Gramática 1.5** we present the verb **gustar** with **me/te/le/nos/os/les.**

There is no mention made at this point of indirect object pronouns or of the other verbs that take them; the goal here is only for students to be able to use **gustar** with pronouns to express likes and dislikes.

1.5   Expressing Likes and Dislikes: *gustar* + Infinitive

> **Gustar** is used to express likes and dislikes.
>
> **Me gusta bailar.** (*I like to dance.*)

> **¿Te gusta patinar?** (*Do you like to skate?*)
> **A Ernestito le gusta jugar al fútbol.**
> (*Ernestito likes to play soccer.*)
> **A Estela y a Ernesto les gusta ir al cine.**
> (*Estela and Ernesto like to go to the movies.*)
> **Nos gusta cocinar.**
> (*We like to cook.*)

A. The Spanish verb **gustar** expresses the meaning of English *to like.* From a grammatical point of view, however, it is similar to the English expression *to be pleasing to someone.**

Me gusta leer.	*I like to read.* (*Reading is pleasing to me.*)

Gustar is usually used with pronouns that tell *to whom* something is pleasing. Here are the pronoun forms.[†]

SINGULAR		PLURAL	
me	*to me*	nos	*to us*
te	*to you (inf. sing.)*	os	*to you (inf. pl., Spain)*
le	*to you (pol. sing.); to him/her*	les	*to you (pl.); to them*

—¿Qué **te** gusta hacer?	—*What do you like to do?*
—**Me** gusta aprender cosas nuevas.	—*I like to learn new things.*
—¿Qué **les** gusta hacer?	—*What do you like to do?*
—**Nos** gusta cocinar.	—*We like to cook.*

B. Since **le gusta** can refer to *you* (*pol. sing.*), *him,* or *her,* and **les gusta** can refer to *you* (*pl.*) or *them,* Spanish speakers often expand the sentence to be more specific. They use phrases with **a** (*to*), such as **a mi papá** (*to my father*), **a Juan** (*to Juan*), or **a los estudiantes** (*to the students*), in addition to using the pronoun **le** or **les.**[‡]

A Carmen le gusta cantar.	*Carmen likes to sing.*
—¿**A usted le** gusta lavar su carro?	—*Do you like to wash your car?*
—No, no **me** gusta.	—*No, I don't like to.*
—¿**Les** gusta acampar **a Guillermo y a Ernestito?**	—*Do Guillermo and Ernestito like to go camping?*
—Sí, **les** gusta mucho.	—*Yes, they like to very much.*

---

*You will learn more about the verb **gustar** and similar verbs in **Gramática 8.2.**
[†]Recognition: **(A vos) Te gusta**
[‡]You will learn more about phrases with **a, le,** and **les** in **Gramática 7.4, 8.2, 10.5, 13.4,** and **13.5.**

C. The verb form that follows **gustar** is an infinitive, such as **hablar** (*to speak*), **leer** (*to read*), or **vivir** (*to live*).

PRONOUN	+	*gusta*	+	INFINITIVE
me				estudiar (*to study*)
te				jugar (*to play*)
le				comer (*to eat*)
nos	+	gusta	+	correr (*to run*)
os				competir (*to compete*)
les				escribir (*to write*)

EJERCICIO 8

¿Qué les gusta hacer a Ernestito y a Guillermo? Complete los diálogos con **me, te, les** o **nos.**

MODELO: AMANDA: Graciela, *¿te* gusta bailar?
              GRACIELA: Sí, *me* gusta mucho bailar.

1.   MAESTRA: Ernestito, ¿_____ gusta andar en bicicleta?
       ERNESTITO: Sí, _____ gusta mucho. Tengo una bici nueva.

2. ERNESTITO: Guillermo, ¿_____ gusta jugar al béisbol?
      GUILLERMO: No, pero _____ gusta jugar al fútbol.

3.   PEDRO: Ernestito y Guillermo, ¿_____ gusta escuchar la música rock?
      LOS CHICOS: ¡Claro que sí! _____ gusta mucho.

EJERCICIO 9

¿Qué le(s) gusta hacer a las siguientes personas?

1. A Ernestito _____ gusta _____.
2. A Estela (la madre de Ernestito) no _____ gusta _____.
3. A Clarisa y a Marisa (las primas de Ernestito) _____ gusta _____.
4. A Ernestito _____ gusta _____.
5. Al perro _____ gusta _____.

SCOPE AND SEQUENCE

Paso A   La clase y los estudiantes

Los nombres de los compañeros
   de clase
¿Quién es?
Los colores y la ropa
Los números (0–39)
Los mandatos en la clase
Los saludos

A.1 Naming and Describing: The Verbs **llamarse** and **llevar**
A.2 Spelling: The Spanish Alphabet
A.3 Identifying People and Things: Subject Pronouns and the Verb **ser**
A.4 Identifying People and Things: Gender
A.5 Responding to Instructions: Commands

Paso B   Las descripciones

Hablando con otros
Las cosas en el salón de clase
Los números 40–69
El cuerpo humano
La descripción de las personas

B.1 Addressing Others: Informal and Polite *you* (**tu/usted**)
B.2 Expressing existence: **hay**
B.3 Describing People and Things: Negation
B.4 Identifying People and Things: Plural Forms
B.5 Describing People and Things: Adjective-Noun Agreement and Placement of Adjectives

Paso C   Mi familia y mis amigos

La familia
¿Qué tenemos?
Los números (10–100) y la edad
Los idiomas y las nacionalidades

C.1 Expressing Possession: The Verbs: **tener** and **ser de (l)**
C.2 Expressing Possession: Possessive Adjectives
C.3 Expressing Age: The Verb: **tener**
C.4 Describing People: Adjectives of Nationality
C.5 Talking about Habitual Actions: Present Tense of Regular **-ar** Verbs

Capítulo 1   Los datos personales y las actividades

Las fechas y los cumpleaños
Datos personales: El teléfono y la
   dirección
La hora
Las actividades favoritas y los deportes

1.1 Counting: Numbers 100–1000 and Dates
1.2 Talking about Habitual Actions: Present Tense of Regular **-er** and **-ir** Verbs
1.3 Asking Questions: Question Formation
1.4 Telling Time: Hours and Minutes
1.5 Expressing Likes and Dislikes: **gustar** + Infinitive

Capítulo 2   Mis planes y preferencias

Los planes
Las clases
Las preferencias y los deseos
El tiempo

2.1 Expressing Future Plans: **ir** + **a** + Infinitive
2.2 Sequencing: Ordinal Adjectives
2.3 Stating Preferences and Desires: **preferir** and **querer** + Infinitive
2.4 Describing the Weather: Common Expressions
2.5 Pointing Out People and Objects: Demonstrative Adjectives

Capítulo 3   Los lugares y las actividades

Los lugares

Las actividades diarias

Las tres comidas

¿De dónde es usted?

3.1 Talking about Location: **estar** (+ **en**) and **ir** + **a(l)**

3.2 Talking about Habitual Actions: Present Tense of Regular Verbs

3.3 Using Irregular Verbs: **hacer, salir, jugar**

3.4 Asking and Answering Questions

3.5 Describing Origin and Location: **ser de/estar en**

Capítulo 4   La vida diaria y los días feriados

Los días feriados y las celebraciones

La rutina diaria

Los estados físicos y anímicos

4.1 Discussing Habitual Actions: Verbs with Stem-Vowel Changes (**ie, ue**) in the Present Tense

4.2 Discussing Habitual Actions: Irregular Verbs

4.3 Describing Daily Routine: Reflexives

4.4 Ordering Events: Infinitives After Prepositions

4.5 Describing States: **estar** + Adjective and **tener** + Noun

Capítulo 5   Las clases y el trabajo

Las actividades de la clase de español

Las habilidades

Las carreras y las actividades del trabajo

Las actividades futuras

5.1 Indicating to Whom Something Is Said: Indirect Object Pronouns with Verbs of Informing

5.2 Expressing Abilities: **saber** and **poder** + Infinitive

5.3 Referring to Actions in Progress: Present Progressive

5.4 Expressing Obligation and Duty: **tener que, deber, necesitar, hay que, es necesario**

5.5 Expressing Plans and Desires: **pensar, quisiera, me gustaría, tener ganas de**

Capítulo 6   La residencia

El vecindario y la casa

Las actividades en casa

Las actividades con amigos

Las presentaciones

6.1 Making Comparisons of Inequality: **más/menos**

6.2 Making Comparisons of Equality: **tan/tanto**

6.3 Talking about Past Actions: Preterite Tense of Regular Verbs (Part 1)

6.4 Knowing People, Places and Facts: **conocer** and **saber**

6.5 Referring to People Already Mentioned: Personal Direct Object Pronouns

Capítulo 7   Hablando del pasado

Mis experiencias

Las experiencias con los demás

Hablando del pasado

7.1 Talking about Past Actions: The Preterite of Regular Verbs (Part 2)

7.2 Relating Past Events (Part 1): Verbs with Irregular Preterite Forms

7.3 More about Relating Past Events (Part 2): Stem-Changing Verbs in the Preterite

7.4 Reporting the Past: Indirect Object Pronouns with **decir**

7.5 Expressing *ago:* **hacer** + Time

Capítulo 8   La comida

Las comidas, las bebidas y la nutrición
La compra y la preparación de la
   comida
Los restaurantes

8.1 Referring to Objects Already Mentioned: Impersonal Direct Object Pronouns: **lo, la, los,** and **las**

8.2 More about Expressing Likes: The Verbs **gustar** and **encantar**

8.3 Making Negative Statements and Questions: *No, never*

8.4 Expressing *one* or *you:* The Impersonal **se**

8.5 Using Stem-Changing Verbs like **pedir** and **servir:** Present Tense and Preterite Forms

Capítulo 9   La niñez y la juventud

La familia y los parientes
La niñez
La juventud

9.1 Describing Family Relationships: The Reciprocal Reflexive Verbs: **parecerse** and **llevarse bien**

9.2 Expressing *for, from, to whom:* Prepositions + Pronouns

9.3 Saying What You Used to Do: The Imperfect Tense

9.4 Describing the Past: The Imperfect and Preterite of "State" Verbs

9.5 Saying What You Were Going to Do: The Imperfect of **ir** + **a** + Infinitive

Capítulo 10   Nuestro planeta

La geografía y el clima
Los medios de transporte
La ecología y el medio ambiente

10.1 Saying What You Have Done: The Present Perfect

10.2 Exclaming: **¡Qué... !, ¡Cuánto/a/os/as... !**

10.3 Expressing *by, through,* Destination, and Time: **por** and **para** (Part 1)

10.4 Describing Actions: Adverbs

10.5 Expressing Reactions: More Verbs like **gustar**

Capítulo 11   De viaje

Los viajes en automóvil
En busca de sitios
Los planes de viaje
Los sitios turísticos

11.1 Giving Instructions: Polite Commands

11.2 Softening Commands (Part 1), The Present Subjunctive Following **querer**

11.3 Expressing Indefinite Future and Present Subjunctive of Irregular Verbs

11.4 Talking About Past Actions in Progress: Imperfect Progressive

11.5 Saying What Was Happening: The Imperfect in Contrast to the Preterite

Capítulo 12   La salud y las emergencias

El cuerpo humano y la salud
Las enfermedades y su tratamiento
Las visitas al médico, a la farmacia y
   al hospital
Los accidentes y las emergencias

12.1 Expressing Existence: **haber**

12.2 Expressing Changes in States: *become, get*

12.3 Making Requests: Indirect Object Pronouns with Commands and the Present Subjunctive

12.4 Relating Unplanned Occurrences: **se**

12.5 Narrating Past Experiences: The Present Perfect, Imperfect and Preterite

Capítulo 13   De compras

Capítulo 14   La familia y los consejos

Capítulo 15   El porvenir

USING *DOS MUNDOS* IN QUARTER AND SEMESTER SYSTEMS

The materials in ***Dos mundos*** provide the basis for a full academic year, or three semesters (30–45 weeks) at the college level. Approximately four hours should be spent on each of the **Pasos**. Each regular chapter can be presented in eight to twelve hours, depending on content and pace. For courses that meet five hours per week, this will still allow for supplementary activities and periodic testing. Do not hesitate to teach the last four chapters in the text (**Capítulos 12–15**) in second-year Spanish. If your beginning language course meets three hours per week, you may need to reserve the last seven chapters (**Capítulos 9–15**) for second year.

The ***Dos mundos*** package may be used in different academic calendars. The amount of material presented should be adjusted, however. We provide schedules for two distinct course paces: standard and intensive. The intensive pace will be followed by many Spanish programs at large universities where many Spanish students are false beginners or have had many years of another foreign language and can acquire new foreign-language material rapidly. The standard pace may be more appropriate if you have large numbers of rank beginners and/or you plan to do many supplementary activities, either your own or those from the *Instructor's Resource Kit.* The following chart shows suggested schedules.

Standard Pace	Intensive Pace
1. Semester system (150 hours of instruction, 5 hours per week, 30 weeks) Semester 1: **Pasos A–C, Capítulos 1–5** Semester 2: **Capítulos 6 –11** **Capítulos 12–15** reserved for second year	1. Semester system (150 hours of instruction, 5 hours per week, 30 weeks) Semester 1: **Pasos A–C, Capítulos 1–7** Semester 2: **Capítulos 8–15**
2. Quarter (trimester) system (150 hours of instruction, 5 hours per week, 30 weeks) Quarter 1: **Pasos A–C, Capítulos 1–3** Quarter 2: **Capítulos 4–7** Quarter 3: **Capítulos 8–11** **Capítulos 12–15** reserved for second year	2. Quarter (trimester) system (150 hours of instruction, 5 hours per week, 30 weeks) Quarter 1: **Pasos A–C, Capítulos 1–5** Quarter 2: **Capítulos 6–11** Quarter 3: **Capítulos 12–15**
3. Semester system (120 hours of instruction, 4 hours per week, 30 weeks) Semester 1: **Pasos A–C, Capítulos 1–4** Semester 2: **Capítulos 5–10** **Capítulos 11–15** reserved for second year	3. Semester system (120 hours of instruction, 4 hours per week, 30 weeks) Semester 1: **Pasos A–C, Capítulos 1–5** Semester 2: **Capítulos 6–11** **Capítulos 12–15** reserved for second year
4. Quarter (trimester) system (120 hours of instruction, 4 hours per week, 30 weeks) Quarter 1: **Pasos A–C, Capítulos 1–2** Quarter 2: **Capítulos 3–6** Quarter 3: **Capítulos 7–10** **Capítulos 11–15** reserved for second year	4. Quarter (trimester) system (120 hours of instruction, 4 hours per week, 30 weeks) Quarter 1: **Pasos A–C, Capítulos 1–3** Quarter 2: **Capítulos 4–7** Quarter 3: **Capítulos 8–11** **Capítulos 12–15** reserved for second year
5. Semester system (90 hours of instruction, 3 hours per week, 30 weeks) Semester 1: **Pasos A–C, Capítulos 1–3** Semester 2: **Capítulos 4–8** **Capítulos 9–15** reserved for second year	5. Semester system (90 hours of instruction, 3 hours per week, 30 weeks) Semester 1: **Pasos A–C, Capítulos 1–4** Semester 2: **Capítulos 5–10** **Capítulos 11–15** reserved for second year
6. Quarter (trimester) system (90 hours of instruction, 3 hours per week, 30 weeks) Quarter 1: **Pasos A–C, Capítulo 1** Quarter 2: **Capítulos 2–5** Quarter 3: **Capítulos 6–8** **Capítulos 9–15** reserved for second year	6. Quarter (trimester) system (90 hours of instruction, 3 hours per week, 30 weeks) Quarter 1: **Pasos A–C, Capítulos 1–2** Quarter 2: **Capítulos 3–6** Quarter 3: **Capítulos 7–10** **Capítulos 11–15** reserved for second year

INTRODUCTION

This *Instructor's Manual* and the annotations (Instructor's Notes) in the *Instructor's Edition* were written to help you use **Dos mundos** most effectively. **Dos mundos** is designed for a course in which the students, by interacting with you and with each other, develop the ability to communicate their thoughts and ideas in spoken and written Spanish.

In this manual we describe each component of **Dos mundos** and suggest how and when to use a specific type of activity or exercise. We firmly believe, however, that the ultimate success of the course and of the students depends on the instructor. Although these materials are provided to facilitate your efforts in creating communicative experiences for your students, the materials alone will not create the experience; only you and your students, interacting in natural, relatively spontaneous interchanges, can do that. You will decide how to weave these activities and materials into a coherent and natural learning experience that ultimately will result in communicative proficiency in Spanish. We will not give lesson plans per se but will propose suggestions and guidelines. In most cases the oral and written activities are to be used as starting points for communication. We hope that the materials will not confine you but rather that you will feel free to interact with your students in the sorts of communication activities that are the basis of second language acquisition.

The Materials

There are two students texts: **Dos mundos** (the main text) and the **Cuaderno de actividades** (Workbook/ Laboratory Manual). In both the main text and the **Cuaderno** there are three preliminary chapters (**Pasos A, B** and **C**) and fifteen regular chapters (**Capítulos 1–15**). Each chapter of the main text contains three sections: the communication activities (**Actividades de comunicación**) with the readings (**Lecturas**), the chapter vocabulary (**Vocabulario**), and the grammar and exercises (**Gramática y ejercicios**). The **Actividades de comunicación y lecturas** are the main focus of the course; they consist of suggestions for oral communication activities for the classroom as well as various kinds of cultural readings that offer more oral interaction and creative writing possibilities. The **Vocabulario** is a reference list that contains the most useful new vocabulary introduced in the **Actividades de comunicación**. The **Gramática y ejercicios** section includes explanations of grammar and word usage, followed by short verification exercises.

Each chapter of the **Cuaderno de actividades,** which is perforated for easy removal of homework exercises, consists of writing activities (**Actividades escritas**), coordinated with the **Gramática** of the main text, a cultural summary activity (**Resumen cultural**) and listening comprehension activities (**Actividades auditivas**). Both the **Actividades escritas** and the **Actividades auditivas** are organized thematically to correspond with the topics of the main text. The **Actividades auditivas** begin with **Los amigos animados,** two animated review selections that appear on the Video, Interactive CD-ROM, Online Learning Center, and also recorded on the audio CDs. These are followed by the recorded thematic segments (conversations, ads, short narratives). In addition to the listening comprehension activities, there are pronunciation exercises (**Ejercicios de pronunciación**), spelling and writing exercises (**Ejercicios de ortografía**), video activities (**Videoteca**), and more readings (**Lecturas**). The **Actividades auditivas, Ejercicios de pronunciación,** and **Ejercicios de ortografía** are used in conjunction with the audio program. Also available is a set of master audio CDs and a complete answer key that contains the answers to the **Actividades escritas,** the **Resumen cultural,** the **Actividades auditivas,** and the **Ejercicios de ortografía,** as well as to the **Comprensión** questions that follow some of the **Lecturas.** The **Dos mundos** package is also accompanied by the *Instructor's Resource Kit* of supplementary activities, a complete *Testing Program,* an interactive CD-ROM program and a **Dos mundos** specific website with activities and links: **www.mhhe.com/dosmundos6.**

The following section discusses second language acquisition theory and the methodological principles that underlie these materials. The remaining sections examine each component of the **Dos mundos** program in more detail and finally provide a chapter by chapter section of expanded Instructor Notes, giving specific suggestions for using the materials in class.

Learning a Second Language

The context of foreign-language instruction in the United States is quite different from that of most of the rest of the world and is even quite different from the situation in Canada. Beginning language students in the United States may choose from among Spanish, French, German, Japanese, Chinese, Italian, Russian, and Arabic. Their decision is usually based on interest in the language because it is widely spoken in the area where they live or where they will travel. By and large, however, it is impossible for students in the United States to determine what language will be of most use to them in the future. This is not true for language students in most other countries. English is the preferred language of study elsewhere because of its usefulness in work, study, and travel.

Taking these facts into consideration, we believe that it is important for students to learn to acquire a language, since it is likely that they will have the opportunity or be obligated to repeat the process with a different language later in their lives. We want then to understand the language-acquisition process and, to that end, we usually conduct an in-class discussion on how humans acquire their first language. Useful areas for discussion include parent talk, baby babbling, comprehension preceding production, one-word stage, early sentences, and error correction. Most of all, we want students to enjoy the process of second-language acquisition. At the end of a Spanish course using *Dos mundos* we want our students to say, "Learning Spanish was great! I really think I could learn another language if I needed to."

The specific techniques that we will recommend in this *Instructor's Manual* are based on our view of the processes involved in classroom acquisition of a second language. Our views have been shaped by research in linguistics, psychology and psycholinguistics, particularly work in first-and second-language acquisition, and by learning theory in general. They are tempered by our years of experience in studying and teaching languages.

Language Proficiency

The central theoretical question in language is what it means to have acquired a second language. To define the product of first-language acquisition is not difficult. For most people, first-language acquisition results in the ability to comprehend and to speak their native language.

Native speakers understand input from a wide variety of sources and under a multitude of conditions, but they cannot understand everything. Sometimes a different accent throws them off, or they are unfamiliar with certain words or subjects. By and large, however, an educated native speaker can understand ordinary conversation, academic lectures, language in cognitively demanding tasks, and dialogue in a movie or news broadcast.

Native speakers can understand more language than they can produce. For the most part, however, native speakers speak their language well enough to satisfy their daily communicative needs. They can tell a story, argue, convince, promise, explain, and accomplish a variety of functions and tasks in their native language.

Educated speakers also learn to read and write their native language, but there is a great deal of variability in their level of proficiency. How well people read and write depends on how much they read, which in turn depends on their exposure to books and print.

However we define proficiency in a second language, it is clear that we cannot base our expectations of our students on the level of proficiency of a native speaker. Very few people who begin their study of a second language after the age of sixteen ever reach that level. We *can* expect students to be able to communicate their ideas and needs to a native speaker and to understand the native speaker's responses without undue stress in the conversation because of a lack of language abilities. We want students' accents to be comprehensible and free of the distortions that prevent native speakers from understanding. We expect that their range of vocabulary will be wide enough so that they will not feel restricted in their conversational topics. Although we do not expect their grammar to be perfect, it should be functional at the level of their communicative needs.

The goal of second-language acquisition in a course using *Dos mundos* is proficiency in Spanish. In terms of the ACTFL oral proficiency scale, students who complete *Dos mundos* (approximately 150 class instructional hours) are usually in the Intermediate range. Some slower students are Intermediate-Low, but most are Intermediate-Mid, and some very good students are Intermediate-High. In addition to achieving a certain level of proficiency, we feel that it is important to lay a good foundation for continued acquisition. This is done by informing students about the language acquisition process: we teach them functional, practical Spanish, pique their interest in the cultures of Spanish-speaking countries, and introduce them to stimulating and accessible reading in the second language.

National Standards in Foreign Language Education

The goal of *Dos mundos* is to provide students with the linguistic and cultural knowledge necessary for communicating successfully with native speakers of Spanish at home and abroad. To this end, *Dos mundos* text and ancillary materials fully support the National Standards for Foreign Language Education.

- **Communication.** During the first several months of study , students using *Dos mundos* interpret spoken and written Spanish and engage in basic interpersonal communication in many semantic areas. By the end of the first year of study, learners can exchange information successfully and present ideas and opinions in both oral and written modes on a wide variety of topics.

- **Cultures.** *Dos mundos* is a rich source of cultural information: fine art, cultural notes, readings, magazine-style sections, and video provide students with an understanding of cultural differences and similarities. **Sobre el artista** and the **¡Ojo!** boxes in the **Actividades de comunicación** section of the text provide brief cultural overviews, while more extended readings—**Lecturas, Ventanas culturales, Ventanas al pasado, Enlace literario,** and the magazine **Vida y cultura**—give deeper insight into Hispanic cultures.

- **Connections.** The many authentic communicative activities and cultural materials in *Dos mundos* give students the knowledge to make broader connections between the Spanish language and Hispanic linguistic and cultural traditions. In **Capítulos 12, 13, 14,** and **15** students are given opportunities to explore service learning options in the community.

- **Comparisons.** *Dos mundos* helps students develop insight into the nature of language and culture. The student and instructor prefaces to the text help learners to understand the process of language acquisition. Concise grammar explanations, frequent re-entry of grammatical concepts and short verification exercises enable *Dos mundos* students to compare and contrast their own language with Spanish. The expanded focus on Hispanic culture gives students many opportunities to compare and contrast Hispanic cultures with their own cultural traditions.

- **Communities.** *Dos mundos* highlights the contributions of Hispanics to their communities in the section entitled: **Ventanas culturales: Nuestra comunidad.** A new section in **Capítulos 12, 13, 14,** and **15, Conexión a la comunidad,** encourages students to work with Spanish speakers in their communities. The **Ventanas culturales** and the **Conexión a la comunidad** encourage professors and students alike to explore Hispanic culture and the Spanish language beyond the classroom. New Internet activities in the *Instructor's Resource Kit* and on the *Dos mundos* website encourage students to make connections with the large community of Spanish speakers. (See also our suggestions for Service Learning on page 110 of this *Manual.*) Our program is committed to attainable and enjoyable language acquisition, as it motivates students to become lifelong learners of Spanish.

AN OUTLINE OF SECOND-LANGUAGE ACQUISITION THEORY

Research in language acquisition during the last fifty years has greatly influenced language teaching methodologies. Various communicative methodologies gradually came to replace both Cognitive Code methodologies (based on conscious manipulation of explicit rules) and the Audio Lingual Method (based on behaviorist approaches to language learning). The following pages summarize some of the findings, discuss how those findings have forged new approaches to foreign language teaching, and establish the guidelines that *Dos mundos* is based upon. Much of the information in this section comes from various books written by Stephen D. Krashen[1], emeritus, University of Southern California and from the book *From Input to Output: A Teacher's Guide to Second Language Acquisition* by Bill VanPatten[2]. Keep in mind that this discussion does not represent some definitive truth about second language acquisition but rather our best understanding of the process that takes place, based on both formal and informal research evidence.

Characteristics of Second Language Acquisition

In order to acquire a second language the learner must create an automatic linguistic system, first by using strategies to comprehend data in the new language and then by using that data to gradually produce utterances while at the same time learning to comprehend ever more complex linguistic data. Second language (L_2) learners go through various stages in this process, constantly adjusting their L_2 system as they take in new communicative input. Learning a set of grammar rules does not give learners linguistic competence; this comes only from dynamic interaction between the L_2 learner and the input that he/she receives.

Similarities and Differences in First and Second Language Acquisition

Both first (L_1) and second (L_2) language learners need to hear and process large amounts of comprehensible input, that is, language with a message that is at the learner's comprehension level. On their way to acquisition of the complete linguistic system, both L_1 and L_2 learners pass through various complex developmental stages, from comprehension, to one- and two-word utterances, to eventual production of phrases and sentences, all the while forming and reforming their own internal grammar of the target language. Research has shown that overt correction of errors has little or no impact on language acquisition and that motivation to communicate plays a pivotal role in language development. All L_1 learners eventually acquire the linguistic system that is their native language, but few L_2 learners ever completely acquire native-like competence in their second language. In addition there is great variation in the abilities of L_2 learners with regard to their new linguistic system, ranging from near-native to limited comprehension and production. Most foreign language educators agree that the goal of L_2 instruction is not to create native speakers but to give students the tools to be able to communicate at various levels with native speakers.

---

[1]For more detailed information, consult Stephen D. Krashen, *The Natural Approach: Language Acquisition in the Classroom,* Prentice Hall, 1996; S. Krashen, *Fundamentals of Language Education,* Laredo, 1992; and S. Krashen, *Foreign Language Education the Easy Way,* Language Education Associates, 1998.

[2]Bill VanPatten, *From Input to Output: A Teachers Guide to Second Language Acquisition,* McGraw-Hill, 2003. This book and others are part of the McGraw-Hill Second Language Professional Series called *Directions in Second Language Learning* and include many books on communicative language teaching, affect in foreign language learning, and other areas of interest to the foreign language educator.

The Importance of Input

Input is the oral or written information in the target language that communicates a message and is intended for the learner, so that he or she is able to comprehend. Acquisition takes place when learners are exposed to many hours of such input; L_1 learners receive thousands of hours of such input. L_2 learners also need exposure to large quantities of input in order to begin creating their new linguistic system. Production (talking and writing) is the result of language acquisition (aural comprehension and reading), not the cause. (We will discuss the positive role of production or **output** below.) Comprehensible input can be aural or written; there is growing evidence that reading is an excellent source of such input.

Application

Early on in the acquisition process learners focus on content words and prefabricated patterns such as **¿Cómo te llamas?** without understanding the meaning of **te** or the **-s** ending. What students will produce depends on what they are able to understand from the input. During oral acquisition activities and readings in *Dos mundos,* students' attention should be on the exchange of ideas and gathering information. Acquisition depends first on understanding new words and grammatical structures used in communicative contexts and then on producing those words and structures in meaningful interactions. Instructors can help make input more comprehensible by slowing their speech down, pausing often, simplifying the vocabulary and structure, emphasizing content words, and making use of gestures, visual aids and sound effects, and using what has been alternately called **caretaker speech** or **teacher talk.** This teacher-talk input is indispensable because no amount of explanation and practice can substitute for real experiences, understanding, and communicating in Spanish.

Implicit versus Explicit Knowledge

Implicit knowledge is the subconscious knowledge that all native speakers have of the grammar of their language. This same implicit knowledge is what the L_2 learner gradually comes to acquire when given enough comprehensible input. Explicit knowledge is the system of language rules that are learned through formal instruction and that can be articulated in some way. Krashen has called these two systems **acquisition** (implicit knowledge) and **learning** (explicit instruction). Implicit knowledge is a subconscious process; the learner is not usually aware that it is happening. Explicit knowledge is a conscious process; learning takes place through practice or drills of some type. When we talk about grammar rules, we are usually talking about explicit knowledge. Many learners use their explicit knowledge as a production strategy in the early stages of acquisition, before their implicit knowledge is sufficiently well developed to allow more fluent production. A student who has learned that **yo soy** = *I am* may initially produce **Yo soy sueño** until he/she has internalized the structure: **Tengo sueño.**

The process of **error correction** does not affect implicit knowledge, but it does affect explicit knowledge. When we make a mistake and someone corrects us, we may change our conscious version of the rule we are using or we may become more likely to perceive structures in the input and thereby acquire them more readily.

Application

The main focus of the chapter activities in *Dos mundos* is on the development of the learner's implicit knowledge through a series of communicative experiences, both oral and written: **Actividades de comunicación y lecturas, Actividades auditivas,** and **Videoteca.** But the study of grammar is also important for many students. Knowing how Spanish words and sentences are put together may facilitate processing the input, and to that end *Dos mundos* includes grammar explanations and exercises (located at the end of each chapter and intended as reference material), as well as a section on **Pronunciación y ortografía** located after the listening activities in the *Cuaderno de actividades.* Overt error correction is reserved for those activities that focus on explicit knowledge (grammar and spelling exercises). **Indirect error correction,** where the correction is woven into the communicative interchange, is used during conversation activities.

Acquisition Order

Both L_1 and L_2 learners acquire the parts of language in a predictable order. Some grammatical structures are acquired early, and others come later. The order of acquisition for first and second languages is similar but not identical. In English, for example, the progressive form *-ing* is acquired well before third-person singular *-s*. In English as a first language, six months to a year may pass between the emergence of *-ing* and *-s*. In English as a second language, the acquisiiton of *-s* may lag many years. Here are some interesting points about acquisition order:

- The order of acquisition appears to be immune to deliberate teaching; we cannot change the natural order by explanations, drills, and exercises.

- The order of acquisition has nothing to do with ordinary notions of "simplicity" or "complexity." Some structures that appear to be simple are acquired late, and some that appear to be complex are acquired early.

- The order of acquisition and the order of instruction are frequently different. For example, students of languages such as French, Spanish, and German only begin to acquire the ability to produce gender agreement automatically in their speech by the end of their first year of study, although they learn the rule and the concept quite early in the course. Thus, it appears that although some grammar rules are learned early and relatively quickly, the ability to use those forms occurs only after long periods of communicative contact.

Application

The basic syllabus for ***Dos mundos*** is semantic (topical-situational in the case of grammar). We identify the situations students are most likely to encounter and the topics they are likely to talk about. The ***Dos mundos*** topical syllabus progresses from those semantic areas most relevant to students (their clothing, their class-mates, the classroom environment), to the outside world, (the university, their community, their activities), and finally to the Hispanic world and less concrete situations. Given a particular situation and topic, we specify some of the linguistic tools necessary for communication; that is, we choose the important vocabu-lary and some of the grammatical forms and structures that students will need to understand others and express themselves on a particular topic in a given situation. We use a grammatical syllabus as the basis for the **Gramática y ejercicios** section. We do not expect language acquisition (implicit knowledge) and the study of grammar (explicit knowledge) to coincide perfectly, however. For example, students may study grammar and do exercises with the past-tense forms in a particular chapter of grammar, but the activities that encourage the acquisition of the past tense must be spread over a much longer period of time. In most cases acquisition seems to occur without any grammar study. This appears to be especially true of syntax: given good input and enough communicative experience, most students acquire the ability to produce correct word order without explicit study of the rules or exercises that practice them.

The Role of Output

Output is oral or written language production with a communicative purpose. Although output cannot create the implicit system that generates communicative language, it may help facilitate long-term acquisition in several ways. Speaking with native speakers or even with other L_2 learners promotes negotiation of mean-ing; if communication breaks down the speaker must rephrase the utterance. The process of negotiating meaning then provides the learner with additional comprehensible input. Language production may also help learners to focus on an area in their implicit system that is weak and to pay more attention to the input they receive during conversational interchanges.

Application

Although input is the critical ingredient for language acquisition, most students of foreign language are also motivated to produce language, initially to converse with native speakers and eventually to exchange written information. The materials in *Dos mundos* give students ongoing comprehensible input (Pre-text activities, **Actividades de comunicación, Lecturas, Ventanas culturales, Ventanas al pasado,** and **Actividades auditivas**), while at the same time providing opportunities for structured output (**Diálogos, Preferencias, Entrevistas, Actividades escritas, Actividad creativa**). As students' implicit and explicit knowledge develops, these materials gradually guide them toward more open-ended output activities (**Diálogos abiertos, Entrevistas, Narraciones, Conversaciones, Del mundo hispano**).

Monitoring Production

Monitoring refers to the corrections and adjustments to speech and written output that we all make as we produce language. Krashen posits that one of the main roles of conscious learning for an L_2 learner is to monitor or edit production. After a learner produces language using the acquired system (implicit knowledge), he/she sometimes inspects it and uses explicit knowledge to correct errors. This can happen internally before the learner speaks or writes or as self-correction after the learner produces the sentence. To use the conscious monitor, Krashen says that three conditions must be met:

(1) **The learner must know the rule.** Language texts do not contain all the rules for a given language, teachers do not always teach all the rules in the text, and even the best students do not learn all the rules or remember all the rules they have learned.

(2) **The learner must have enough time.** In real conversation people rarely have enough time to think about rules unless the topic is very familiar and the rules are well-known and very simple.

(3) **The learner must be focused on form and thinking about correctness.** While focusing on form may improve accuracy a little, it also can disrupt communication. Focusing on form is time-consuming, which often makes learner speech irritating to listen to. In addition, thinking about correctness while the other person is talking makes it difficult to attend to meaning.

Application

Because monitoring with a formal knowledge of grammar learned through drill and exercise is so difficult in real communicative contexts, acquisition-oriented activities and readings play a central role in *Dos mundos* materials. Students are evaluated primarily on their comprehension and on their communicative ability, rather than on the grammatical correctness of their spontaneous speech. Grammar exercises, in which students are asked to pay close attention to correct application of grammar rules (to monitor their output), are done primarily as written homework, to allow adequate time for reflection on those rules. Other written activities also give students time to monitor their output. The conditions necessary for monitoring remind us that the ability to produce written forms should never be equated with the ability to use those forms in natural speech.

Affective Factors

Attitudes and feelings play an important role in our ability to acquire another language. If a student is anxious or does not perceive the target culture in a positive way, he or she may understand the input, but what Krashen has called the **affective filter** will prevent him or her from acquiring language from input.

When a foreign-language student identifies positively with the target culture, he or she will acquire even those aspects of language that are not crucial for communication but that mark the student as a member of the group that speaks the language (morphological endings, intonation, and the like). When the student feels like a member of the target culture, the affective filter diminishes. Some researchers have posited that the affective filter appears to increase in strength around puberty, which may help to explain why young children typically do better at language acquisition in the long run.

Application

It is of utmost importance that students be relaxed and interested in the activities in which they participate and that they feel comfortable with their classmates. Classroom interactions should be carried out in a supportive, rather than a competitive, environment. Opportunities for group work in *Dos mundos* encourage student interest and involvement in activities that relate directly to their lives and the world around them.

GUIDELINES FOR USING THE NATURAL APPROACH

Research on second language acquisition has given rise to various communicative teaching methodologies including Total Physical Response (TPR), the Natural Approach, task-based learning, immersion, and content-based instruction. The materials in *Dos mundos* are based primarily on the Natural Approach, which in turn incorporates elements of TPR. The next section outlines the guiding principles of the Natural Approach as they apply to *Dos mundos.* Instructors may also want to incorporate elements of other communicative approaches into their teaching.

Comprehension Precedes Production

The ability to produce language is the result of implicit knowledge, the knowledge that develops from prolonged exposure to comprehensible input. Thus, students' ability to use new vocabulary and grammar is directly related to the opportunities they have to listen to and read that vocabulary and grammar in meaningful and relevant contexts. Opportunities to express their own ideas must *follow* comprehension. We have attempted to include introductory comprehension activities for all major semantic word groups and grammatical forms and structures before requiring students to produce speech containing those words, forms, and structures. See in particular the Pre-Text Oral Activities and *Instructor's Edition* notes that begin each chapter, as well as the notes accompanying the illustrated displays that begin each section of the communication activities. Ultimately, however, it is your responsibility to ensure that new words and grammatical forms and structures are introduced for comprehension before students are expected to use them.

Speech Emerges in Stages

Speech is allowed to *emerge* in the Natural Approach. Although students are never prevented from speaking, there is no pressure on them to produce language beyond their capacity.

There are two reasons to concentrate on developing comprehension and not requiring beginners to speak Spanish immediately: (1) Their anxiety levels will be lower, and (2) their comprehension of spoken Spanish will develop faster. According to our experience, students who are not required to produce Spanish immediately feel more comfortable with the language and pronounce it better when they do begin to speak.

Beginners in the Natural Approach are allowed to pass naturally through three stages.

- Stage 1: Comprehension
- Stage 2: Early Speech
- Stage 3: Speech Emergence

In Stage 1 (**Paso A**) students need not respond in the target language. During this pre-speech stage teachers use TPR and ask questions that can be answered with **sí** or **no,** a classmate's name, or a gesture. In Stage 2 (**Pasos B** and **C** and **Capítulo 1**) students respond with single words or short phrases, and by Stage 3 (**Capítulos 1** and **2**) they are able to understand and produce longer utterances. Keep in mind that students will continue to pass through these same stages with the new material of each chapter and that vocabulary and structures presented in a particular chapter may not be fully acquired until several chapters later.

Speech Emergence Is Characterized by Grammatical Errors

When students start putting words together into sentences, they make many errors. These errors will *gradually* disappear with more comprehensible input. We do not expect students to wait until they have Spanish completely under control before they are allowed to use it. Because explicit knowledge only supplements implicit knowledge, correction appears to play a limited role. Consider what must happen for error correction to work: The learner must notice the correction, understand the correction, adjust his or her version of the conscious rule, and arrive at a better version; this is difficult to do while focusing on meaning.

Early speech errors that occur during the communication activities do not necessarily become permanent, nor do they affect students' future language development. It is perfectly acceptable to let students make errors as they negotiate meaning in interaction with the instructor, with peers, and with native speakers. During classroom activities instructors should pay attention primarily to factual errors and simply respond to student utterances in a normal communicative way. Some teachers are concerned that uncorrected errors will become permanent. Such "fossilization" is a real phenomenon, but it is not a problem for Natural Approach classes. It occurs among second-language learners who live and work in the environment of the new language for many years. It usually takes several years of daily language use for mistakes to become so ingrained as to be truly fossilized. Although we do not expect students to speak the target language without errors, we do expect steady improvement in their speech throughout the course. We feel that one way of *preventing* fossilization of incorrect forms is by providing a great deal of comprehensible input, through aural input in class and through reading.

Students Must Engage with Language-Acquisition Activities

Students must actively interact with the materials. Students are more likely to participate if they believe that learning a second language has potential value, purpose, and use for them; if the process seems attainable; if they are free from anxiety; and if their classroom experience is enjoyable.

Teacher Expectations of Student Success

Although students will make many errors, we fully expect them to acquire quite a bit of Spanish in the course of the year. Adult learners need to be given clear messages that not only are they expected to learn to understand and to talk, but that they are capable of doing so. They need to be made consciously aware of how they learned to master their first language. With the **Actividades de comunicación** in *Dos mundos,* students are able to be successful at communicating in Spanish within a few weeks.

Students Acquire Language Only in a Low-Anxiety Environment

A low-anxiety environment is essential for language acquisition. Research shows that the most anxiety-provoking practices are error correction and forcing students to speak before they are ready. On the other hand, the least anxiety-provoking practices are those that engage the students in truly interesting, comprehensible input (whole-class discussions, interacting with classmates, problem solving, listening to interesting stories, silent readings, self-selected reading).

A very effective way of ensuring a relaxed environment is to make sure that students are engaged in communicative activities that they enjoy and in which they feel they can express their ideas in the target language without fear of correction or reprimand. The goal is for them to express themselves as best they can and enjoy and develop a positive attitude toward their second language experience.

Group Work Encourages Interaction and Creates Community

As soon as students feel ready to produce in the target language, let them begin working in pairs and small groups. We suggest doing some pair work very early on, starting at the end of **Paso A,** and using it frequently thereafter. Pair work allows many more students to speak the target language during the class period and gives students confidence in speaking. Pair work also allows students to take responsibility for their progress. Most students enjoy interacting with others on a personal basis, and this creates a sense of classroom community that contributes to a low-anxiety environment. Group work also gives you the opportunity to move quickly from group to group, making sure that the activity is going well, answering questions, and contributing to the discussion.

Speaking Helps Language Acquisition Indirectly

In addition to the focus on comprehensible input, the Natural Approach encourages student output in both whole-class and group-work situations. Speaking helps language development *indirectly* in several ways:

- It encourages comprehensible input, via conversation.
- It gives students the important feeling of participating in real language use, which contributes to identification with the target culture.
- It lowers speaking anxieties by giving students the experience of communicating.
- It allows students to "play with" their newly acquired language.
- It prepares them for communicative interactions with native speakers outside the classroom. This in turn will provide them with more comprehensible input.
- It also helps create a sense of community as the instructor and students share opinions and life experiences in groups or whole-class discussions.

Grammar Plays a Supplemental Role

Formal knowledge of grammar does not contribute to language fluency and makes only a limited contribution to accuracy, as a monitor. Some grammar study is justified to develop a monitor because for second language learners acquisition does not typically do the entire job; even those who have a great deal of comprehensible input may have small gaps in their competence. Under the right conditions, language users can use their explicit knowledge to fill these gaps.

There are other reasons for grammar study. It can lead to a greater appreciation of the structure of a language and can be good introduction to the field of linguistics. Some language students derive great satisfaction when they learn about what they are acquiring. In addition, very adept learners may be able to use grammatical knowledge to make the input they hear more comprehensible. Keep in mind that explicit knowledge does not turn into implicit knowledge; real acquisition occurs only through continued comprehensible input.

All activities in *Dos mundos* can be done without previous grammar study; indeed, the most benefit is derived if activities are done in a purely communicative way, with both teacher and students focusing entirely on meaning. Previous study of the corresponding grammar section(s), however, will be helpful to students interested in the structure of language.

The Goal of a Spanish Course Using *Dos mundos* Is Proficiency in Communication Skills

Proficiency, or communicative competence, is the ability to understand and convey information, feelings and opinions in a particular situation for a given purpose. We might determine, for example, that a student is proficient in one area if he or she is able to ask a native speaker how to get from one location to another and understand directions given by the native speaker. Accuracy is but a small part of proficiency; in no sense is it the only goal of a communicative course or even a prerequisite for the development of communicative proficiency.

In any particular foreign-language course, there may be additional goals; reading and writing, for example. For this reason, and because reading is a rich source of input, we have extensive marginal notes on the use of various reading materials in *Dos mundos.* In these materials, there will always be more oral and written activities than you will be able to use in a year-long, college-level course. How many of these materials you use depends on the goal you and your students have for the course. The most important point, however, is that proficiency develops from comprehension and communication experiences, not from covering a certain amount of material in this or any other textbook.

TEACHING COMPREHENSION AND SPEAKING

Your class activities should contain both comprehensible input and interactional activities that allow students to progress through the natural stages of acquisition: comprehension, early speech, and speech emergence. The purpose of this section is to clarify the relationships between the acquisition process, comprehension, and speaking, with an overview of the use of particular teaching techniques to aid in the development of communicative proficiency.

Comprehension

The student who begins a ***Dos mundos*** Spanish course concentrates first on the development of listening skills. It is important, then, to understand how beginning students interpret the utterances they hear in the instructor's speech. The immediate goal in the first few classes is to develop students' ability to use comprehension strategies. Beginning students are able to comprehend an utterance if they engage with the topic, recognize the meaning of key words in the utterance, and are able to use context to derive the meaning of the utterance itself: Comprehension = engagement + key words + context.

Looking at comprehension in this way implies that students need several kinds of experiences in the classroom. Input must consist of utterances in a meaningful and interesting context; that is, the instructor must use body language, gestures, intonation, and other aspects of paralanguage, as well as visuals, props, and anything else available to make the meaning of the utterance clear. Students must also perceive topics as relevant to their needs in the new language.

Students will pay attention to the words emphasized by the instructor. Several techniques can draw attention to the most important parts of an utterance:

- You may speak a key word louder than the words that surround it: **La mujer lleva una *falda* negra.** Emphasis is on **falda,** pronouncing the word louder, perhaps drawing it out longer, while pointing to a skirt or a picture of a skirt.

- You may pause slightly before saying the key word. Pointing to a picture: **Miren lo que lleva este señor. Esto es un... traje de baño.**

- Repetition and re-entry of the key word also draws students' attention to it. Point to what one student is wearing: **Ashley lleva una blusa blanca... Esta blusa es blanca; no es roja, no es azul, es blanca. Ashley lleva una blusa blanca.**

Good listening skills will develop from communicative experiences, not from the rote memorization of vocabulary and grammar.

The task of the instructor is to use the key word meaningfully. The task of the student is to attend to the input in such a way that the meaning of the key word is linked to its form in Spanish. How does the linking of form and meaning take place? The key element in acquisition of vocabulary appears to be communicative experiences. We link words to meaning by hearing or reading them used in contexts. Context includes:

- the use of visuals (pictures, drawings, posters, advertisements, and so on)

- the use of the real object or item

- the use of movements (such as acting out words and situations)

In addition, affective factors can help students acquire new words:

- the associations of words with a particular classmate (that is, the fact that a particular classmate has long brown hair and blue eyes and wears glasses helps associate meaning with the words for *brown, hair, blue, eyes,* and *glasses*)

- the association of new words with the interests of classmates (for example, acquisition of **cocinar** with its meaning is easier if someone in the class particularly likes cooking)

- the unusualness of something in a picture or a visual
- the use of humor to draw attention to certain words

Linguistic factors can also help:

- words made more salient by being spoken louder or by pausing slightly before the word
- words with particular sounds, word length, and rhythm
- similarities with other languages a student knows (cognates, borrowings, or invented similarities)

Cultural factors also play a part, that is, words may be acquired during cultural discussions or experiences that involve the use of slides, movies, videotapes, games, parties, skits, and so on.

Instructors should not expect a word to be completely acquired after one use or even after several uses. Research suggests that vocabulary acquisition does not occur all at once, but in small increments. It typically takes many meaningful occurrences of a word for complete acquisition to take place. Neither rote memorization nor repeating lists of words aloud help the acquisition process. The responsibility of the instructor is to create vivid experiences and provide stimulating reading that will help students form strong associations.

Teacher-Talk

Since second language acquisition theory posits that input plays the major role in acquisition, the input the instructor supplies to students in the form of teacher-talk is extremely important. This input has certain characteristics:

1. It focuses on meaning. Everything in the input is aimed at getting across meaning—that is, information about some topic or situation being addressed.

2. It is comprehensible. Students are able to follow the main ideas of the input.

3. It is slightly above students' current level of competence. This means that students understand enough of the key words and structures to be able to interpret new vocabulary and structures by using what they do understand and the context of the input (that is, knowing about the topic under discussion, looking at visual aids, attending to gestures, and so on). Not *every* utterance coming from the teacher must be above the students' current level of competence. If instructors simply make input comprehensible and interesting, a great deal of what they say will be at the appropriate level.

4. It is interesting and relates to students' experiences. The instructor must use knowledge about the students themselves to personalize the discussion that results from the communication activities.

5. It allows for spontaneous and innovative student responses without being threatening. The attitude of the instructor during the give-and-take of the input must be one of attention to meaning. Any attempt students make to communicate is accepted in a positive fashion.

6. It is simplified. All language learners, including children acquiring a first language, must have access to simplified input. In this context, *simplified* means many things. The speed of the input is somewhat slower than regular adult-to-adult, native-speaker input. It is more clearly enunciated. The focus is usually maintained on a single topic longer than normal, and the information may be repeated in several forms. The range of vocabulary and structures used in the input is limited without being artificial. (Note that many of these alterations will happen naturally as you communicate with your students.)

7. It is varied and natural. Since the focus is always on the message, the instructor reacts naturally to students' responses, thereby creating new situations and additional information in the input. In this way, the instructor re-enters frequently used vocabulary and structures many times without having to plan a specific review.

Good teacher-talk is essential for the success of communicative language teaching. If in-class interaction is artificial and overly controlled, students will not acquire Spanish.

Speaking

Although early emphasis in **Dos mundos** is on the development of implicit knowledge through comprehensible input, most students also want to practice speaking Spanish. In addition to the affective and motivational value of speaking, when students begin to respond in Spanish, class interactions and activities become much more interesting, and there is greater potential for variety than when students simply listen to and indicate comprehension of input. **Dos mundos** provides many opportunities for students to express themselves in Spanish.

Proficiency in speaking emerges in stages. Stage 1 is the comprehension stage. In Stage 2, students are encouraged to respond with single words or short phrases. It is important that you formulate questions so that students are asked to produce only words that they have had a chance to acquire. The idea is to avoid "translation searches" in which students go through a thought process like, "*dog*—how do you say *dog* in Spanish?" for each word and grammatical form they wish to produce. For this reason, we begin speech production in Stage 2 with either/or questions: **¿Lleva Kathy una falda negra o azul? ¿Tiene este señor bigote o barba?** Even simple interrogatives such as **¿Qué es esto?** or **¿Dónde están los señores?** should be attempted only when we are relatively sure that students have enough vocabulary to produce the correct word. The following is a sequence of question types, increasing in complexity, that provide opportunities for encouraging speaking in Stage 2.

1. Yes/no questions

2. Either/or questions

3. Simple interrogatives (**¿Qué? ¿Dónde? ¿Cuándo? ¿Quién?**)

4. Open sentences (**Este señor lleva un...**)

5. List of words (**¿Qué vemos en esta foto?**)

The transition from the production of single words to longer phrases and more complete sentences in Stage 3 is facilitated by dialogues and interviews. In the model dialogues we use key words in short, complete sentences. The open dialogues are particularly effective because they provide the grammatical context, and students only have to provide words that have already been acquired.

As students move to Stage 3, there will be more situations in which they will be unable to retrieve a word in Spanish, either because they have not heard it enough to acquire it fully or because they simply have never encountered it. In either case, it is natural that they think of the English word first and ask: **¿Cómo se dice _____ en español?** Such spot translations are not damaging per se, but we want to avoid situations in which each utterance is new and must be translated one word at a time.

We recommend that you not push students into Stage 3 too quickly; allow them to answer with short replies until they are ready to attempt more complex responses. When students are pushed to respond using words and grammar they have not yet acquired, they invariably fall back on their native language to formulate a reply and then translate word for word. This probably does no great damage to the acquisition process, but it requires a great deal of mental energy and is unnecessary.

In Stage 3, when students do begin to produce Spanish, they will make a number of errors: errors of pronunciation, word usage, grammar, and discourse. As we noted earlier, errors are a normal part of the acquisition process, and we do not recommend direct correction of speech errors during class interactions. Error correction interrupts the exchange of ideas and creates affective barriers to acquisition even when it is done in a positive manner. Adults do not normally correct other adult second language learners' mistakes in real-life conversations, so error correction will not be a source of feedback on students' speech in or outside of class. Since learners will not acquire what they do not hear or read in input, it is suggested that you use student responses as a basis for a more complete and correct version of what they wish to express. We call this "expansion of student responses" and will discuss it in more detail under *Expanded Instructor Notes*.

TEACHING READING AND WRITING

Reading and writing play an important role in *Dos mundos*. In the following sections we describe how reading and writing are treated in the text and suggest how to teach these skills.

Reading

There are two reasons for students to learn to read Spanish. One is a practical consideration: Students learn to read in order to understand and enjoy texts written in Spanish—signs, ads, instructions, magazines, newspapers, books, and so on. The other is more theoretical: Reading provides the comprehensible input that contributes directly to the acquisition process. From the point of view of the language instructor, there are other reasons to read: Reading is a rich source of cultural information and stimulates discussion, creating the possibility for more comprehensible input and student interactions.

The are four main reading skills: scanning, skimming, intensive reading, and extensive reading. We scan the text for specific information. It is a very useful skill for travelers, who often need to scan advertisements, signs, and menus for pertinent information, even though they are not able to understand everything. We skim a text to get the main ideas. It is often a good idea to skim readings before attempting to read them intensively. Intensive reading is a close reading: We attempt to understand each utterance and, in some cases, even each word. We use intensive reading techniques to study a text carefully: to read a contract, for example, or to analyze literature. Extensive reading is usually pleasure reading: We read for content and supporting material but not for detail. Too often in a foreign-language course students are taught only to read intensively; in some cases, they simply translate without ever learning how to read. It is through extensive pleasure reading that we gain the vocabulary and grammar we need for more advanced language proficiency. (For more information on the role of reading in language acquisition, see S. Krashen, *The Power of Reading,* Libraries Unlimited, Englewood, Colorado, 1993.)

The most important point to remember about reading in Spanish is to remind students to focus on the meaning, to get absorbed in the information or the story. Readers do not need to know every word to understand a text; in fact, if students skip some words they don't know, they may actually acquire vocabulary faster, because they will acquire many more words from context. Of course, if there are too many words in a text that readers don't know, the material is too far above their level, and something else needs to be selected.

We strongly advise students to read as much self-selected material in Spanish as possible: newspapers, comic books, magazines, short stories, and novels. Even if they are only able to get some meaning out of these texts, they will improve their Spanish enormously. We offer a wide range of readings in *Dos mundos*. Some are in the main text, others in the **Lecturas** of the *Cuaderno de actividades. Dos mundos* contains more readings than do most introductory texts. When students learn to read for the main ideas without translating to English, they are able to read a great deal of text quite rapidly. You do not need to assign every reading in *Dos mundos;* we hope that, once they realize that they can read Spanish rapidly, students will want to read on their own. Some instructors use readings that are not regular assignments as makeup work for students who have had to miss class.

All readings are "glossed"; that is, English or simpler Spanish equivalents of difficult key words appear at the beginning of the reading in a **Vocabulario útil** box, or at the bottom of the text in footnotes. New vocabulary from the readings, however, is not included in the chapter reference vocabulary. Most new words from the readings are found in the Spanish-English Vocabulary at the end of the text.

The readings in *Dos mundos* are presented under the following categories:

- **Readings with a Strong Focus on Culture.** The wide range of cultural materials in *Dos mundos* provides opportunities to reflect on the similarities and differences between the culture of the student and the cultures of the Spanish-speaking world. Brief readings called **Ventanas culturales** are windows to the culture and society of the Hispanic world, while **Ventanas al pasado** address various historical aspects. All **Ventanas** have a follow-up pair activity and accompanying instructor notes provide suggestions for activities. There are four categories of **Ventanas culturales: Nuestra comunidad, La lengua, La vida diaria,** and **Las costumbres.**

- The **Lecturas** in the main text and the **Lecturas** and **Notas culturales** in the *Cuaderno de actividades* feature descriptive narratives or fiction about interesting aspects of Hispanic culture. They are all preceded by the **Pistas para leer** box, which presents questions, clues, and useful reading strategies such as scanning, visualization and cognate recognition. Follow-up activities include **Comprensión,** which tests general understanding of the material, and **Un paso más... ¡a escribir!,** a creative writing assignment related to the topic of the reading. Some of the **Un paso más** activities are labeled **¡a conversar!,** as these are intended for whole-class interaction and conversation. The descriptions in **¡Ojo!** offer insight into the customs of the Spanish-speaking world. Finally, three **Vida y cultura** magazine sections are included in *Dos mundos.* This magazine, with articles on topics such as holidays, music, art, food, and history appears after **Capítulos 4, 9,** and **15.**

- **Journalistic texts.** This category includes ads, bills and short articles on topics of interest taken directly from Hispanic newspapers and magazines. Most of these readings are incorporated directly into various **Actividades de comunicación** or serve as additional realia with accompanying *Instructor's Edition* notes about how to expand their use in class. Remind students that they do not need to understand every word in the text to complete the associated task or to search for the requested information.

- **Literature.** We believe that literature is best read for pleasure and information, and we hope that students will enjoy the literary material in *Dos mundos.* Each chapter of the text includes an **Enlace literario** featuring poetry and fiction selections by well-known Spanish, Latin American, and U.S. Latino writers. All **Enlaces** are preceded by an introduction to the piece and the author, and followed by a creative writing activity: the **Actividad creativa.** This **Actividad creativa** allows students to develop their writing skills in Spanish, and encourages them to associate the reading of literature with an active participation in the creative process. Other literature selections include several short stories under the heading **Cuento** and excerpts from novels.

All the **Lecturas,** the **Notas culturales,** and the **Cuentos** are preceded by a list of useful vocabulary and reading clues in the **Pistas para leer** box. These readings also feature optional comprehension questions and creative writing or conversation activities. Other suggestions for post-reading activities are included in the Instructor's Notes and the *Instructor's Manual.*

Introducing Reading

The reading material in *Dos mundos* may be considered parallel to the communication activities, in that they provide input and a basis for interaction. Students using *Dos mundos* begin to read almost immediately. During the first oral input of Stage 1 (the Pre-Text Oral Activities), many instructors write some of the key words of the input on the board. This practice allows students to begin the process of connecting Spanish sounds to familiar letters—if not consciously, then intuitively. The reading involved in these activities is minimal and silent. We do not recommend that you ask students to read these words aloud because in Stage 1 they will not have had enough input to produce Spanish sounds correctly for what look like "English" letters. For beginners, the likelihood is great that reading aloud will result in rather serious pronunciation distortions.

As students engage in the **Actividades de comunicación** in the **Pasos** (Stages 1 and 2), they will have more opportunities to hear words and to match them with the printed versions. In addition, they can work through the exercises on pronunciation and orthography in the *Cuaderno de actividades.* Those exercises explicitly point out the sound-letter correspondences of Spanish. The emphasis during this stage, before formal readings begins, is on extracting meaning from the printed word without translating into English.

The first short readings in **Capítulo 1** are the **Ventana cultural: Nuestra comunidad: Rigoberta Menchú** and the **Ventanas al pasado: Frida y Diego.** We recommend that you read both of these in class to familiarize students with the process of reading in a second language. Begin by asking them to review the **Vocabulario útil** box and then to skim the passage quickly without reading each sentence. Emphasize that they are not to translate into English, but rather to attempt to get meaning directly from the Spanish.

Read the **Ventana** aloud slowly. Pause at the highlighted words and give students a chance to glance again at the English translation. Stop at the end of each paragraph and paraphrase what you have read. At the end you might ask brief comprehension questions like: **¿Cuál es la meta personal de Rigoberta Menchú? Sí, quiere justicia para los indígenas de Guatemala. ¿En qué año recibe ella el Premio Nóbel de la Paz? Sí, en 1992.** Review the **Ahora... ¡ustedes!** questions before pairing students to discuss. Circulate helping students with vocabulary as they ask and answer these questions.

"El interrogatorio" by Virgilio Piñera is the first **Enlace literario** in *Dos mundos.* We suggest that these literary selections be read in class so that you may guide students through the material. Read the introduction first and then go over the glossed words with the students. Tell them to skim the piece and look for any information that would help them understand what is taking place: two people are talking. Ask questions like: **¿Qué pasa aquí? ¿Quién habla? ¿Hay una persona o dos personas? Son dos, ¿verdad? Es un diálogo. ¿Y quiénes son estas personas?** (Provide the answer yourself and teach the words **juez, acusado** and **personaje.**) **Pues... hay un juez y un acusado. Son dos personajes. Uno hace preguntas y el otro las contesta, ¿verdad?** Now read the selection aloud, ideally using a different voice for each character. Pause at the glossed words so students have time to look at the English translation. Always prepare students for the **Actividad creativa** and have them do all initial work for this writing assignment in class. (See section on *Teaching Creative Writing,* page 108.) You may want to do the **Actividad creativa** of the first three or four chapters in class before assigning it as homework.

The first **Lectura** in **Capítulo 1** is **La pasión por los deportes.** This **Lectura** lends itself to the practice of scanning as a reading strategy. Have students scan the title, photos, and highlighted words. Then review the **Pistas para leer** and the **Vocabulario útil.** Now read aloud, pausing to paraphrase. Use exaggerated intonation and gestures to make meaning clear. Read key words and cognates slowly, but quickly pass over function words and phrases not essential to main points. Pause and add comments or ask questions to aid comprehension. Your objective is to demonstrate that students can answer brief comprehension questions without understanding every word in the reading. Now have students reread the text silently. Remind them to concentrate on comprehension without translating.

Interesting discussion following the reading can provide excellent aural input and facilitate understanding of the material. Do the **Comprensión** activity with the class and assign **Un paso más...** (UPM) as written homework. **UPM** consists of personalized questions and situations that further explore the topic and stimulate students' participation and creativity. Innovative and engaging formats have been provided for these post-reading activities. Some will focus on writing, **¡a escribir!**, and some on conversation, **¡a conversar!** When presented in conversation format, the activity is intended for interaction between you and your class. An additional activity, **Ahora... ¡usted!,** is included for each **Lectura** in the section titled *Expanded Instructor Notes: Chapter Goals, Techniques for Providing Input and Additional Activities.* This variety of post-reading activities will allow you to pick and choose which ones suit your needs, possibly assigning **Comprensión** as homework and reserving **Un paso más... ¡a escribir!** for an in-class writing activity; or using **Comprensión** for a class discussion and **UPM** as written homework.

Reading Strategies

The readings selected for *Dos mundos* were designed with two purposes in mind: to provide comprehensible input and to give students confidence in reading a foreign language. To achieve these two objectives, any reading—especially those assigned for homework—should be previewed by the instructor. Before assigning any longer reading, the instructor should spend a few minutes preparing students. Be sure to:

- create interest in the topic of the reading.
- integrate any difficult new vocabulary in your lesson and classroom activities.
- offer students a short synopsis of content.
- assign specific tasks, rather than just saying, "Be prepared to discuss the reading" or "Answer the questions."

Whenever possible, while reading in class with the whole group, incorporate the following strategies without calling direct attention to them. After you have used them successfully several times, many students will begin to apply them effortlessly to their independent reading.

1. **Cues.** Look at the title, photos, illustrations, and any other cues outside the main text for an introduction to what the reading is about.
2. **Cognates.** Scan the text for cognates and familiar words. Use cognates to make predictions about content, to guide students' imagination, and to help them anticipate.
3. **Main idea.** Pay attention to the first paragraph: it will present the main idea of the reading. The remaining paragraphs develop the main idea with more details.
4. **Context.** Use context to make intelligent guesses regarding unfamiliar words.
5. **Visualize.** Picture the story instead of trying to translate it in your mind as you go.
6. **Global Reading.** Read several times. First reading, focus on the main idea. Second reading, clarify the main idea and notice important details. Third reading, answer questions and relate content to your own experiences.
7. **Active Reading.** Be an active reader. Anticipate, predict. An active reader asks him- or herself questions: Why is this said? Who says it? An active reader predicts the outcome and incorporates clues to reformulate predictions as he or she continues to read.

Teaching the *Lecturas*

The readings in the **Actividades de comunicación y lecturas** section of the main text are supplemented by the **Lecturas** and **Notas culturales** of the *Cuaderno de actividades.* It is a good idea for students to read the **Lecturas** and **Notas culturales** in the *Cuaderno de actividades* or other self-selected reading since they provide input and reading practice. Instructor's Notes for each of the **Lecturas** and **Notas culturales** in the *Cuaderno de actividades* are at the end of this *Manual.*

Supplementary Reading

Research evidence shows that self-selected and free voluntary reading play an important role in first language acquisition. We believe that free voluntary reading is also great source of input for second language learners. We recommend Spanish-language newspapers, comic books, and magazines. Scholastic, Inc., publishes a series of magazines in Spanish at four different levels. These magazines have language tailored to the interests and language levels of beginning and intermediate students and include a variety of very short, well-written articles, recipes, and stories with full-color photos. Many instructors like to keep a supply of *Geomundo, Vanidades, Selecciones de Reader's Digests, PC Magazine en Español, Ser Padres,* and *Américas* in their classroom and set aside fifteen minutes once a week for Silent Sustained Reading. For second- or third- semester classes you may also want to use readers in the *¡A leer! Easy Reader Series: Cocina y comidas hispanas* and *Mundos de fantasía* or novels from the *Storyteller's Series: Viajes fantásticos, Ladrón de la mente,* and *Isla de luz.*

Writing

We include writing activities in ***Dos mundos*** for two reasons. First, writing is satisfying and, like speaking, it lets students feel like members of the Spanish-speaking world. Second, writing helps us organize our thinking. When we write something down, thoughts that are vague become more concrete, and we can edit our thoughts and come up with better ones.

The first steps in learning to write Spanish begin during the Pre-Text Oral Activities of Stage 1 (**Paso A**), in which students may copy key words from the board into vocabulary notebooks. The dictation exercises of the orthography sections of the ***Cuaderno de actividades,*** especially in the first few chapters, are helpful in clarifying the more difficult sound-letter correspondences. Writing activities in **Paso A** of the ***Cuaderno*** require only words or short phrases, and most of them involve copying simple words. Writing in **Paso B** of the ***Cuaderno*** requires simple words and some complete sentences. Students are given explicit directions and guidelines on how to compose the sentences. Some instructors assign students to write out the answers to grammar exercises and **Comprensión** for readings. Writing grammar exercises can be helpful, but these are manipulative activities. "Creative" writing, in which students express themselves directly in Spanish, is required in the following activities:

- **Actividad creativa.** These post-**Enlace literario** activities allow students to engage creatively with the literary selection.

- **Cuéntenos usted.** This culminating activity asks students to prepare a very brief story about an experience in their lives.

- **Un paso más... ¡a escribir!** These post-reading activities allow students to work alone or in groups to reflect creatively on the reading.

- **¡Dígalo por escrito!** These activities give pairs or groups a specific writing task that often involves preparatory oral work.

- **Actividades escritas.** These writing activities are present in every section of the ***Cuaderno de actividades.*** Some of them have a grammatical focus, while many others are open-ended.

Teaching Creative Writing

You can start creative essay writing at the end of Stage 2 (**Paso C** or **Capítulo 1**), even though students are not yet speaking in complete sentences. This kind of activity provides some of the satisfaction of writing and also provides valuable input. Since the class topics have been the students themselves, choose the following theme for the first essay. Ask for a volunteer to be the person the other student will describe. Write the title of the essay on the board, and have students copy it: **Nuestro compañero de clase, Guillermo.** Then ask students to brainstorm what they want to write about Guillermo by giving you words and phrases. Write their output on the board as they give it to you, including minor form corrections such as gender and number agreement: **pelo negro, estudiante alto, le gusta nadar, ojos azules,** and so on. After you have five to ten descriptive phrases on the board, have students pick the one to start with. Suppose they say **estudiante.** You respond orally: **Sí, Guillermo es un estudiante de la clase de español.** Write that sentence on the board. Suppose the next response is **pelo negro.** Write: **Tiene el pelo negro.** Here is an example of the first essay generated in a class.

> **Guillermo es un estudiante de la clase de español. Tiene el pelo negro y los ojos azules. Es alto pero no es gordo. Tiene una novia que se llama Araceli. Guillermo vive en un apartamento con tres estudiantes. A Guillermo le gusta ir a la playa y correr.**

After you have written this essay together, ask students to write in class a second one, about another classmate or a friend. Circulate among students, helping them individually as necessary—at this stage they will be unsure of the "filler" words: **es, tiene, a, pero,** and so on. We suggest that you do two or three group essays with the class before assigning the first composition from the text.

Each chapter of the main text contains suggested topics for short essays, poems, letters, diary entries, and other personal narratives. These suggestions appear in the activities **Un paso más... ¡a escribir!, Actividad creativa, ¡Dígalo por escrito!,** and **Cuéntenos usted.** We recommend that students do some type of creative writing once a week. Naturally, it is impossible for you to collect, correct and grade all writing assignments. When you do collect them for a grade, the following procedure is recommended to help students learn to edit their writing. Have students turn in a draft, then circle errors on the draft that students should be able to correct on their own. Be sure to limit their corrections to rules that students have studied in the grammar sections.

Keep in mind that correction (editing) helps students produce a more accurate composition, but it is not directly responsible for language acquisition. Editing should take place after the student organizes his or her ideas clearly on the page. Students should not be too concerned with grammatical accuracy while they are writing for meaning.

The first creative writing assignment appears in the **Actividades comunicativas y lecturas** section of *Dos mundos,* **Capítulo 1,** under **Datos personales** on page 62. The assignment is based on the **Enlace literario,** an excerpt from a short story by Cuban writer Virgilio Piñera. This story is written in dialogue form, a technique that facilitates understanding of the text. Once the piece has been read in class, go over the **Actividad creativa.** Tell students about the playwright: **Piñera escribe sobre personas extrañas y situaciones absurdas.** Emphasize **extrañas** and **absurdas.** Now write a sample dialogue in class based on the story and with your students' help. Tell students: **Ahora vamos a escribir un diálogo «extraño» entre un juez y un acusado.** List on the board the questions provided, leaving space between them for the answers. You could also present the model as theater:

JUEZ:	**¿Cómo se llama?**
ACUSADO/A:	... (Make up an interesting Spanish name.)
JUEZ:	**¿Quiénes son sus padres?**
ACUSADO/A:	... (These could be historical figures or celebrities.)
JUEZ:	**¿Dónde nació?**
ACUSADO/A:	... (This could be a real or fictional place.)

Try to declare something interesting and/or comical at the end, in response to the question **¿Tiene algo que declarar?** This could be a simple remark such as **¡Nada, señor!** or **¡Nada, caramba!,** or a more elaborate response such as **¡Soy una profesora de español fantástica!** Now read the directions in the **Actividad creativa** to the class, placing emphasis on **¡Usted es el personaje que el juez interroga en el cuento!** Add, **Entonces, ¡usted es el acusado!** Encourage students to write simple responses. Discourage them from looking up too many words. The next day, set up drama reading groups where students listen to each other's dialogues.

The first writing assignment for an essay appears in the **Actividades escritas** section of the *Cuaderno de actividades,* **Capítulo 1,** under **Datos personales,** page 41. In the first part we provide a model essay describing Estela Ramírez. In the second part we give the same information about another character in list form (name, address, telephone number, and so on). Students are asked to write a paragraph incorporating the information given. Finally, they are asked to write a paragraph describing one of their friends.

TEACHING CULTURE

Dos mundos offers a wide variety of resources for teaching culture. These include the fine art, **Sobre el artista** and time line sections on the chapter opener page, **Ventanas culturales, Ventanas al pasado, ¡Ojo!** boxes in the **Actividades de comunicación,** various culturally oriented **Lecturas,** realia-based **Actividades de comunicación,** and the **Videoteca.** In addition, the **Vida y cultura** section at the end of **Capítulos 4, 9,** and **15** provides in-depth cultural information in an appealing magazine format. Also, many pieces of realia and photographs have been chosen to serve as points of departure for discussions of Hispanic culture. In the *Instructor's Edition* Notes there are many suggestions for teaching culture with these paragraphs and realia. Most of the vocabulary displays and many of the communication activities also provide cultural insights. We recommend that you include cultural content frequently in your class activities, relating language and culture as a natural part of your input.

As you and your students read, discuss both similarities and differences between the Hispanic and English-speaking worlds. Use the **Videoteca** in the **Cuaderno de actividades** to explore culture in the Hispanic world. Students will get additional cultural input from the **Escenas culturales** and the **Escenas en contexto** included in the sixth edition of the video program. We hope that with our materials students will acquire a deeper understanding of their own culture and of the various Hispanic cultures. Ideally, they will come to see that all cultures are essentially approaches to common human situations.

Culture and Community

As technology and immigration continue to shrink our national borders, many more students seek contact with Spanish speakers beyond the classroom. Students may have already explored bilingual communication options on the Internet. The Internet activities in the *Instructor's Resource Kit* provide a guided start to exploring Hispanic culture through the World Wide Web.

Other students may prefer a hands-on approach to cultural understanding and for these individuals we recommend community involvement. Many regions of the United States have flourishing Hispanic communities where business and leisure activities are conducted in Spanish. These communities present opportunities for students to become involved through participation in cultural events at museums, concerts, and holiday celebrations. Additionally, service learning provides students a venue for performing useful service to their communities and to society, and connects their classroom experiences to social responsibility.

Service Learning and Acquisition of Spanish

Service learning enables students to interact in Spanish with native speakers in authentic communicative situations. Service learning supports all five of the National Standards for Foreign Language Education by giving students the opportunity to use the target language for real communication in culturally authentic situations.

In this edition of *Dos mundos* we have chosen to spotlight the community service of many Hispanics in **Ventanas culturales: Nuestra communidad** and **La vida diaria** (Rigoberta Menchú [p. 61], Frank Guajardo [p. 98], Reuben Martinez [p. 252], Carlos Santana [p. 316], Juan Luis Guerra [p. 384], Soraya [p. 416], and Amalia Hernández [p. 487]. Students in several classes that use *Dos mundos* are providing educational opportunities for young Nicaraguan women through the nonprofit organization, **Círculo de Amigas.** Active letter writing supports the language acquisition process of this project. See the **Vida y cultura** magazine on page 336 of *Dos mundos* for more information.

In addition, **Conexión a la comunidad** in **Capítulos 12, 13, 14,** and **15** provide students with opportunities to use their Spanish in real-life volunteer settings in their own communities. For an in-depth look at the how service learning can bring Spanish language learners and Hispanic cultures and communities together, see *Construyendo Puentes* (Building Bridges), *Concepts and Models for Service-Learning in Spanish,* eds. Josef Hellebrandt and Lucía T. Varona, American Association for Higher Education, 1999.

TEACHING PRONUNCIATION

Unlike the pronunciation of our first language, which we seem to learn effortlessly, good pronunciation of a second language is usually considered by learners to be difficult. The degree to which students of Spanish develop good pronunciation varies greatly; a very small number can barely make themselves understood. Some learners will be able to pass for native speakers of Spanish, but most students will speak with an American English accent. It is normal and is even expected by native speakers of Spanish. In fact, a relatively poor accent in Spanish is usually understood by native speakers.

We would like students using *Dos mundos* to develop good pronunciation habits. By "good," we mean that their pronunciation of Spanish will be close enough to that of native speakers so as not to call undue attention to the mispronunciations. Although poor pronunciation is comprehensible, it distracts the native speaker from understanding what the learner wants to express. Unfortunately, student pronunciation depends on factors largely beyond the instructor's control. These factors include present motivation for learning Spanish, past association of Spanish with people and events, listening acuity, ability to imitate, and other factors not yet well understood.

We suggest that students be urged to concentrate first on listening carefully and avoiding repetition. One of the major benefits of Stage 1 input activities is that they allow students to hear Spanish sounds in context so that they can develop a "feel" for Spanish pronunciation before they attempt to produce it. We feel that this listening period is especially important for developing good rhythm and intonation. Classroom practices that will help students develop a feel for the rhythm and intonation of Spanish include simple rhymes and songs and children's poetry. Good sources of these materials are **Lectorum,** www.lectorum.com (1-800-345-5946) or **El almacén de libros de Nana,** www.nanasbooks.com (1-800-737-6262), a family-run business of children's books and audio CDs in Spanish. In particular, we recommend the book and audio CDs by José Luis Orozco entitled *De colores and Other Latin American Folksongs for Children* (ISBN 0-8136-0706-x).

Even when a solid listening stage is provided, many students still experience problems in recognizing and producing certain sounds. For example, only a few students can pronounce a trilled r without explicit practice. A timely hint to avoid aspirating the sounds *p* [p], *t* [t], and *c* [k] can also be helpful. For this reason, a complete set of pronunciation exercises is included in the *Cuaderno de actividades.* Some students don't need or even profit by these pronunciation exercises, but many others find them useful.

We do not use class repetition drills or direct error correction to improve pronunciation. For students who need help with their pronunciation, special, discreet attention from you while they work in small groups or pairs may be sufficient. Others may need individual help during your office hours.

THE TOOLS OF PROFICIENCY: VOCABULARY AND GRAMMAR

The four skills—listening, speaking, reading, and writing—are the primary focus of *Dos mundos.* Two tools are essential for students to become proficient in any of these skills, however: vocabulary and grammar. Here we describe how each functions in *Dos mundos.* Since vocabulary is far more important than grammar, we will teach it first.

Teaching Vocabulary

The indisputable fact is that if learners do not know the meaning of words, they will not understand Spanish. And if they do not understand the input, they will not acquire! Our hypothesis is that the building block of language acquisition is the individual meaning-form pair. This means that much of the students' effort will go toward storing words and their meanings. The following are some resources and techniques that help students attend to key words and that make them meaningful.

- a clear and relevant context
- interesting visuals
- body language and gestures
- voice modulation
- emphasis on key words
- dramatic pause

Our general approach to vocabulary acquisition is to use new words in the Pre-Text Oral Activities, in the topical displays, and then in the communication activities and readings. Much of the vocabulary is repeated in the audio activities. Thus, the words that students need to talk about themselves and their interests will recur frequently enough to be acquired without resorting to rote memorization.

Instructors should ask students to keep vocabulary notebooks. During the Pre-Text Oral Activities and the communication activities, write key vocabulary items on the board and have students copy these words into their notebooks. (Students often include a first-language translation in their vocabulary notebooks for reference.) In the early stages, they are responsible for nothing more than recognition of meaning; that is, they need not produce or spell the words correctly. Aim to introduce, for recognition, twenty to forty new key vocabulary items per classroom hour. Remember that students can make very fast progress in the early stages of the NA because they only have to recognize the meaning of words.

Although we have provided a vocabulary list for reference and review in each chapter (**Vocabulario**), all new words introduced during the communication activities and written on the board can be copied by students into their vocabulary notebooks. In our experience teaching with *Dos mundos* these lists normally include about one-third more vocabulary than the lists in the text. Most of these extra words will be reintroduced, of course, many times in subsequent activities and will finally appear formally in one of the later chapters. This preview of vocabulary speeds up considerably in later chapters, since students will always encounter words they are familiar with, even when dealing with new topics.

The vocabulary list for each chapter contains the words that students should be able to recognize when used in context. We do not expect students to produce all these words in their speech. Usually students begin to use words in speech long after they are introduced in a particular chapter, and in fact, words that are only recognized in a particular chapter will be produced spontaneously during an activity in a subsequent chapter. The **Vocabulario** includes the most important new words from the **Actividades de comunicación,** but not words from realia, authentic texts, or other readings. When doing the **Actividades de comunicación** in class, keep in mind that even vocabulary words that previously have been active may need review. It is always best to ask **¿Hay vocabulario que no comprenden?** before pairing students to work together. We have repeated some words in chapter vocabulary lists in the **Repaso** section of the **Vocabulario** when they fit well into the thematic categories of a particular chapter or when they will be used by the students in activities for a particular topic. Close cognates are listed under the heading **Palabras semejantes.** The examples and exercises in the **Gramática y ejercicios** sections are based mainly on these vocabulary lists. When new words are used in the exercises, a margin note is provided. These vocabulary lists are recorded on separate *Vocabulary CDs,* which students may listen to if they need to hear the words pronounced in isolation.

Teaching Grammar

While grammar is clearly secondary to vocabulary in expressing meaning, we do not want students to acquire pidgin Spanish. Using **Dos mundos,** students in early Stage 3 may still begin activities with a reduced and simplified output, but gradually during the course their speech improves and becomes more grammatical. We believe that this improvement comes primarily from the input students hear in class and from what they read. On the other hand, **Dos mundos** does include the study of grammar for these reasons: (1) learned rules can be used to edit written production; (2) adult students get satisfaction from knowing the rules; and (3) some students can use conscious knowledge of rules to improve their listening comprehension.

The grammar and exercise sections of the text present the grammar rules that students will use to monitor their written work. There are short explanations of the rules of morphology (word formation), syntax (sentence formation), and word usage (lexical sets). (Orthographic and pronunciation rules and practice are found in the *Cuaderno de actividades.*) We have tried to reduce explanation and detail since we believe that excessive study and memorization of grammar rules and exercises are not very helpful to beginning students. We feel that grammar in **Dos mundos** is more than adequate for a first-year program. If individual students want more grammar practice, you may refer them to the **Expansión gramatical** at the end of the *Cuaderno de actividades.* Above all, students should not get the impression that the material presented in the grammar is to be completely learned. The grammar explanations and exercises serve as an introduction, a guideline, a reference—nothing more. The exercises are not meant to teach the grammar, but rather to verify comprehension of the explanation. Only real communicative experiences will result in acquisition of grammatical forms and structures. The acquisition of grammar takes a long time; students should not think that a conscious mastery of Spanish grammar is a prerequisite to communication with native speakers of Spanish.

The specific way you use the **Gramática y ejercicios** will depend on your own teaching style and your students' learning preferences and background. Some instructors prefer to assign the grammar and exercises before they begin the corresponding section in the **Actividades de comunicación y lecturas;** others assign parts of the grammar and exercises as they are working on a particular section; still others use the grammar and exercises as a follow-up after they have completed the corresponding section of the **Actividades de comunicación y lecturas** in class.

Students should be aware that the sections in the grammar usually (but not always) relate to the activities they are doing in class. We emphasize, however, that the **Gramática y ejercicios** sections are not responsible for developing the ability to use grammar in spontaneous speech. On the other hand, for many adults a clear grammar explanation, even if it does not really help the acquisition process, is affectively very satisfying. Only in a specific class situation can you judge the appropriate time and emphasis to be given to grammar assignments. We suggest that you avoid detailed grammar explanations in the classroom whenever possible. They rarely help more than a few students and invariably take away valuable time from language input and acquisition activities. More detailed comments on specific grammar points are found in the section *Expanded Instructor's Notes: Chapter Goals, Techniques for Providing Input and Additional Activities,* beginning on page 130 of the *Instructor's Manual.*

Most of the grammar exercises are short. We usually recommend that they be done in writing, as homework, because in writing students have time to focus on form. Many instructors assign the grammar exercises as homework and check them quickly during the following class period. We recommend that you distinguish carefully between an exercise in which the focus is on grammar and an acquisition activity in which the focus is on the message. Otherwise, students will get the idea that they should focus on grammar in all communication activities. Note that while grammar errors are not corrected directly in activities (but rather by naturally expanding the conversation), errors in the verification exercises are self-corrected using the answer key since the focus is indeed on grammar and correctness. The answers to all grammar exercises are in Appendix 4 of the student text.

The CD-ROM to accompany *Dos mundos* has more interactive grammar activities that students may do outside of class to supplement their formal knowledge of Spanish. Additional grammar exercises are also available on the *Dos mundos* website.

Syllabus

We recommend a comprehensive syllabus that students can use as a guide throughout the course. The sample syllabus included here is for first-semester Spanish for a course that meets 75 hours over 15 weeks, taught at Standard Pace. You will need to adapt this syllabus to your own teaching situations, and you may extend or modify it for use in second- or third-semester Spanish.

SPANISH 1
FALL 2005
Monday/Wednesday 8:00–10:30

Text: ***Dos mundos,*** Sixth Edition and ***Dos mundos, Cuaderno de actividades,*** Sixth Edition by Terrell, Andrade, Egasse, and Muñoz.
Dos mundos Audio CDs for Spanish 1
Dos mundos CD-ROM
Dos mundos **Website: www.mhhe.com/dosmundos6**

Office: _____   **Office Hours:** _____

Telephone: **email:**

Grade: Your grade in this class will be based on the following criteria:

Participation   _____%

Homework   _____%

Chapter Exams   _____%

The grading scale used in this class:

90–100%	A
80–89%	B
70–79%	C
60–69%	D
59% and below	F

Attendance: This class requires your participation and attendance is mandatory. If you do not need to attend class in order to pass the chapter exams, then you belong in a more advanced Spanish class. You may miss 15 hours of class, equivalent to six (6) classes. Your instructor may drop you for any absence above 15 hours. Late arrival to class will count toward missed classes.

Native Speakers: This beginning Spanish class is far below the level of any native speaker of Spanish. If you do not wish to learn another language and choose to be in this class in order to meet a college require-ment, keep in mind that your instructor will **only give you credit for what you accomplish in this course, and not for what you already know.**

Participation: Class participation is a vital part of your language learning experience and it is _____%
of your grade in this course. All students enrolled in Spanish 1 begin the semester with 100% in participation. Each missed class lowers that participation grade by 10% points: **1 miss = 90%, 2 misses = 80%,
3 misses = 70%, 4 misses = 60%, 5 misses = 50%, 6 misses = 40%, 7 misses = drop or F in course.**
Your participation grade is also influenced by: 1) coming to class prepared, 2) your use of Spanish to
converse with both your classmates and your instructor, and 3) classroom courtesy.

Assignments: This is a college-level transfer course. In order to succeed you will need college level skills in
reading, writing, listening, speaking, and note-taking.

This course is worth five (5) units. Plan on studying between 8 and 12 hours per week outside of class.

There are several types of assignments:

These assignments are collected:

- *Actividades escritas* section of the *Cuaderno de actividades*
- One **Lectura** or **Enlace literario** per chapter

These assignments are *not* collected:

- The *Ejercicios de gramática* from the *Dos mundos* text book
- The *Actividades auditivas* and the *Ejercicios de pronunciación y ortografía* from the *Cuaderno de actividades* are assigned before the end of each chapter.
- The *Ejercicios de gramática, Actividades auditivas* and *Ejercicios de pronunciación y ortografía* all have answer keys. Although these exercises and activities are not collected, you are encouraged to seek feedback from your instructor.

ASSIGNMENTS ARE NOT ACCEPTED LATE! DO NOT TURN IN LATE ASSIGNMENTS!

For every chapter, you will receive a sheet detailing assignments and exams for that period. Always check
your assignment sheet; it is your responsibility to hand in work on time and to complete future assignments
even if you are absent. When your work is returned, examine all corrections carefully since they will help
you to edit your written Spanish. Your assignment grade is calculated as a percentage of the total assignment
points for the semester.

Exams: There will be four (4) chapter exams in this course, one at the end of **Pasos A** and **B,** one after
Paso C and **Capítulo 1,** one after **Capítulos 2** and **3** and one after **Capítulos 4** and **5.** The last exam will
be given on the day of the scheduled final exam. Each exam will have spelling, listening comprehension,
reading, culture, vocabulary, and writing components. **You may miss and make up only one exam per
semester.** Any other misses will be calculated as 0. You must let me know on or before the day of the exam.
Make-up exams are given during instructor's office hours within one week of original exam date and may
be given as essay exams. All exams will be returned for review within two weeks and then kept by the
instructor for three months.

Final Grade: You may e-mail me with this request.

Disability Accommodations for Spanish Classes: If you have a disability that might prevent you from fully demonstrating your academic abilities, you should meet with the Disabled Student Program staff in room _____ as soon as possible to initiate disability verification and discuss appropriate accommodations. It is also your responsibility to make me aware of any special needs you may have relating to this class.

Group Work: Working with other students in study groups is an extremely effective means of studying. Not everyone in the study group needs to be at the same proficiency level: teaching others is a very powerful way to learn material yourself. Make sure, however, that you do not simply copy another student's work and turn it in as your own. When working in groups all participants must vary their work so that each assignment reflects individual work.

Academic Honesty: Cheating is not tolerated on either exams or assignments. Turning in essays that you did not write, for which you had considerable direct help from someone else, or which have been translated by a translation service or computer program will be considered cheating. Anyone copying from others, allowing others to copy their work, or using information fraudulently obtained may receive an "F" in this class.

Classroom Courtesy: Please turn off (or set to vibrate) and put away (purse or backpack) all pagers and cellular phones while in the classroom. If your cell phone rings during class you will immediately take a pop quiz.

When your professor is talking, you and other students need to listen. When your professor provides time for pair and/or group work, you need to work with your partner or group. This is not the time to talk to your professor about matters not related to the assigned activity, work on other assignments, or talk in a language other than Spanish: these matters must be handled during office hours or by appointment. You will have a break midway through the class session. Your professor will ask you to leave the class if you engage in disruptive behavior.

Class Procedure and General Goals: The primary focus of this first semester of Spanish is to develop your ability to understand native spoken and written Spanish and to increase your skill at expressing yourself in basic situations. Listening comprehension and reading are the bases for the sound acquisition of a foreign language. Remember that as children learning your first language, you had lots of time to listen before you attempted to speak. Don't be impatient with yourself when you find that you can understand far more than you can produce. This is natural; your speaking and writing abilities will always lag slightly behind your ability to understand.

You cannot expect to acquire native-like competence in a foreign language in one or two years. You *can* expect to be able to communicate with native speakers of Spanish even though you make mistakes. The goal in this course is communicative competence, not grammatical perfection. This class will use reading and writing activities to enhance your grasp of vocabulary and to provide you with opportunities to express yourself in Spanish.

Classroom time will be devoted almost solely to activities that will allow you to practice your skills of understanding and interacting in Spanish. Classroom time will not be spent doing grammar drills, translating, or listening to lengthy explanations of grammar. Please read all assigned grammar explanations and complete all assigned exercises. If you feel that you need additional help with grammar, see your instructor outside of class.

TENTATIVE CLASS SCHEDULE	
August 23, 25	Paso A
August 30	Paso B
September 1	Paso C
September 8	**Exam Pasos A and B**
September 13, 15, 20, 22, 27	Capítulo 1
September 29	**Exam Paso C and Capítulo 1**
October 4, 6, 11, 13	Capítulo 2
October 18, 20, 25, 27, November 1	Capítulo 3
November 3	**Exam Capítulos 2 and 3**
November 8, 10, 15, 17, 22	Capítulo 45
November 24, 29, December 1, 6, 8	Capítulo 5
December 13	**Exam Capítulos 4 and 5**

Course Objectives: At the end of this semester you can reasonably expect to be able to understand and communicate in the following areas:

- **You and the Other Students in the Classroom Setting:** Names, colors, clothing, description of people, classroom commands, classroom objects, body parts, numbers 0–100 and age, greetings and leave-taking
- **Family and Favorite Activities:** Immediate family, possession, languages and nationalities, favorite activities and sports
- **Preferences:** Making plans, classes, days of the week, preferences, weather
- **Activities:** Places in a city or university, daily activities, foods, origins
- **Daily Life and Holidays:** Holidays and celebrations, daily routine, states of being and emotions
- **Classes and Careers:** Classroom activities, abilities, careers and work activities, activities in progress, future plans

Using the *Dos mundos* Text

Each chapter of *Dos mundos* has four parts:

1. **Actividades de comunicación y lecturas** (Communication Activities and Readings): To be used primarily in class. The communication activities section consists of innovative classroom activities and readings. The classroom activities will be done in class with your instructor and other students. The readings may be written by the authors or selected from Hispanic magazines and newspapers. These readings will be assigned. One or more of these readings may be selected for the chapter exam. The audio recordings for some of these readings are included on the audio CDs and on the Online Learning Center.
2. **En resumen** (Summary): Activities that summarize the chapter material.
3. **Vocabulario** (Vocabulary): A list of all the vocabulary from the **Actividades de comunicación** section. You may use these lists as a reference. A *Vocabulario Audio CD* is available in the IVC library.
4. **Gramática y ejercicios** (Grammar and Exercises): To be used outside of class for explanations of structure. You will not need to turn in these assignments. Correct these exercises using the answer key

in Appendix 4 in the back of the text. Additional grammar points are in the **Expansión gramatical** in the back of the *Cuaderno de actividades.* You will not be formally tested on grammar, but it is a good idea to do exercises as assigned in order to keep up in class.

Vida y cultura (Life and Culture) is a cultural magazine following **Capítulos 4, 9,** and **15.** Each magazine includes articles on various aspects of Hispanic culture from a variety of countries.

The *inside front cover* of your text includes useful classroom phrases and expressions of courtesy and maps of Latin America. Use this as a ready reference when you need to ask questions, make comments, or make polite requests in Spanish.

The *inside back cover* of your text includes a map of Spain and data about the Spanish-speaking world. Additionally, you will find Verb Charts (Appendix 1), Grammar Summary Tables (Appendix 2), a Guide to Spelling and Accent Marks (Appendix 3), the Grammar Key (Appendix 4), a Spanish-English Vocabulary, and an Index at the back of your text.

Using the *Dos mundos Cuaderno de actividades* (Workbook)

Each chapter of the *Cuaderno de actividades* has six parts:

1. **Actividades escritas** (Writing Activities): Do these exercises in the workbook. Choose one of the essay activities **¡A escribir!** to hand in at the end of each chapter. Please write this essay on a separate sheet of paper.

2. **Resumen cultural** (Cultural Summary): These activities allow you to review the cultural information from **Sobre el artista, Lecturas, Ventanas culturales, Enlaces literarios,** and **¡Ojo!** sections of each chapter. This information will be included in your chapter exams.

3. **Actividades auditivas** (Listening Activities): Activities recorded on audio CD for use primarily outside of class.

   Los amigos animados: This section consists of one or two review listening activities presented in animated format on the video, CD-ROM, and website to accompany *Dos mundos.* They are followed by short comprehension questions.

   ¡A repasar! (Let's Review!): Listening selections that review the material in the chapter.

4. **Pronunciación y ortografía** (Pronunciation and Spelling Exercises): Auditory and written exercises on a chapter audio CD immediately following **¡A repasar!** These exercises will be assigned, but will not be handed in. A portion of the chapter exam will be devoted to spelling.

5. **Videoteca** (Video Activities): In addition to the **Los amigos animados,** the Videoteca also includes **Escenas culturales** with scenes from all 21 Spanish-speaking countries and **Escenas en contexto,** vignettes that correspond to the chapter themes. Each segment has a list of useful vocabulary, a brief synopsis of the action, and viewing activities. These may be done in the library or in class.

6. **Lecturas** (Readings): Will be assigned or read in class. Reading is an excellent way of acquiring more vocabulary and is also of great help in internalizing grammatical structures you have studied. One or more of these readings may appear on the chapter exams or the final exam. The answers to the questions that follow these readings are also in the key at the back of the *Cuaderno de actividades.*

Correct all of these exercises and activities using the key at the back of the *Cuaderno de actividades.* Use the **Ejercicios de ortografía,** the **Actividades auditivas,** the **Resumen cultural,** and the **Actividades escritas** to prepare for the spelling, listening, culture, and essay portions of your chapter exams. You will not need to bring your *Cuaderno de actividades* to class unless directed to do so by your instructor.

Additional Components

Dos mundos Audio CDs

Each chapter Audio CD contains the **Actividades auditivas** and **Pronunciación y ortografía.** Audio CDs are available with your new package of book and workbook, or may be purchased separately. The audio is also available digitally on the *Dos mundos* website as *premium content.* Use the passcode at the beginning of your text to gain access.

Lecturas and *Enlace literario* Audio CDs

This audio component comes with the audio program and is a collection of readings from the text. See selections with the headphones icon.

CD-ROM

An interactive CD-ROM is provided with your purchase of the first semester materials or is available for purchase separately. The CD-ROM is useful for review or extra practice.

Video Program

The video program, available on CD for student purchase, includes all *Videoteca* segments for *Dos mundos.* This set is available at bookstores, but it is *not* required class material. You may also view an additional video component on the Internet at **www.mhhe.com/dosmundos6.** Under Online Learning Center, click on *Student Edition,* choose a chapter, then click on *Entrevistas.* These are collections of interviews with native speakers of Spanish.

Your Responsibilities in This Class

All humans under normal conditions acquire one or more languages, but it is not possible to acquire Spanish in 75 to 150 hours of in-class instruction. You must take responsibility for your out-of-class learning. In addition to completing all assignments on time, we recommend that you read Spanish-language magazines or stories, watch TV, or converse with native speakers one to three times weekly. Take every opportunity to use your new skills in Spanish: read bilingual product labels, start a journal in Spanish, write notes and lists to yourself in Spanish, spend time with other students of Spanish, speaking only Spanish. Above all, make your extra activities fun and incorporate them into your daily life. Your instructor can open the door to Hispanic language and culture, but only you can enter.

Specific tasks:
- Read the syllabus, fill out the student data page, and sign the syllabus agreement.
- Attend regularly and speak Spanish in class.
- Bring your text, *Dos mundos,* to every class meeting.
- Take vocabulary notes in class from the words your instructor writes on the board. This vocabulary may appear on chapter exams.
- Do the **Ejercicios de gramática** (*Dos mundos*) at home. Correct all grammar exercises with the key in Appendix 4.
- Do the **Actividades escritas** (*Cuaderno*) for writing practice. Turn in **Actividades escritas** on time. It is your responsibility to read ahead on the assignment sheet and know when work is due.
- Listen and respond to the **Actividades auditivas** (Listening activities) in the *Cuaderno.*
- Read and listen to as many **Lecturas/Enlaces literarios** as possible.
- Take all exams when they are given.

Syllabus agreement

SPANISH 1 - FALL 2006

Please complete, sign, and return this form to your instructor

Name _____   Major: _____

Home Phone (_____)_____   Work/Cell Phone (_____)_____   e-mail: _____

Is a language required for your degree? _____   How many semesters? _____

Have you ever studied Spanish? _____   If yes, for how long? _____

What other foreign language(s) have you studied? _____   For how long? _____

Is Spanish spoken in your home and/or at work? _____   How frequently? _____

Is there anything about yourself that you want me to know? _____

_____

Is there anything you want to know about me or the class? _____

_____

I have read the syllabus for Spanish 1, and I agree to abide by the guidelines set forth. These guidelines include attendance as part of my grade. I understand that enrolling in this course and purchasing the text and materials in no way guarantees a passing grade or credit for the course. Grades and transferable credit are conferred only upon meeting the standards set forth in this course syllabus. Furthermore, I understand that grades cannot be changed after they have been assigned and an Incomplete is given only under emergency situations, not for routine failure to complete the requirements of the course.

Student's Signature _____   Date _____

Student Responsibility for the Learning Process

Students benefit more from communicative instruction when they are aware of the process of language acquisition and the many techniques for helping that process along. See the sample syllabus for the paragraph to the student, Your Responsibilities in Class. We also recommend a guided whole class discussion during the first two weeks that helps student to come up with strategies for language acquisition. We then provide them with a checklist of the most important learning strategies and ask them to meet with us once during the semester to discuss their progress. The checklist below was developed by Professors Jeffra Flaitz and Karine Feyton of the University of South Florida and presented at ACTFL in 1995. We have modified it to fit *Dos mundos* classes and reproduced it here with the gracious permission of the authors. Our students report that it is very helpful.

What language-learning strategies are you using?	✓ Yes, I do this.
Re-listen to language CDs in the car.	
Highlight my textbook.	
Review material immediately before and after class.	
Study before I go to sleep at night.	
Watch Spanish language television and/or DVDs.	
Initiate conversations in Spanish with my instructor or other native speakers.	
Complete all assignments.	
Write down new vocabulary in my notebook.	
Study my notes.	
Ask for help from the instructor.	
Practice speaking by myself.	
Use new vocabulary as soon as I can.	
Read ahead in the textbook.	
Try to speak spontaneously instead of translating everything in my head.	
Talk to my classmates in Spanish as best I can.	
Participate voluntarily in class.	
Study with a friend.	
Review corrected homework.	
Make and use flashcards.	
Uses rhymes and pictures to remember things.	
Use mnemonic devices to remember vocabulary.	
Eavesdrop on people speaking Spanish.	
Attend class regularly.	
Learn about Hispanic culture.	
Guess the meaning of new words before looking them up.	
Do some outside reading in Spanish.	
Review past material in both the main text and the *Cuaderno.*	

Modes of Address

We recommend that you address students with **usted** and that students also use **usted** with you. The use of **tú** between a student and instructor would be culturally inauthentic in most Hispanic institutions of higher learning. In addition, if the instructor uses **tú** with the students, they will have few opportunities to hear **usted** in the input. The pronoun **tú**, introduced in **Paso B**, should be used in all cases when students talk to each other. The text uses **usted** when addressing students. There are many opportunities in the interviews, dialogues, and other student-oriented activities to practice the use of **tú.** We do not include the pronouns **vosotros/as** or **vos** in the activities or exercises, since these pronouns of address have a more limited distribution and can be acquired later if needed. **Vosotros/as** and its verbs forms are included in all verb paradigms, and **vos** forms are footnoted in the grammar explanations. Both **vosotros/as** and **vos** are discussed in more detail in the **Expansión gramatical** at the end of the *Cuaderno de actividades.* In the authentic language of the **Actividades auditivas**, vosotros/as is used by Spaniards and **vos** by Argentineans.

Selecting Class Activities and Making Lesson Plans

Lesson plans are not provided for *Dos mundos,* as we believe it is important for the instructor to feel free to use these materials to supply exciting input and to allow the development of interesting interactions with and among the students. The activities in *Dos mundos* are not meant to be covered as in a traditional textbook but rather are intended as springboards for meaningful interactions using the target language. In this way the lives and experiences of your students can help determine the course of the activities and discussions that take place.

It is very conducive to a communicative language environment if the classroom can be decorated by instructors and students. Birthday charts, calendars, posters, poetry, and student work help create an environment that communicates language to students. If the instructor interacts with these materials on a frequent basis, it will help create classroom community and motivate students to take responsibility for their own learning.

A typical instructional hour consists of three to seven interactions. These interactions are selected from the Pre-Text Oral Activities, the thematic displays, **Actividades de comunicación, Actividades adicionales** (**AAs**) (see *Expanded Instructor Notes: Chapter Goals, Techniques for Providing Input and Additional Activities* on page 130), **Lecturas, Ventanas culturales, Ventanas al pasado, Enlaces literarios,** and **Actividades escritas.** In addition, you will want to include games, skits, presentations, videos, slides, movies, and your other favorite input and interactive activities. In general, the grammar explanations and exercises, as well as the listening comprehension, written activities, and pronunciation and orthography sections of the *Cuaderno de actividades* are meant to be used as homework assignments. Students like to have a follow-up of some sort on homework in class, however. In most classes you will want to save a small amount of time for grammar discussions and perhaps check one or more of the exercises that students have written. The sequence of class interactions is not fixed, but here is one possibility that you may want to try in a 50-minute class.

- 5 minutes   warm-up/review with picture file (PF)
- 10 minutes   comprehensible input based on new display
- 20–25 minutes   **Actividades de comunicación** + **AAs**
- 5–10 minutes   pre-reading, reading, songs, or video
- 5 minutes   grammar questions

The length of the interactions is not fixed either. Some may be as short as one minute while others may last up to twenty minutes. Generally, students' attention starts to wander after about ten minutes on most interactions. For this reason, you must determine both the length and the presentation order of the interactions you select for a particular class period. The thematic divisions of each **Actividades de comunicación y lecturas** section are ordered as logically as possible, and the activities within a topic are ordered from input activity to output. In most cases, however, there is enough flexibility to change; many experienced instructors skip to various thematic sections within a chapter as seems appropriate to their particular class.

We have tried to provide more than enough materials for a variety of interactions for each topic. For some topics you may wish to add other activities (see the *Instructor's Resource Kit*), and for others you may wish to omit several activities. There may even be entire topics (and vocabulary and grammar items) that you decide to omit as not relevant to your students' needs.

Picture File

A good picture file (PF) is essential for use with **Dos mundos.** It is created with real pictures from magazines and newspapers. A 50-photo PF is available for use with **Dos mundos,** Sixth Edition. If you wish to supplement it, cut pictures from magazines or newspapers. Trim them to eliminate English and other distracting elements. Paste or tape them to heavy construction paper. If possible, laminate them to protect them while they are handled. Some instructors request that their students bring one picture per week as part of a "show-and-tell" session. In this way, a large picture file is built up quickly and without too much work or expense.

The pictures in your PF will be more useful if they fulfill certain requirements:

1. Each picture should focus on a particular thing or event but also contain other items or events to lend interest. Flash cards with a single item (for example, a banana) are less useful, since they do not lend themselves to much more than a flash-card drill.

2. Each picture should be interesting or eye-catching. It should contain something that will invite students to pay attention as you talk about it.

3. Each picture should be large enough to be seen easily. Attention wanders quickly if the input cannot be related to the visual being used.

We recommend that in making a PF you save all pictures that students bring in and group them for use later. Searching for a particular item or category is too time-consuming.

The PF is useful in various ways at different levels. In Stages 1 and 2 the pictures have several functions. First, they bring the outside world into your classroom and help create images and situations with which your students can engage. Second, they make the input comprehensible. In some cases there are new words that we do not wish to associate with students in the class (for example, adjectives such as *fat, thin* and *ugly*). In other cases, it is difficult in class to dramatize a new item adequately (for example, activities such as camping, sailing, and cleaning). The third function is one of associating. Often, particular characteristics of a picture (the background, the people in the picture, or something that they are doing that draws one's attention) will aid students in associating the meaning of a new word or structure with its target-language form. In Stage 3, pictures are used to stimulate creative writing. Pictures also may be used for quizzes, especially in the initial stages of language acquisition. Finally, pictures may be useful for creative writing assignments for individuals, groups, or the whole class.

Homework

Homework assignments should vary depending on the students, their goals in the course, and the time available for outside study. In many foreign-language classes in the United States, the class hour is the only chance students get to interact in the target language. For this reason, class hours should be reserved almost entirely for communicative activities. Activities that take more time, such as long readings, listening to recorded materials, written exercises, and reading grammar explanations, should be done outside class whenever possible. Sometimes this is not possible; students may not have access to CD players, and working adults may not have time to read and study outside class. In some cases, students may not have the background to read and study grammar on their own. In such situations you will want to include some of these activities in the class hour. A good rule of thumb is two hours of homework per week for every hour in class (the Carnegie unit). Do not lose sight of the basic principle of a communicative language class: communication skills are acquired through comprehensible input and the communication of meaning with others. Classroom interaction can be an ideal situation for acquisition to take place.

Evaluation

Good tests are ones that encourage acquisition; that is, to prepare for the test is to obtain more comprehensible input. According to this view, reading comprehension, listening comprehension, and interaction are good tests, because the best way to prepare for them is to extensively read and interact with people who speak the language. The testing emphasis in any course will vary. In some classes you may want to test only listening comprehension and speaking. In others you may be interested in developing the reading skill but will not feel that your students need to be tested on writing skills. The *Testing Program* includes sample exams and a bank of questions in the areas of listening comprehension, reading, vocabulary, grammar, composition, and conversation.

Affective Filter

We have described acquisition as a process that takes place when certain requirements are met. One is that students be exposed to high-quality, comprehensible input. The other is that they be able to use the target language in a low-anxiety environment. How you go about lowering affective filters will be a part of your own teaching style, and each instructor is different. Here are some general guidelines that seem to work for most instructors in creating a positive affective environment in the classroom.

- Each student should feel that the instructor takes a personal interest in his or her progress. Learn your students' names immediately, and begin to accumulate personal information about each one. (A student information card filled out the first week of class can help you get to know your students. [See the last page of the sample syllabus.]) Use this information to make comments during the communication activities to link the information in the activity to students' own interests and experiences.

- Foster a sense of classroom community, and encourage students to become acquainted with one another through pair work.

- Encourage all attempts to communicate. Limit direct error correction to the grammar exercises or to formal essays; such correction should not occur during the communication activities or during any conversation in which the focus is on meaning rather than structure. Praise attempts at guessing and risk-taking in both comprehension and speech production. Promote creativity and risk-taking as more important than any error students might make.

- Encourage a positive attitude about eventual success. The goal of a first-year course is to communicate with native speakers, not to be able to understand and speak the target language as fluently as a native speaker.

- Help your students set realistic, useful, and attainable goals. Most students will not be able to develop a perfect accent, nor will they be able to monitor extensively enough to correct all errors in their speech. On the other hand, through perseverance, all students can be proficient and successful communicators in a new language.

- Make the class enjoyable. Smile, laugh, react, share, explain—but, most of all, enjoy yourself. Language acquisition—and instruction—does not need to be a chore.

- Appeal to students' desire to learn. Add cultural information (in the target language) in all activities. Recount your own experiences, travels, and encounters. Give PowerPoint™ presentations, show movies, and videotapes, play music. Bring newspapers and magazines to class. Play games. Read and tell picture-book stories to students. Familiar folk- and fairytales are great for beginners. Make the course a cultural as well as a linguistic experience.

USING THE COMMUNICATION ACTIVITIES

Pre-Text Oral Activities

The Pre-Text Oral Activities are found in the margins of *Dos mundos, Instructor's Edition,* most often on the first page of each chapter and also in the section titled *Expanded Instructor Notes: Chapter Goals, Techniques for Providing Input and Additional Activities,* page 130. They are meant to be done before you begin the communication activities of the chapter, but since they introduce vocabulary and structures used in the entire chapter, you may decide to integrate them with the chapter's **Actividades de comunicación.** The purpose of the Pre-Text activities is for you to use new words in a communicative context, inviting interaction with students. Most chapters have Pre-Text Oral Activities, but the Pre-Text Oral Activities of **Pasos A, B,** and **C** are especially important, as they represent the first comprehensible input that students will hear; they also set the tone and pace of the class. Due to space considerations, the **Pre-Text Oral Activities** of **Pasos A, B,** and **C** continue on the last page of the **Gramática y ejercicios.** In a few other chapters the **Pre-Text Oral Activities** are also on the last page of the chapter. Many of the Pre-Text Oral Activities require use of your picture file.

Chapter Organization

Each chapter consists of three to four themes, with a vocabulary display for each and two or more activities and/or readings that support the theme. There are fifteen types of recurring activities in *Dos mundos.* We will describe each one in order of appearance in the text.

Vocabulary Displays

Each thematic section of a chapter of *Dos mundos* begins with a visual display containing new vocabulary that will be useful in doing the **Actividades de comunicación** for that section. These displays generally have a **Lea Gramática...** note to let students know which sections in the **Gramática y ejercicios** correspond to a particular topic. The Instructor's Notes include suggestions for the introduction of the vocabulary and/or grammar.

Diálogos (Dialogues)

Two kinds of dialogues appear in the **Actividades de comunicación** of *Dos mundos:* (1) model dialogues and (2) open dialogues.

1. *Diálogos* (Model Dialogues). These fixed-content dialogues are meant to be models for conversation. They often introduce new vocabulary and phrases that are difficult to introduce in classroom conversation. The model dialogues are not designed to be memorized, nor it is necessary to vary their content. See **Paso A, Actividades 1, 2,** and **8.**

2. *Diálogos abiertos* (Open Dialogues). These are patterns used to create dialogues. Read the entire pattern aloud, asking students to supply words and expressions to fill in the blank spaces. Some useful words and expressions may precede the dialogue in a **Palabras útiles** box. It is sometimes helpful, especially in longer open dialogues, to put lists of additional possible words for each blank in columns on the board. Less creative students can pick and choose from the lists to fill in the blanks. Have students practice the dialogue in pairs, and encourage them to create their own versions by changing the dialogue in any way they want. Then ask *volunteers* to perform the dialogue for the class. See **Paso B, Actividades 3** and **9.**

For all dialogues we suggest the following steps: Read through the dialogue aloud, with the class following along silently. Read slowly and role-play both parts, changing your voice to match the gender and situation of the characters if possible. Ask students to identify words and phrases they do not understand. Explain new words and forms, and then have students practice the dialogues in pairs. Many instructors find that the "read, look up, and say" technique is useful; that is, students read a line silently to themselves and then (not looking at the book) look up at their partner and say the line meaningfully. In this way they do not "read" the dialogue to each other, and the effect is more like real conversation.

The role of the dialogues in **Pasos A** and **B** is primarily affective in nature—students like to be able to speak some Spanish at the very beginning of the course; otherwise they sometimes feel they are not making progress. Dialogues are also quite useful when students have a need to use the language outside the classroom and cannot "wait for acquisition." They provide expressions that students need in conversations right away. Consequently, the dialogues in **Pasos A** and **B** are made up of stock phrases like **Buenas tardes, Hasta luego,** and so on. You can introduce most of these expressions via the **Diga** command during the TPR input activities: **Digan «Buenos días», digan «Hola».** By the end of **Paso B,** you will expect most students to be able to do two- to three-line dialogues with these expressions. (Keep in mind that dialogues in *Dos mundos* are not meant to be memorized.)

Asociaciones (Associations)

These activities match a person or a situation with a description or solution. There is often more than one appropriate choice or match; encourage students to supply options not included in the list. In later chapters, the **Asociaciones** are often fairly involved and require students to read carefully before making choices. Follow up each set of matched items with expanded conversation and appropriate personalized comments. See **Paso A, Actividad 3.**

Identificaciones (Identification Activities)

These usually involve a person or an object that must be matched with a brief description. Often these have a correct answer. See **Paso A, Actividad 5,** or **Paso B, Actividad 1.**

Intercambios (Interactions)

These are usually tables or lists of information that students scan for particular pieces of information. Look at the **Intercambio** in **Paso B, Actividad 6.** In this **Intercambio,** students state the prices of illustrated items. It is important that students understand how to substitute words using the sentence pattern. First, ask students to scan the items. Then use the pattern and ask questions, substituting the various items illustrated: **¿Cuánto cuesta la silla? ¿Cuesta $57.59 o $47.59 la mesa?** and so on. Then have students work in pairs, using the structure suggested in the text. In other **Intercambios,** students are able to choose the questions they will ask. For example, in the **Intercambio** in **Actividad 2** of **Capítulo 1,** students ask each other questions about the place and date of birth of several of the characters in the text. Student 1 chooses either the place or date; Student 2 must understand the question and find the answer in the table. In Stage 3 the **Intercambios** are based on more complex information than in earlier stages, and allow for more freedom of selection by the students.

Descripción de dibujos (Description of Drawings)

These activities derive their input or output from a series of small drawings that simulate communication. The first **Descripción de dibujos** is in **Paso B, Actividad 7,** and requires students to listen to the instructor's descriptions of the drawings and select the appropriate one. In subsequent chapters students are often paired to describe the drawings to their partner. See **Capítulo 2, Actividad 16.**

Entrevistas (Interviews)

Model questions and possible answers first, writing possible answers on the board for reference. Have students work in pairs, one asking the questions and the other answering. The interviewer may take notes on the interviewee's answers. Students then switch roles and follow the same procedure. In the follow-up, ask students to give the class information on the person they interviewed. See **Paso B, Actividad 11.**

En resumen (Summary Activities)

This culminating section at the end of **Actividades de comunicación y lecturas** starts with **De todo un poco** in **Paso B,** and adds **Dígalo por escrito!** and **Cuéntenos usted** in **Capítulo 1.**

- *De todo un poco.* These activities are meant to expand and integrate the chapter topics in a communicative way. They may be one of various types of activities and usually involve pair or group work.

- *¡Dígalo por escrito!* These creative writing assignments summarize the chapter topics.

- *Cuéntenos usted.* These activities are intended to help students to tell their own short stories about life experiences.

Del mundo hispano (From the Hispanic World)

These activities consist of various sorts of realia-based forms, advertisements, or articles taken from Spanish-language newspapers and magazines. They serve to develop scanning skills and, particularly in Stage 3, are useful as a point of departure for comprehensible input and oral interaction. See **Capítulo 1, Actividad 8.** Introduce each **Del mundo hispano** by asking simple questions that require students to scan the realia for information: **¿A qué hora es el programa** _____**? ¿En qué canal se presenta el programa** _____**?** Comment on and explain key words, then have students do the interaction or answer the questions in the text in pairs. In the follow-up, add personalized questions.

Preferencias (Affective Activities)

In these activities, students are asked to express a personal opinion. Students are given a statement and three or more ways to complete it. See **Capítulo 1, Actividad 10.** For example, **(No) Me gusta...** might be followed by choices such as **acampar, patinar,** and sometimes an empty set of question marks to cue students to complete the statement with an item of their choice. Normally students need only answer **sí** or **no** to each choice. The **Preferencias** activities have an optional follow-up, **Y tú ¿qué dices?,** in which students work with a partner to react to their partner's statement. A vocabulary box with possible reactions is provided. The **Y tú, ¿qué dices?** section is not intended to be the sole focus of the activity nor to replace the input provided by the instructor in the whole-class discussion. If you choose to do the **Y tú, ¿qué dices?** section, make it clear to students that they do not have to ask questions of each other but rather make statements based on their preferences and use the phrases provided to make comments on their partner's statements.

Although students are introduced to affective activities in Stage 2 (**Capítulo 1**), the range of possible responses is limited. The emphasis is not on a particular answer but rather on commenting (or explaining) why the students picked (or created) a particular response. Follow up by comparing (or explaining) comments on your own experiences. Try to remember as much information as you can about the likes and dislikes, favorite activities, experiences, and so forth of each student, in order to bring up this information in other relevant situations. In affective activities, stress positive attributes.

Narración (Narration Series)

Each narration series consists of a set of eight to sixteen sketches that form a connected narrative. These series use grammatical structures that are presented in the grammar section of the chapter; they can, however, be done by students who have not studied the grammar sections.

Each series has a particular focus. For example, the narration series in **Capítulo 2** is used to illustrate infinitives after **ir + a;** the one in **Capítulo 3** practices daily activities, and so on. Do not rely excessively on the grammatical focus, and do not expect students to produce the new form correctly after doing the narration series. (Once students are comfortable narrating a particular series, the situation and structure may be varied. For example, after doing **Actividad 2** in **Capítulo 2** in the third person singular, you may want to use the first person singular and narrate your own weekend plans. See *Expanded Instructor Notes* in **Capítulo 2** for a detailed description of teaching a narration.

Conversación (Discussion)

These are usually sets of guideline questions on a particular topic. The instructor asks the questions and students volunteer their opinions. These activities provide opportunities for students to express themselves more freely on topics in which they are interested. Thus, they are designed to generate conversation and interchange. Encourage students to elaborate on each response, make comments, and ask *each other* questions that expand responses. See **Capítulo 2, Actividad 13.**

Definiciones (Definitions)

In these activities, the definition is usually given and students must supply only a word. In most activities, however, the words to be supplied are often new, as are many of the words used in the definitions. Therefore, you may want to preview each definition activity, usually by using your PF to highlight the new key words. Definition activities can be done as whole-class interactions, or first in pairs followed by whole-class discussion. As you match definitions with words, work with the whole class to define in Spanish some of the important terms in the definitions themselves. See **Capítulo 2, Actividad 15.**

Orden lógico (Logical Sequence)

These activities are designated to be done with the whole class or in pairs, and require students only to order activities or events. Sometimes there is a correct order; at other times the order is flexible. See **Capítulo 4, Actividad 5.**

Encuestas (Poll)

Encuestas ask for students' opinions and lend themselves to a general discussion of class opinions. We encourage you to take a poll of "all students in the class who . . ." and to expand discussion as you write this information on the board. See **Capítulo 5, Actividad 11.**

Situaciones (Situational Dialogues)

These consist of a description of a particular situation, followed by several introductory lines for a possible dialogue on the situation described. They are meant to allow students more flexibility in language use and in role playing. Read over the situation with the whole class, explaining new vocabulary and making sure that students understand the setup. Then divide the class into pairs and ask each pair to create their own dialogue. Remind them to keep the dialogues short and interesting. They should use vocabulary they know well and avoid looking up new words in the dictionary, as new words will simply confuse other students when the dialogue is performed for the class. Give students time to practice the situations in pairs or small groups, then let volunteers perform their dialogue. Most students prefer to use notes. See **Capítulo 13, Actividad 10.**

Using the *Videoteca*

Each chapter introduces the **Videoteca** on the chapter-opening page under **Multimedia Resources.** In-depth **Videoteca** activities are found in the *Cuaderno de actividades* and include **Los amigos animados,** with questions in the **Actividades auditivas** section, **Escenas culturales,** and **Escenas en contexto,** each with post-viewing questions. These activities may be done in class if time permits, and, indeed, we recommend that **Paso C** and **Capítulo 1** be done with the whole class so that students become familiar with the process. Later on, **Videoteca** activities may be assigned as homework or for extra credit. The video scripts are in the section *Video Program to accompany* **Dos mundos,** beginning on page 183 of this *Instructor's Manual.*

EXPANDED INSTRUCTOR NOTES: CHAPTER GOALS, TECHNIQUES FOR PROVIDING INPUT AND ADDITIONAL ACTIVITIES

Paso A

Goals

Paso A has four goals: (1) to convince students that they will understand the Spanish you speak in class; (2) to help lower their anxiety by letting them get to know their classmates; (3) to begin binding meaning to key words in the input; and (4) to teach students to listen primarily to key words and context. All activities are designed to make input comprehensible. To provide comprehensible input you will use three principal techniques that do not require students to produce Spanish words: Total Physical Response (TPR), student centered input, and picture file (PF) input. Each technique is described in detail in this section.

By the end of **Paso A** students should understand your "teacher talk." They will recognize the meaning of about 250 words when used in context. Above all, students will learn to understand words, grammatical forms, and structures they have not previously heard or studied. Keep in mind that not every word that you use nor every word in the communicative activities will be listed in the end of chapter **Vocabulario.** The chapter **Vocabulario** includes thematic and comprehension vocabulary that will help your students understand and converse with native speakers. In addition, remember that students may not remember every word you introduce, so they may need to review words prior to beginning an activity.

Input Techniques in Stage 1

Total Physical Response (TPR)

TPR, as used in the Natural Approach, is adapted from a methodology developed by James Asher, Professor of Psychology at San Jose State University in California.[1] During Stage 1, TPR in its simplest form consists of commands given by the instructor that students then act out. (In Stage 2 and particularly in Stage 3, students may also give commands to each other and/or to the instructor.)

The first time TPR is introduced, briefly explain in English what you are going to do and what you expect of the students. Tell the class that you are going to teach them to follow instructions. Assure them that they will learn to recognize the meaning of the commands gradually during the next few class periods. Introduce each new command one at a time, reviewing each one frequently. Have students listen first and watch you do the action. For example, begin with **Por favor, pónganse de pie.** Say the command clearly, and stand up while saying it. Then say **Siéntense,** executing the command yourself. Repeat the sequence several times; then have students do the command with you. Then give the command and have students practice it with the class, and test comprehension by giving the command and having the class perform it alone. Remind students that "cheating" (looking around at classmates to see what actions they are performing) is allowed.

Here is a sample TPR sequence: **Pónganse de pie, caminen, sí, lentamente. Ahora, corran, corran rápidamente. Siéntense de nuevo y ahora pónganse de pie, corran, caminen lentamente y salten una vez. Ahora salten dos veces. Dénse una vuelta y miren hacia arriba. Ahora regresen al asiento y siéntense.** An average TPR activity last from three to seven minutes and introduces from five to fifteen new commands.

---

[1]For details see Asher, J., *Learning Another Language through Actions: The Complete Teacher's Guide;* and Ray, Blaine, *Look I Can Talk! A Step-By-Step Approach to Communication Through TPR Stories,* Sky Oaks Productions, Inc., Los Gatos CA, 1993, 1995; and Olliphant, Jo Ann, *Total Physical Fun: Strategies and activities for teaching language through cooperative play,* Sahmarsh Publications, 1991.

Student-Centered Input with Names as Responses

This technique is used to introduce new words or grammatical forms and structures in the comprehension mode. Students indicate comprehension by answering with their classmates' names or, in some cases, with **sí/no.** Several topics can be used as a basis for input in **Paso A.** We describe each separately; in your speech, however, they should be mixed.

1. **Color and length of hair.** A cue that aids students in remembering names consists of drawing their attention to each other's physical characteristics (use only positive characteristics). For example, Jean Clark might be **una muchacha de pelo largo** or Jim Armstrong **el muchacho de pelo castaño corto.** As you speak, write key words on the board; students may copy these words into their vocabulary notebook. The key words in these examples are **pelo, largo, corto,** and **castaño.** Pick characteristics that seem especially positive and easy to remember.

2. **Facial characteristics.** Often the fact that a male student has a **barba** or **bigote** will provide identification clues. Eye color and glasses are distinguishing features also.

3. **Clothes.** Articles of clothing plus color words are an easy identification tool. For example, Judy Lindstrom might be **la muchacha de la blusa amarilla.** Use key words like **blusa, camisa, pantalones, vestido, falda,** plus a few color words such as **rojo, azul, verde,** and **blanco.** Form changes for gender agreement do not normally interfere with comprehension. Write the words on the board in either masculine or feminine form, as they occur in conversation; if the students are particularly knowledgeable about grammar, write adjectives on the board in double form: **bueno/a.** Use both **de (la muchacha de los pantalones azules)** and **(que) lleva (Miguel lleva una chaqueta negra)** for clothing.

Here are several techniques for introducing these topics.

1. Ask the student his or her name directly: **Usted, señorita, ¿cuál es su nombre?** Then make some comment about an identifying feature—hair or eye color, clothing, and so on. For example, suppose the student's name is Linda McClure: **Miren a Linda. Linda** (or **la señorita McClure) lleva una falda roja.** (Point to the skirt.) **Es una falda roja, ¿verdad?** (Point to other red things.) **¿Quién es** (or **¿Cuál es el nombre de..., ¿Cómo se llama...) la muchacha de la falda roja?** Students answer with the student's name: **Linda.** Expand each response: **Sí, Linda es la estudiante de la falda roja** (or **que lleva una falda roja).**

2. Ask the class to find a student with the characteristics you announce: **¿Dónde hay una muchacha de pelo rubio?** (use mime techniques to illustrate the meaning of **dónde.**) Students need only point to those female students with blond hair (there may be several). Pick one of them and ask her name. Then the procedure continues as in (1) above.

Use both procedures and switch back and forth from one to the other. Suppose, for example, that we already know Valerie Nguyen as **la muchacha de la falda verde;** you can then ask if there is another student in the class with a green skirt. If there is, then that student's name is learned together with some other characteristic. Laurie Avant, who is wearing **una falda verde,** may also be wearing **un suéter blanco.**

With this technique you can usually introduce about twenty new words in a twenty-minute activity. Make sure the class understands what you are saying by using frequent review questions that require only a student's name as an answer: **¿Quién es la estudiante que lleva una falda roja?** and so on. Remember that the goal of the activities in Stage 1 is to give students the opportunity to interpret meaning by using key words and context: Comprehension = key words + context.

Picture-File Input with Names as Responses

As we noted in the Picture File section on page 124, you will rely heavily on your PF throughout *Dos mundos.* The PF is very helpful in making the input in Stage 1 comprehensible. Suppose, for example, you hold up two pictures, one of a man and one of a woman. Here is some possibile input: **Aquí tengo dos fotos.**

En esta foto hay un hombre y en esta foto hay una mujer. ¿Entienden? Un hombre aquí (pointing) y una mujer aquí (pointing). In addition, using your PF in **Paso A** allows you to introduce adjectives like **feo** and **gordo** without referring to students in the class. If the pictures are interesting, a PF holds students' attention and lowers anxiety levels.

This technique consists of (1) describing a picture or something in a picture, (2) passing the picture to a student to hold, and (3) asking the class: **¿Quién tiene la foto de _____?** Sample input: **En esta foto hay un carro. ¿Ven el carro? Es un carro muy grande** (mime the meaning of **grande**), **¿verdad? (Sí.) Ahora le doy la foto del carro grande a Barbara. Barbara tiene** (mime) **la foto del carro grande. Ahora, yo les pregunto, ¿quién tiene la foto del carro grande?** **y ustedes responden...** (wait for students to figure out that you want to say the student's name) **Barbara. Sí, Barbara tiene la foto del carro grande.**

Each time you introduce a new picture, review (in random order) others that you have previously handed out. Vary your question format so that this does not become an oral activity drill. Sample input: **¿Quién tiene la foto de una casa pequeña? (Mark.) Sí, Mark tiene la foto de una casa pequeña. ¿Y el gato blanco? El gato blanco lo tiene Doug, ¿verdad?** (Keep in mind that using object pronouns in context will not prevent students from understanding the input.) You can usually introduce from five to fifteen new pictures in a single fifteen- to twenty-minute activity.

We suggest that you return to your PF to review the pictures you have shown several times during each class period throughout **Paso A.** Each time you review, be sure to include one or two new pictures that contain familiar items; otherwise students will tire of talking about the same picture, even whey they still need more input that contains the same words.

Here are some suggestions for the use of the PF for **Paso A:** (1) common things in students' daily life (**casa, carro, bicicleta,** and so on); (2) pets (**perro, gato**); (3) people (**hombre, mujer, padre, madre, muchacho, muchacha, niño, niña,** and so on); (4) colors (**azul, rojo, amarillo,** and so on); (5) descriptive adjectives (**grande, pequeño, bonito, feo, joven, viejo,** and so on).

Expanding Student Responses

Many instructors expand what students say. For example, if the instructor asks, **¿Quién es la muchacha de la falda roja?** and the students answer **Margie,** the logical expansion is **Sí, Margie lleva una falda roja.** The expansion is easily understood because of its discourse position. This expansion is then followed by another question related to the first: **¿Es corta la falda de Margie? (Sí.)** The expansion is **Sí, es corta, no es larga,** and so forth.

Here are other examples of expansion to be used in Stage 1.

- **¿Quien lleva un suéter azul? (Roula.) Sí, hoy Roula lleva un bonito suéter azul. ¿Quién más lleva un suéter hoy? (John.) Sí, John lleva un suéter también. Pero el suéter de Roula es azul. ¿Es azul también el suéter de John? (No.) No, es rojo.**

- **Hay tres muchachos que tienen bigote, ¿verdad?** (Hold up three fingers.) **(Sí.) ¿Quiénes son? (Paul, Hoang, Alex.) Sí, Paul tiene bigote, Hoang tiene bigote y Alex también tiene bigote. Hay tres estudiantes de bigote en la clase. ¿Hay mujeres en la clase que tienen bigote? (No.**—students usually laugh) **¿Por qué? Porque las mujeres no tienen bigote, los hombres tienen bigote.**

Note that words like **más, también, pero, por qué, porque,** and **hay** have all been introduced and understood in context.

An expansion can also be a grammatically correct rephrasing, by the instructor, in response to a student's grammatically incorrect utterance. For example, if a student says, **yo lleva una camisa blanco,** an instructor may say, **¿Usted lleva camisa? Sí, y su camisa es blanca. Yo llevo una camisa negra.** Note that in the instructor's response the discourse remains natural; the expansion is not an artificial correction and does not disturb the flow of conversation. Rather, it adds input. If this kind of expansion comes easily to you, we recommend that you use it. If not, don't worry; students will have many chances to acquire the correct form from other input they hear and read.

132

Optional Grammar

These classroom grammar activities or discussion points may be used to expand upon grammar explanations and exercises done at home.

A.1 Write the appropriate pattern on the board with blanks for names and have students practice asking each other's names in a whole-class autograph activity. All students circulate with pen and paper. Each student asks five classmates their names and has them sign their paper (**Firma, por favor**). Follow up by asking: **¿Quiénes son los estudiantes de su lista?** or **¿Cómo se llaman los estudiantes de su lista?**

Paso B

Goals

The purpose of **Paso B** is to continue to provide comprehensible input that will help students acquire basic interpersonal communication abilities. Continue to emphasize development of students' ability to comprehend Spanish, but also encourage them to respond with single words and short phrases. In some activities, students will work with classmates in pairs or small groups. The semantic focus continues to be on identification and description of common items and people in students' environment.

Input Techniques in Stage 2

Either/Or Questions

The most important question technique for making the transition from Stage 1 and Stage 2 is the "choice" question. The Pre-Text Oral Activities of **Paso B** use the vocabulary introduced in **Paso A** but encourage students to produce a word or phrase in Spanish.

- **Numbers.** As numbers have been introduced for comprehension in Stage 1 (*Pre-Text Oral Activities, Dos mundos,* page 21), use the following activity to make the transition to Stage 2. Begin by including the numbers from one to ten in your input. Count the students, walking around the room pointing to each one and counting slowly. Students should mostly listen, but some will want to count along, and some will say the numbers aloud. Repeat the procedure several times—go forward and backward, always giving the same student the same number. Hold up fingers, and count to ten slowly. Continue until most of the students have joined in voluntarily. Hold up fingers and ask either/or questions like **¿Son dos o tres? ¿Son cinco o siete?** Always expand answers: **Sí, es verdad, son tres,** and so on. Continue until numbers through ten are easily recognized by most students. Ask either/or questions, so that each time students respond, the response is simply a repetition of what you have just said: **¿Son siete o diez? (Diez.)**

- **Colors and clothes.** Talk about students and their clothing, as you did in **Paso A** by mixing questions that require a student's name as the response (**¿Quién lleva una chaqueta azul?**) and **sí/no** questions (**¿Lleva Tom un suéter amarillo?**). Then every fifth question or so use an either/or question: **¿Es azul or roja la chaqueta de Ann?** Students respond with a single word, which you expand: **(Roja.) Sí, la chaqueta de Ann es roja. ¿Son azules o negros los zapatos de Ahmed? (Negros.) Sí, son negros. Los zapatos de Ahmed son negros.** Attend to the semantic correctness of students' responses, and simply expand the responses that have grammatical errors: **¿Es blanca o amarilla la blusa de Lucy? (Blanco.) Sí, la blusa de Lucy es blanca.**

Open Sentences

Use the descriptive adjectives introduced in **Paso A** and your PF to encourage production: **En esta foto tenemos una señorita. Es muy...** Students might say **joven/vieja, bonita/fea, delgada/gorda,** according to the picture. Expand the responses: **Este hombre es... (Gordo.) Sí, es un hombre gordo y un poco feo, ¿verdad?**

Lists

Ask for a volunteer to stand up. Direct attention to the clothes the student is wearing: **¿Qué lleva Mike? (Pantalones.) Sí, lleva pantalones. ¿De qué color son los pantalones de Mike? (Verde.) Sí, son verdes, ¿verdad? Lleva pantalones verdes. ¿Qué más lleva? (Camisa.) Sí, lleva una camisa. ¿Es azul la camisa que lleva Mike? (No, amarillo.) Sí, la camisa no es azul, es amarilla.**

Interrogatives (¿Qué? ¿Cuántos? ¿Quién?)

Use your PF to talk about people and their appearance. Include photos of famous people: **¿Quién es esta persona? (Ben Affleck.) ¿Es hombre o mujer? (Hombre.) Sí, es hombre. Es actor, ¿verdad? (Sí.) ¿Qué ropa lleva Ben Affleck en esta foto? (Pantalones.) Sí, lleva pantalones. Describa los pantalones que lleva. (Azul.) Sí, son azules. ¿Son nuevos? (Viejo.) Sí, son viejos, no son nuevos. ¿Lleva zapatos? (Sí.) ¿Cuántos? (Dos.) Sí, lleva dos zapatos. ¿De qué color son sus zapatos? (Negro.) Sí, son negros. Los zapatos de Ben Affleck son negros.**

All these question techniques should be mixed naturally in the input. Whenever students give a response that is correct, but that contains a grammatical error, you should attend to the semantic correctness of the response; when natural, you can give the appropriate grammatical form in the expansion.

Actividades adicionales (AAs)

Actividades adicionales (AAs) are included for each chapter of ***Dos mundos*** starting with **Paso B. AAs** suggest ideas and possibilities for oral interaction between the instructor and students without reference to the text. The **Actividades adicionales** are meant to provide additional comprehensible input using language similar to that used in the other components of the chapter. You will need to decide when your students are ready for a particular AA. (New vocabulary presented in **AAs** is *not* included in the **Vocabulario** nor in the exams of the *Testing Program*. If you wish, you may add classroom-generated vocabulary to your versions of quizzes and exams from the *Testing Program*.)

Las cosas en el salón de clase y los números 40–69

AA 1 (TPR). Use classroom objects with commands such as **muéstreme un libro (una silla, un cartel), toque la puerta (una camisa azul, la silla, el libro del profesor / de la profesora), camine hacia la puerta (hacia una chica rubia), recoja el libro (un bolígrafo), ponga un bolígrafo (un lápiz, un libro) en la mesa (el piso).** Remember that you can also give commands in sequence: **Tome un libro de la silla de la persona a su izquierda, póngase de pie y ponga el libro en el escritorio de la profesora, etc.**

AA 2 (whole-class). Mix either/or questions with **sí/no** questions as in the following example. Holding an eraser say: **Esto es tiza, ¿verdad? ¿Es esto una pared o un reloj?** Expand all responses: **¿Es esto un lápiz o un bolígrafo? (bolígrafo) (Sí), es un bolígrafo. No es un lápiz. Esto es un lápiz.** Review the numbers 0 to 39 using techniques described in the margin notes of **Paso A,** on page 5. Introduce the numbers 40 to 69 by first producing them while students read along in the display. Distribute cards with random numbers from 40 to 69 written on them. Ask: **¿Quién tiene el 44?** The class answers with the name of the student. See IRK for **Los números: ¡A practicar!** Introduce **¿Cuánto cuesta?** with photos of items or actual items. Place the photos in the chalkboard tray and write prices above them, or put price tags on items and place them on a table on desk at the front of the room. Suggested items: notebook, book, pen, pencil, radio, watch or clock, chair, articles of clothing, plant, telephone, or any other items that might be priced under $70.00. Go over each item, telling students: **El teléfono cuesta $59.29. Las botas cuestan $45.69.** Then ask questions that require one-word answers: **¿Qué cosa cuesta $38.00?** The whole class answers: **(la) silla.** Students may be paired up to practice the question-answer pattern. **¿Cuánto cuesta el radio? (cuesta) 55 dólares.** You may want to teach both **dólares,** and **centavos.**

La descripción de las personas

AA 3 (individual; whole-class). (See IM. Affective Activities.) Instruct students to write the names of five classmates on a separate sheet of paper and, under each name, write the numbers 1–5 to answer these questions: **1. ¿Tiene el pelo rubio/rojo/negro/castaño? 2. ¿Tiene el pelo largo/corto? 3. ¿Tiene barba/bigote? 4. ¿Tiene los ojos azules/castaños/verdes/negros? 5. ¿Lleva lentes?** Have them answer the questions with a single word for each student named.

Follow-up: Ask questions like: **¿Cuántos compañeros tienen barba? ¿Cuántos tienen ojos azules? ¿Tiene _____ pelo corto o largo? ¿De qué color son los ojos de _____?**

AA 4 (individual; whole-class). Give students a list of famous people (for example, Albert Einstein, Saddam Hussein, Celia Cruz, Shakira, Matt Damon, Hillary Rodham Clinton, Chris Rock, Christopher Columbus, Che Guevara, and William Shakespeare) and ask them to write a single descriptive word (adjective) that comes to mind when they think of that person. Share volunteers' responses on the board, if possible. Introduce the expression. **¿Cómo se dice _____ en español (inglés)?**

Optional Grammar

B.3 Use your PF to make a series of negative statements: **Esta señorita no lleva vestido. ¿Lleva pantalones? Los pantalones no son rojos. ¿Son verdes?**

B.4 Use input based on pictures from your PF to help students acquire plural agreement: **¿Hay cinco niños en esta foto? ¿Son grandes estos niños? ¿Son pequeños? ¿Llevan pantalones? ¿Son bonitos los pantalones?**

Paso C

Goals

The goals of **Paso C** are (1) to continue to expand listening comprehension, and (2) to enable students to discuss family and friends, including age and nationality. The verb **tener** is introduced both with possession and with age, as is the present tense of **-ar** verbs. (A more complete presentation of the present tense appears in **Capítulo 3.**) Students will still make many errors in speech and will only gradually string three, four, and five words together spontaneously.

La familia

AA 1 (whole-class). Have the whole class look at the family tree and give family terms to match your definitions: **la esposa de mi padre (madre), la madre de mi madre (abuela), el hijo de mi madre (hermano), el padre de mis hijos (esposo), etc.**

AA 2 (whole-class). Make a family tree using all the students in the class. If the class is large, you will need to make large families and create divorces with ex-spouses to use all the students. When all relatives are labeled with names. Ask questions such as: **¿Cómo se llama el _____ de _____? ¿Quién es la _____ de _____?**

¿Qué tenemos?

AA 3 (whole-class). Bring articles of clothing from home. Teach or review the Spanish words for each article, then pass them to various students. Use TPR techniques to ask students to give their article of clothing to other students: use **llévele, déle,** and **traígame.** Then ask: **¿Quién tiene _____? ¿Tiene John el/la _____?**

Los idiomas y las nacionalidades

AA 4 (whole-class). Write the names of some of the countries on the chart on pages 43–44 on the board. Then write either a nationality (**alemán/alemana**) or a famous person of that nationality on cards or strips of paper, and tape them to students' backs. Have students circulate, asking others to help them identify their nationality (and/or eventually identifying the famous person). Write **¿Soy chino/a?** And other possible **sí/no** questions on the board for reference. When students have identified their nationalities, instruct them to gather under the appropriate country label on the board. Ask questions such as: **¿Cuántos alemanes hay? (tres) Sí, hay tres. Y ¿cuántos españoles hay? (cinco) Sí, hay cinco.**

Optional Grammar

C.1 Have each student bring in a common object from home. First identify the object: **¿Qué es esto? ¿Es un(a)... ? Bien. Ryan tiene un(a)...** Identify all the objects and then ask questions such as: **¿De quién es el/la... ?** And **¿Es de Ryan el/la... ?** Students should answer with **de** + name.

C.5 Write on the board the five forms of **hablar,** followed by various languages (or use any other regular **-ar** verb). Tell students that you will begin sentences, and they must choose the correct verb to end the sentences: **Nora y su madre no... (hablan chino). Mi hermana y yo... (hablamos inglés).**

Capítulo 1

Goals

Capítulo 1 has two goals: (1) to enable students to understand and give personal information and (2) to enable them to understand and use a relatively large number of infinitives with **gustar** to express likes and dislikes. Semantic areas are personal data such as birthdays, addresses, telephone numbers, and recreational activities. Most infinitives introduced will recur in the input of subsequent chapters. A brief introduction to **-er/-ir** verbs is included so that students will have a better idea of verb endings and person/number agreement, but emphasis on present-tense forms is postponed until **Capítulo 3.**

Input Techniques in Stage 2 Pre-Text Oral Activities

Association Activities

Association activities have three goals: (1) providing input that contains new vocabulary and grammar, (2) associating new vocabulary with individual students, and (3) lowering the affective filter. In these activities, certain information is associated with a particular student. The instructor and students try to remember with whom the information is associated. Initially, the information for association is relatively simple: birthplace, place of current residence, classes a student is currently taking, major, and so forth. Association activities are used in the Pre-Text Oral Activities to introduce many areas of vocabulary and structure, in particular, infinitives (**Capítulo 1**), present indicative (**Capítulo 3**), and preterite (**Capítulo 6** and **Capítulo 7**).

Infinitives

You may have to use a little English to explain how this association activity will function. Ask each student to think of a favorite thing he or she does. Use **me gusta...** structure, so that the examples will be given in the infinitive (not present participle) form: *to eat ice cream, to sleep, to play tennis,* and so on. Each student must think of a different favorite activity, although related activities (*to play football, to play basketball*) are acceptable. As they give a favorite activity, write the Spanish equivalent on the board and pronounce each word or phrase several times for all class members to hear. For example, suppose a student has said, I like to ski; you say: **A Robert le gusta esquiar—esquiar, le gusta esquiar.** Then try to add comments like

¿Dónde le gusta esquiar? This question can be answered with just a place, usually with an English name—for example, Snow Summit. Follow up with questions like: **¿Está cerca de aquí Snow Summit? ¿A cuántas horas en carro? ¿Es un buen lugar?** Then return to the original sentence by asking a question: **¿A quién le gusta esquiar? (Robert.) Ah sí, a Robert le gusta esquiar. Y ¿a quién le gusta cocinar? (Betty.) Sí, a Betty le gusta cocinar y a Robert le gusta esquiar.**

When you do these activities, it is sometimes helpful for the instructor to use more or less complete predicates (of course, students need not). This way students will also have a chance to acquire nouns that normally accompany the verbs. In addition, it is usually easier to remember the meaning of a verb if there is a common noun associated with it. For example, students will remember **comer helado de chocolate** more easily than just **comer** or **helado.**

You cannot know in advance which verbs students will select. They tend to pick activities common in English-speaking countries but not so widely practiced in Spanish-speaking countries such as backpacking and paintballing. It is often difficult to find Spanish equivalents for these activities. If you believe that an expression is very difficult in Spanish or that it is not appropriate, ask the student to select another activity. Continue the association activity for as long as you maintain student interest, usually about twenty minutes.

During subsequent class periods, review the activities that students have selected, and add associations for the rest of the students in the class. Start out with simple questions: **¿A quién le gusta esquiar? (Robert.) ¿Le gusta cocinar a Sheila? (Sí.) Y ¿a quién le gusta dormir? (Mike.) Sí, a Mike le gusta dormir. A Jim le gusta montar a caballo, ¿verdad? (Sí.) ¿A Jean le gusta ir a la playa con amigos? (No, Stacy.) Sí, a Stacy le gusta ir a la playa con amigos, pero a Jean le gusta leer.** Rewrite all the predicates on the board. As you review, ask for information from the students who did not give you an activity in the previous class. Students may add the new predicates to their vocabulary notebooks as you write them on the board. Ask only questions that can be answered with names of students or **sí/no.** You should have as many different infinitives as there are students in the class by the end of this review.

During this and other association activities, maintain the focus on the comprehension of meaning. For example, discuss the various activities with questions like: **¿A quién le gusta _____? ¿A quién no le gusta _____? ¿A cuántos hombres les gusta _____? ¿A cuántas mujeres les gusta _____?** Weave these questions together with comments and other related questions. This is still a comprehension activity, but students can respond using single words, especially nouns and adjectives they have heard enough to have acquired. You should not ask questions that require infinitives in the answer, but some students may begin to use them voluntarily. Ask questions like the following: **¿A quién le gusta manejar? (A Jim.) ¿Tiene usted carro? (Sí.) ¿Qué marca? (Toyota.) ¿Es francés el carro Toyota? (No.) Es japonés, ¿verdad? ¿Quién más tiene un carro japonés? ¿A quién le gusta manejar motocicleta? ¿Lleva casco?** (mime **casco**), and so forth.

Finally, in subsequent class periods, students may be given the opportunity to produce the new verb forms in whole-class discussions. Ask questions exactly as in the preceding activities, but this time integrate the question: **¿Qué le gusta hacer a (Robert)?** For example: **¿A quién le gusta cocinar? (Martha.) Sí, a Martha le gusta cocinar. Y a Steve le gusta cocinar también, ¿verdad? ¿Qué le gusta cocinar a Steve? (Italiana.) Sí, a Steve le gusta preparar (cocinar) comida italiana. Y a Mónica, ¿qué le gusta hacer? (Correr.) Sí, le gusta correr para hacer ejercicio. ¿Cuándo le gusta correr? (Mañana.) Sí, le gusta correr por la mañana. ¿A quién le gusta acampar? (Jean.) Sí, a Jean le gusta acampar. Y a Lucy, ¿qué le gusta hacer? (Cantar.) Sí, a Lucy le gusta cantar. ¿Y a Dave le gusta cantar también? (No.) No, verdad, a Dave le gusta divertirse en las fiestas,** and so forth.

Either/Or Questions

Likes and dislikes. Use your PF to talk about activities that people like to do: **A este señor le gusta montar en bicicleta. Y a esta niña le gusta jugar al béisbol.** After you have introduced twenty or more activities hold up photos and ask: **A esta señora, ¿le gusta nadar o ver la televisión? (Nadar.) Sí, le gusta nadar;**

está nadando en una piscina. ¿Prefiere leer o correr este muchacho? (Correr.) Sí, está en el parque con su perro. ¿A ustedes les gusta correr o prefieren leer?

Las fechas y los cumpleaños

AA 1 (whole-class; pair). Write about fifteen dates on the board. Ask for the three volunteers to come up and point to the dates as you read them. (Write out numbers by hundreds from 100 to 1000 on the board or overhead as reference.) Then dictate dates to students to write on a sheet of paper. Have them pair off and give "point-to" commands: **Muéstreme mil novecientos cincuenta y ocho.**

Las actividades favoritas y los deportes

AA 2 (whole-class). Have students guess whether these statements are true for you. **Mis actividades favoritas: En mi tiempo libre me gusta... 1. ver la televisión 2. ir al cine 3. hablar por teléfono 4. leer 5. estudiar 6. jugar al voleibol 7. comer en restaurantes chinos 8. correr.**

AA 3 (whole-class). Favorite activities: Ask both positive and negative questions about recreational activities. Use your PF and include both previous activities and any important new ones that by chance have not yet come up in the input. Integrate other comprehensible input into your conversation about these pictures. For example: **¿Qué hay en esta foto? (mujer) Sí, hay una mujer. ¿Cómo es ella? (bonita, joven) Sí, es muy bonita y joven también . ¿Dónde está? (playa) Sí, esta en la playa. Entonces, ¿a ella le gusta ir a la playa? (sí) Y en esta clase, ¿a quién le gusta ir a la playa?** (Several students respond positively.) **¿A qué playa les gusta ir?**

AA 4 (whole-class). Use pictures of people doing activities as the basis for the input. Ask, **¿A usted le gusta _____?** Students answer **sí** or **no.** Review about 50 pictures rapidly, then pass out several pictures to each student. Pair students and write a question/answer pattern on the board. **¿Te gusta _____? Sí/No, (no) me gusta _____.** Explain that **te gusta** is informal for **le gusta.** Have students practice asking questions with their partner and with another pair. Continue the activity until each pair has asked and answered about 20 questions.

AA 5 (individual; whole-class). Ask students to think of interesting things members of their family like to do. They can give information in English if they wish. Write the pattern on the board: **A mi _____ le gusta _____.** Ask questions to see how much information students can remember about each other's family. For example. **¿Qué le gusta hacer al padre de Mike?**

AA 6 (individual). Have students write down as many weekend activities as they can in two minutes. Then have them select from these activities and write a small composition using the following rubric: **Los fines de semana, me gusta _____. Los viernes por la noche, me gusta _____. Los sábados (domingos) por la mañana / por la tarde / por la noche, me gusta _____. También me gusta _____ con _____. No me gusta _____.**

AA 7 (group). Divide students into groups of six. Students make up cards with fictitious names but their real address and hobbies. The group secretary then reads the cards aloud and the group guesses who it is.

En resumen

AA 8 (group; whole-class). Using **De todo un poco** as a model, divide students into groups of two or three and ask them to write questions for famous people. After all groups finish, ask for volunteers to read questions while you write them on the board in categories. Then have the whole class try to answer them.

Lectura   La pasión por los deportes

Ahora... ¡usted! (This section provides additional follow-up to the **Lectura** of each chapter.)

¿Cuáles de estos deportes se mencionan en la **Lectura**? ¿Cuáles le gusta practicar a usted? Indique si le gusta practicarlos mucho, a veces o nunca.

	mucho	a veces	nunca
el ciclismo	☐	☐	☐
el fútbol	☐	☐	☐
el fútbol norteamericano	☐	☐	☐
el béisbol	☐	☐	☐
el esquí	☐	☐	☐
la natación	☐	☐	☐
el ráquetbol	☐	☐	☐
el baloncesto	☐	☐	☐
el tenis	☐	☐	☐
el montañismo	☐	☐	☐

Optional Grammar

1.1 Dictate students' birthdays or famous dates in history and have students write down the dates in numerals.

Ejercicio 1 The answers to this exercise in the answer key are written out to enable students to check themselves, but normally large numbers are not written out in Spanish or English.

1.3 Remind students that Spanish does not use *do* or *does* to form questions and that one simply inverts the verb and the subject.

Capítulo 2

Goals

The purpose of this chapter is to expand students' ability to understand and produce longer utterances. They will learn to use **ir + a, querer,** and **preferir** + infinitive to discuss plans, desires, and preferences. Ordinal numbers and weather expressions are also introduced.

Los planes

Narration Series (Narración)

Actividad 2 In this series we introduce a narrative with the verbs in the infinitive form after **va + a.** Drawings 1–5 are activities that Carmen is going to do in the morning, 6–12 are afternoon activities, and 13–16 are evening activities. Begin with Drawing 1: **Miren el cuadro uno. Esta muchacha se llama Carmen y éstas son las actividades que ella va a hacer hoy. En el cuadro uno, es la mañana. Carmen va a dormir hasta las nueve. Está muy cansada.** Personalize with questions such as: **En nuestra clase, ¿a quién le gusta dormir hasta las nueve o diez? ¿A quién le gusta despertarse a las seis o siete?** Then continue: **Miren el cuadro dos. Carmen va a desayunar pan tostado con café. ¿A quién en nuestra clase le gusta**

desayunar pan tostado con café? En el número uno Carmen va a... (pause to give students a chance to finish the sentence) (**dormir**). **Sí, va a dormir hasta las nueve; está cansada.** Continue to introduce new drawings one at a time, using the sequencing words provided; then review all the previous ones. As you introduce each drawing, you can write the infinitive or the entire sentence on the board (students may copy them in their vocabulary notebooks). The idea is not to memorize the exact sentences given by the instructor but to comprehend and then renarrate the set of drawings. You may divide this activity into several parts to be done in different class hours. After sufficient input from you, have students work in pairs to retell the narrative completely. By now most students will be able to narrate the entire series using only the drawing as a guide.

One variation is to have one student ask a question and another answer. For example: **¿Qué va a hacer Carmen en el cuadro tres? Va a hablar por teléfono.** A follow-up activity is to write a class composition based on the narration series. The whole class retells the narration to the instructor, who writes the composition on the board. Once students see that they can indeed write a composition, you can ask them to use the one on the board as a model and write one about a famous person, a classmate, or the instructor. Note that narration series are not grammar exercises. The purpose is to give the teacher a chance to present new input and give students the satisfaction of language production and interaction. Most chapters have at least one narration series.

Las clases

AA 1 (whole-class). Have the whole class match an item from column A with a subject from column B. **Empareje una cosa de la columna A con una de las materias de la columna B. A:** un poema, un microscopio, un mapa, las ecuaciones, una computadora. **B:** la geografía, la biología, la literatura, la física, la informática.

Las preferencias y los deseos

AA 2 (whole-class; individual). Use an association activity to introduce **quiero/quiere** + infinitive. Have students think of one thing they would like to do this weekend. Write each student's activity on the board, as in the **me/le gusta** introduction. Then ask, **¿Quién quiere _____?**

AA 3 (whole-class). See IRK for TPR: **Las actividades favoritas y las preferencias.** Use the entire class and selective TPR to add variety and provide more comprehensible input about favorite activities. Include forms from previous chapters: **naden, bailen, duerman, patinen, esquíen, jueguen al (golf, tenis, etc.), cocinen, tomen (café), escriban, lean, escuchen, coman, hablen por teléfono, dibujen, saquen fotos, toquen (la guitarra), monten a caballo, caminen,** etc. Repeat this activity on different days, varying the sequence.

AA 4 (whole-class; individual). Use photos from your PF to show people doing different activities. Ask: **¿A usted le gusta _____?** for each activity. Then ask: **¿Prefiere _____ o _____?**

AA 5 (pair). Use your PF to review sports terms. Pair students. Each student should find out which sport his/her partner plays or watches. Write the following interview questions on the board: **¿Qué deporte prefieres practicar? ¿Qué deporte prefieres mirar?**

El tiempo

AA 6 (whole-class). Ask students about local weather during various months: **¿Qué tiempo hace en agosto donde usted vive?**

Lectura   *De paseo*

Ahora... ¡usted!

1. ¿Tiene la ciudad donde usted vive un lugar donde la gente pueda ir a pasear? ¿Qué lugar es? ¿Qué le gusta hacer a usted allí normalmente?
2. ¿Qué le gusta hacer en su tiempo libre? ¿y por la noche?
3. Generalmente, ¿planifica muy bien sus actividades y su tiempo? ¿Por qué?

Optional Grammar Activity

2.1 Practice **ir + a** + infinitive with simple interviews. Write on the board: **¿Qué vas a hacer esta noche (después de clase, el sábado, el próximo fin de semana, durante las vacaciones de... , el próximo... , durante el/la...)?** Pick two or three to use as interview questions; students may report their partner's plans back to the class.

Capítulo 3

Goals

The purpose of this chapter is to allow students to communicate about daily activities, locations, and places in a city or on campus where those activities take place. To expand daily activity vocabulary this chapter presents basic foods. Students will also learn how to talk about origin and express nationalities of the Spanish-speaking world. Regular, nonreflexive conjugations are reintroduced (Review **C.5** and **1.2**) along with three irregular verbs: **hacer, salir** and **jugar. Estar en** and **ser de** are introduced. (For a more detailed contrast see Grammar **14.2.**)

Input Techniques Stage 2 - Pre-Text Oral Activities

Origin Association Activity

The goal is to identify the birthplace of each student. First write on the board: **¿De dónde es _____?** and **Soy/Es de... .** Give your own birthplace: **Yo soy de Texas, de Austin, Texas. ¿De dónde son ustedes? Mark, ¿de dónde es usted? (New York.) ¿De Nueva York? (Sí.) De Nueva York, ¡qué interesante! Mark es de Nueva York.** Then add some comment about the location to help with the association: **Nueva York es muy grande, ¿verdad? (Sí.) ¿Quién es de Nueva York? (Mark.)** Then proceed to the next student: **¿De dónde es usted, Roger? (Chicago.) De Chicago, de Illinois, ¿verdad? Roger es de Chicago y Mark es de Nueva York. Leah, ¿de dónde es usted? (Atlanta.) De Atlanta. Y ¿quién es de Nueva York? (Mark.) Y Roger, ¿de dónde es Roger? (Chicago.) Sí, de Chicago. ¿Quién es de Atlanta? (Leah.)** Continue until the class has associated new information with fifteen or so students. During the following class period, review the fifteen that were introduced, and complete the association for the rest of the students.

Present Indicative Association Activity

The present-tense forms in the input will be first- and third-person singular forms, since these are the most common forms and those which the students will find most useful. You need not artificially restrict your speech, however; if the context is clear enough, the use of plural forms will not impede comprehension. Our experience is that most students will have no trouble *learning* the present-tense endings (although for some with no prior language experience the concept of verb endings may take some time to grasp). These forms are *acquired* later, however; that is, students will not be able to use them successfully until they have had multiple opportunities to hear these forms used in communicative contexts. In this association activity, students receive some comprehensible input that contains these conjugated verbs forms, which may begin the acquisition process.

Begin by concentrating on recognizing the meanings of a relatively large number of new verbs in the third-person singular form. Ask students to think of a single activity they normally do every day and to name that activity in English. Write the Spanish equivalent on the board, using the student's name. For example: **Jim estudia, Martha limpia su cuarto, Hoang va a la playa,** and so on. After several activities have been written on the board, review by asking: **¿Quién va a la playa? ¿Quién estudia?** Students need only look at the board or their notebooks to respond. Then erase the names so that students have to associate the activities with a particular student. If there are any questions on verbs, either answer them briefly and/or refer the student asking the question to sections **3.2** and **3.3** in the **Gramática y ejercicios** section.

With daily activities, some (true) reflexives will be suggested: *I take a bath, I brush my hair,* and so on. For this association activity, treat **se** as if it were simply a new word, not a part of a new pronoun set. Since several of the examples will be somewhat different from English (*He brushes his teeth* = **Se lava los dientes**), a short explanation you might give is that **se** is used in Spanish whenever the action is done to oneself. Details about reflexive pronouns will only confuse most students at this stage. If the entire activity is strongly focused on the actions themselves (that is, if you maintain interesting input about the various daily activities), the details of reflexive pronouns and verb use will not cause problems. If the focus is on the meaning, irregular verbs should not cause a problem in this activity; students will not notice the "irregularities."

In subsequent classes, utilize the first-person singular forms. Review the daily activities associated with each student. Write at least fifteen verb forms on the board. Then look at four or five forms and react to them personally; for example: **Mark juega al tenis. Yo juego al tenis también.** Continue reacting truthfully to the first few sentences on the board, writing the first-person singular forms beside the third-person singular verb forms already on the board. When you introduce **me,** say that it means *myself.*

Finally, later activities require production of the first- and third-person singular forms and introduce the first- and third-person plural forms for comprehension. See the notes in the margins of the *Instructor's Edition* for expansion activities.

Las tres comidas

AA 1 (whole-class). Use your PF to review **Me gusta(n)** + basic foods. Ask students: **¿Le gusta(n) el/la/los/las _____?** Share your own likes and dislikes: **A mí también/tampoco me gusta(n).**

Los lugares

AA 2 (whole-class). With the participation of the whole class, draw a map of your campus on the board. Have students help you label school/departmental buildings (*facultades*) and other locations on campus as you ask **¿Dónde está la Facultad de Bellas Artes? ¿Dónde está la piscina?** (Students may point or come up and locate places on the board.)

Las actividades diarias

AA 3 See the IRK for TPR sequences on daily activities. Have students pantomime with you possible activities after work or school.

AA 4 (whole-class). Review the daily activities associations from the Pre-Text Oral Activity 3 on page 115 of the text. Write each on the board; after you have 8–10, go through the list and react personally: **Yo también _____. Yo no _____, pero yo _____.**

AA 5 (whole-class). Have students think about each activity they usually do from waking up in the morning to going to bed at night: **Vamos a hablar de las actividades típicas de un día. Por ejemplo, en la mañana...** As students suggest activities (in English or Spanish), write these in the third-person form on the board. After you have 10 or so daily activities on the board, ask questions using the hour as an organizing principle. **¿A qué hora _____ usted? (a las _____) ¿A qué hora sale usted para la escuela? (a las**

nueve) Note: Answers should be restricted to times in order to avoid requiring production of conjugated verb forms before students are ready.

AA 6 (whole-class; pair). Have each student think of one thing a relative or friend does during the day. Each student must use a different activity. Write each verb form on the board (including as much of the predicate as you need to have it make sense). Leave space beside each predicate to write the **-o** form. React personally to each yourself, and, as you do, write all **-o** forms: **lava ropa (lavo); maneja su carro (manejo).** Then pair students and give them the following pattern to create questions; remind them to be truthful (or suggest they tell outrageous lies!). Have them pretend they don't know each other well and must use the **usted** form: ¿_____ **usted? Sí, (yo)** _____**-o. (No, no** _____**-o.)** This activity will provide input with first-person singular, but does not expect students to always produce correct forms.

AA 7 (pair). Write on the board a list of fifteen daily activities using the first-person singular form. Have each student select ten activities that he/she does and write them on a sheet of paper. Then pair students so they can compare lists. One student reads the first activity: **Yo estudio todos los días.** The second student searches his/her list to see if there is a match. If the second student also does the activity, he/she responds: **Yo también (estudio todos los días).** If the second student has not included it in his/her list, he/she responds: **Yo no estudio todos los días.** Let students work about ten minutes on this activity while you circulate, commenting and participating.

AA 8 (whole-class). Encourage students to talk about their activities with others. Ask: **¿Qué hace usted con sus hermanos? ¿con sus padres? ¿con sus amigos?,** and so on.

¿De dónde es usted?

AA 9 (individual; whole class). Have students sit in a semicircle and participate in a chain activity. Each student says where he/she is from: **Soy de** _____ and where the person to the left of him/her is from: **Y** _____ **es de** _____. Occasionally stop and poll the whole class: **¿De dónde es** _____**?**

¡Cuéntenos usted!

MODELO: Mi lugar favorito es un museo de arte en la calle séptima en la ciudad de San Francisco. Tarda sólo 30 minutos ir a ese museo. Normalmente no hay mucha gente y es un lugar tranquilo. Tiene exhibiciones de arte contemporáneo latinoamericano. Me gusta ver el arte y leer la historia de los artistas. Prefiero ir con amigos y luego tomar un refresco en el café que está al lado del museo.

Lectura La presencia vital de los hispanos

Ahora... ¡usted!

Usando **Comprensión B** como guía, describa a algunos de sus amigos hispanos. Si no tiene ningún amigo hispano, describa a dos hispanos famosos que no se mencionan en la lectura.

Optional grammar

3.1 Use your PF to provide more input on the use of **estar** for location. Pass out five pictures to each pair of students. One student asks: **¿Dónde está el/la** _____**?** and the other answers. Then they switch roles for the next picture.

Use your PF to ask contrasting questions: **¿Dónde están ahora? ¿Adónde van a ir después?**

3.5 Practice adjectives of nationality by making open statements.

1. Un hombre de Cuba es _____ .   2. Una mujer de España es _____ .

3. Los hombres de Francia son _____ .   4. Las mujeres de Italia son _____ .

5. Un hombre de Costa Rica es _____ .   6. Una mujer de México es _____ .

7. Las mujeres de Colombia son _____ .   8. Los hombres de Chile son _____ .

9. Una mujer de Perú es _____ .   10. Un hombre de Paraguay es _____ .

Capítulo 4

Goals

Capítulo 4 provides opportunities to understand and talk about topics related to common activities. It focuses on three areas: (1) holidays, celebrations, and associated activities, (2) grooming activities (which in Spanish are expressed with reflexive constructions), and (3) physical and mental states. All of these topics typically involve use of present-tense verbs: regular, irregular, and stem-changing. In addition, **Capítulo 4** introduces **estar** + adjetives and **tener** + noun constructions used to describe states of being.

Los días feriados y las celebraciones

AA 1 (whole-class; pair). Write several activities related to holidays on the board and ask students to name the appropriate holiday. Suggestions: **1. Estamos con la familia. Cenamos todos juntos y miramos el árbol en la casa. 2. Salimos con el novio / la novia. 3. Le damos regalos a mamá. 4. Recibimos regalos y cumplimos un año más. 5. Vamos a fiestas, tomamos y comemos mucho. Esperamos la medianoche.** Later, if you think students are ready, write holidays on the board and ask them to work in groups to make a list of activities appropriate for those days.

La rutina diaria

AA 2 (whole-class). See the IRK: **Actividad de firma: La rutina.** Have everyone circulate and ask questions. Limit each student to three questions or this will become an interview activity. After 5–10 minutes, ask the class who does certain activities.

Los estados físicos y anímicos

AA 3 (TPR). See the IRK for TPR: **Los estados físicos y anímicos.** Sample sequence: **Ustedes tienen frío; pónganse un abrigo. Tienen calor ahora; quítense el abrigo. Tienen prisa; miren el reloj. Recojan sus cosas y corran. Tienen sueño, tomen café o duérmanse. Tienen hambre; coman un taco. Están tristes; lloren. Están enojados; griten. Están alegres; canten.** See the IRK for additional activities.

¡Cuéntenos usted!

MODELO: Mi día feriado favorito es el Día de Acción de Gracias. No es una fiesta religiosa en mi familia, pero es una fiesta muy alegre. Lo celebro con amigos y familiares y tenemos una gran cena el cuarto jueves de noviembre. Preparamos mucha comida: pavo, camotes, ensaladas y varios pasteles. Después de comer algunos ven un partido de fútbol norteamericano en la televisión y otros dan un paseo por el barrio. ¡Yo prefiero pasear!

Lectura   *¡Grandes fiestas!*

Ahora... ¡usted!

1. ¿Cuál de las fiestas mencionadas en la Lectura encuentra más interesante? ¿Por qué? ¿Le gustaría ir a esa fiesta algún día?

2. ¿Conoce algunas fiestas o celebraciones de otros países? ¿Ha estado en otro país durante una fiesta especial? ¿Cuál, por ejemplo?

Optional grammar

4.4 You may wish to point out that the infinitive is used after all prepositions in Spanish.

4.5 Mention that **estar** implies "state of being" and that the familiar question **¿Cómo esta usted?** means "What is your state of being at this moment?" Write these two questions on the board: **¿Cómo está** (name of student volunteer)? and **¿Cómo es** (name of same student)? Brainstorm with the whole class for at least five adjectives to classify the person in each question. Emphasize that **estar** corresponds to present (transitory) state and **ser** to inherent qualities. Place adjectives unambiguously under one question or the other without going into detail about their contrastive uses. (For example, place **nervioso** with **estar** even though it could be used with **ser.**)

Capítulo 5

Goals

This chapter focuses on classes, abilities, careers, and future plans. These topics will provide an opportunity to hear grammar constructions from previous chapters again. In addition, indirect object pronouns and demonstrative adjectives are introduced.

Las actividades de la clase de español

AA 1 (TPR). See the IRK for TPR: **Las actividades en el salón de clase.** Sample sequence: **Abran los libros, ciérrenlos, hablen con sus compañeros, escuchen al profesor / a la profesora, pregúntenle al profesor cómo está, tomen apuntes, estudien para un examen de español, piensen, levanten la mano, contesten la pregunta del profesor / de la profesora, copien la tarea de la pizarra, vengan a la pizarra, borren la pizarra, díganle "Hasta mañana" al profesor, salgan de la clase.** See the IRK for additional activities.

AA 2 (whole-class). Talk about classes students are taking. Then introduce professions as follows: **¿Si una persona estudia _____, qué quiere ser? Quiere ser _____.** Use photos from your PF to teach new classes (or careers) and professions. The careers listed below are not included in the **Vocabulario: arquitecto/a (arquitectura), escritor(a) (literatura, periodismo), psicólogo/a (psicología), sociólogo/a (sociología), veterinario/a (veterinaria).**

Las habilidades

AA 3 (whole-class). Use student talent and pictures to introduce common musical instruments such as **piano, guitarra, flauta, violín.** Discussion may be extended to include types of music and popular groups **(conjuntos, banda,** etc.). Find out who plays what instruments and who enjoys what kind of music. Use the pattern **Sé/Sabe tocar _____.**

AA 4 (whole-class). Have students speculate on what a person with a broken leg can and cannot do: **¿Qué (no) puede hacer una persona sana que tiene una pierna rota?** Possible questions: **¿Puede mirar la television? ¿Puede correr? ¿Puede leer? ¿Puede patinar? ¿Puede caminar? ¿Puede escribir la tarea? ¿Puede cocinar? ¿Puede explorar el Internet? ¿Puede nadar? ¿Puede dormir? ¿Puede bailar? ¿Puede pensar? ¿Puede saltar?**

AA 5 (pair). Write the following options on the board: **(a) Sí, muy bien. (b) Sí, bien. (c) Sí, un poco. (d) No.** Then have students ask each other: **¿Sabes _____?** Suggestions: **1. bucear 2. dibujar 3. patinar 4. esquiar 5. cantar 6. bailar 7. jugar al boliche 8. coser 9. diseñar sitios Web**

Las carreras y las actividades del trabajo

AA 6 (TPR). See the IRK for TPR: **Las carreras y las profesiones.** Have students imagine they are members of certain professions, then tell them to perform the following activities. Sample sequence: **Ustedes son médicos; receten medicinas. Son meseros; sirvan la comida. Son enfermeros; cuiden al paciente. Son peluqueros; córtenle el pelo de un compañero. Son cocineros; cocinen. Son cajeros de un banco; cuenten el dinero. Son pilotos; piloteen el avión. Son bomberos; apaguen el incendio. Son amas de casa; limpien la casa. Son choferes de taxi; manejen y escuchen la radio.** See the IRK for additional activities.

AA 7 (whole-class). Give students a definition of a profession and let them guess the profession. Possibilities: **1. Trabaja en una escuela. Da clases. 2. Trabaja en un hospital. Receta medicinas. 3. Recibe el dinero en un restaurante. 4. Hace planos para construir casas y edificios. 5. Atiende a las personas que tienen problemas con la ley. 6. Trabaja en un taller y lleva uniforme. 7. Cura a los animales enfermos. 8. Apaga los incendios.**

AA 8 (TPR). Use TPR to give commands to individuals or small groups of students. Then ask the rest of the class: **¿Qué está(n) haciendo?** See the IRK for TPR: **Las actividades del momento.**

AA 9 (TPR in small groups). Divide students into groups of two or three. Each member of a group is to think of an activity and pantomime it while asking: **¿Qué estoy haciendo?** (This sentence can be written on the board for easy reference.) The other student(s) in the group respond(s): **(Estás) Durmiendo,** etc.

AA 10 (individual). Have students write help wanted ads: **Se necesita mecánico, experiencia necesaria. Horario de 8 a 5, lunes a viernes. Tiene que hacer reparaciones generales.**

Las actividades futuras

AA 11 (whole-class). Introduce the expression **me gustaría** + infinitive by asking students what they would like to do this weekend. Use photos from your PF and ask if they would like to engage in those activities. Use mostly **sí/no** and either/or questions: **¿Le gustaría ir a la playa?¿Adónde? ¿Todo el día? Mike, ¿qué le gustaría más, salir al cine con los amigos o salir a una discoteca con una amiga?**

¡Cuéntenos usted!

MODELO: En mi trabajo ideal soy dependiente en una tienda de equipo electrónico. El sueldo es de $45.00 la hora y sólo trabajo de las 10:00 hasta las 2:00 todos los días. Mis responsabilidades son ayudar a los clientes, vender equipo electrónico y jugar con los nuevos videojuegos.

Lectura   *El lenguaje del cuerpo*

Ahora... ¡usted!

1. Haga (o describa) algunos gestos que caracterizan a los norteamericanos o a las personas de su país de origen. ¿Qué significan?

2. ¿Conoce algunos gestos similares a los de los hispanos pero que significan otra cosa? ¿Cómo son y qué significan?

Optional grammar

5.1 Practice indirect object pronouns with verbs used in the classroom, asking **sí/no** questions: **¿Qué hace el profesor? ¿Les explica la gramática a los estudiantes? ¿Les habla a los estudiantes en inglés? ¿Qué hacen los estudiantes en la clase? ¿Le hablan al profesor en inglés? ¿Le hacen preguntas al profesor sobre la lección? ¿Les hablan a los otros estudiantes cuando el profesor está hablando?**, etc.

5.5 Review **gustar** and point out that pronouns are the same: **me, te, le, nos, os, les.** It also helps some students if you compare reflexive and indirect object pronouns, since they differ only in the third person: **se/le(s).** Have students name things (not activities) they like. Give the Spanish equivalent and write the words on the board: **A _____ le gustan las cuidades grandes. A _____ le gusta Nueva York.**

You may wish to take this opportunity to summarize all the auxiliary verb + infinitive constructions to date: **gustar, ir + a, querer, preferir, pensar, tener ganas de, quisiera,** and **gustaría.**

Capítulo 6

Goals

The input and interactions in **Capítulo 6** are related to where students live and their activities there. You should attempt to make some simple cultural comparisons whenever possible. This chapter also introduces topics that encourage use of past-tense singular forms.

Preterite (Pre-Text Oral Activities)

Explain that you are going to talk about your previous day's activities. Write at the top of the board: PAST = **PASADO.** (This is, of course, explicit grammatical information, but it will make the discourse more comprehensible for some students.) By now students will realize that the goal of these activities is to find out interesting details about their instructor and classmates, not to *learn* verb forms. In case there are questions, refer students to **Gramática 6.3.** Students are to ask you questions to find out if you participated in certain activities the previous day. For example, a student may ask in English, "Did you run? Did you study? Did you watch television?" React truthfully to each question, and answer in Spanish: **Sí (No), yo (no) corrí.** Write each new verb on the board (students may copy into their notebooks). When responding to the question, expand the context. For example, in the answer to the question "Did you run?" You may wish to explain when you ran, how far you ran, if you like to run, how often you run, and so forth. The discussion after the initial answer **corrí** and "when and where" often will involve only short answers without a verb form or with a verb form in the present or in a construction with the infinitive. The purpose of this activity is not to contrast the present and past, and no effort should be made to emphasize this contrast. Use of both present tense and verb + infinitive structures is often a natural outcome of this activity and should not be avoided when it comes up. This is also the case in real conversation; a question is asked about a past action, and then the focus shifts to the present: "Did you run last night?" **Sí, corrí. Corro todas las tardes. Me gusta correr por la tarde,** and so forth. Spend about twenty minutes on this activity the first time it is introduced. *Optional In-Class Grammar Discussion:* call students' attention to the stressed vowel at the end of the verb forms.

The initial association activity related to the instructor's activities should be repeated during several class periods. The second time, students will understand the format of the activity and many of the forms immediately, so many more questions can be asked in the twenty minutes. You should aim for at least forty verb forms. (If students try to ask the questions in Spanish, remind them that the form for third-person preterite questions is different and that they shouldn't try to use it yet.)

In subsequent class periods, give students the opportunity to hear third-person singular forms and to produce first-person singular forms. Narrate activities you did the previous day, and write the forms (first-person singular) on the board as you talk. Then ask individual students if they did those activities. Write on the board: **¿Qué hizo usted?** (*What did you do?*) They answer, of course, using the forms written on the board (or others, if they wish). By now they have heard many first-person forms through your input. As you ask the questions, write the third-person singular forms beside the first-person singular. After you have completed twenty or so verbs, go back and ask questions to see if students remember who did what: **¿Quién fue al cine? (Ruben.) ¿Quién se quedó en casa?,** and so on. Note that students hear third-person singular forms in this activity but do not produce them.

Then do the following listening comprehension activity. Ask for a single volunteer. Tell the student to answer either **sí** or **no** with no elaboration. Then begin asking questions such as: **¿Trabajó usted quince horas ayer?** The answer usually will be **no**. Continue asking questions that will probably evoke a negative response. Make the questions long enough that a specific context is involved. For example, do not say simply **¿Habló?** or **¿Se bañó?** but rather **¿Se baño por la mañana?** or **¿Habló por teléfono con sus padres?** After five or six questions, ask a question that will produce an affirmative response. Then ask for a new volunteer. Continue in this way, moving on to another student as soon as you get an affirmative answer.

Optional In-Class Grammar Activity: If you have asked students to copy the first-person verb forms into a notebook, ask them to look at their list. By this time they should have fifty to one hundred verbs. Ask students to write the third-person singular forms besides the first-person singular forms. Have each student work with a partner and complete the pairs for the entire list. Go from group to group, helping with this grammar activity.

El vecindario y la casa

AA 1 IRK. (whole-class; individual). We suggest using the **Descripción de dibujos** activity of Professor Martínez's floor plan as a pre-text activity. Have students look at Professor Martínez's house plan: **Miren el plano de la casa de la profesora Martínez.** Read each description aloud and have the class answer **Cierto** or **falso.**

AA 2 (whole-class). Use your PF to talk about common animals, especially pets **(gato, perro, pez, pájaro, vaca, caballo)** and related words **(collar, correa, jaula, pecera, acuario,** etc.**).** Discuss different attitudes toward pets in Hispanic countries. See **Ventanas al pasado: La historia de las mascotas** for more information.

AA 3 (whole-class). Use your PF to talk about the most important appliances and furniture in a house. With each item use descriptive adjectives including color, size, shape, price, etc. Ask students if they have similar articles in their homes. If so, have them describe them and compare to the ones in your pictures.

AA 4 (whole-class). Write on the board the names of five to six rooms in a house. Have students think of all the furniture that they would have in an ideal house. Ask questions like: **¿Por qué quiere un(a) _____? ¿Para qué sirve un(a) _____?**

AA 5 (whole-class). Use your PF or various appliances and gadgets and have students invent prices. Use the expression **¿Cuánto cuesta el/la _____?** Put photos in the board tray and label with appropriate prices. Ask questions using comparisons: **¿Cuál cuesta más, el reloj despertador o la tetera? (tetera) Sí, tiene razón, la tetera cuesta más, cuesta $42.59. ¿Cuál cuesta menos, la plancha o el tocacompactos?**

(plancha) **Sí, la plancha cuesta solamente $26.79.** Alternate questions with comparisons using **más, menos,** and **tanto** with questions regarding actual cost: **¿Cuánto cuesta el televisor a colores?** Continue until students have had an opportunity to hear many comparative questions and statements.

AA 6 (group). Divide students into groups of three to four and ask them to make a list of as many **aparatos electronicos** as they can think of in two minutes. Then have them assign prices to these items. **(Decidan un precio para cada aparato.)** Ask for volunteers from each group to come up and write two or three items and prices on the board. After five to six items, elicit general classroom discussion about appliances students have, prices, and stores.

AA 7 (whole-class; pair). Use the twenty-question game format to guess names of furniture and other household items. You should do the guessing the first two or three times. Leave the classroom and let the class decide on an object. Ask students up to twenty questions: **1. ¿Es para el baño? (no) 2. ¿Es para el dormitorio? (no) 3. ¿Se usa en la cocina? (sí) 4. ¿Sirve para lavar ropa? (no) 5. ¿Es para cocinar algo? (sí) 6. ¿Es grande? (no) 7. ¿Se usa por la mañana? (sí) 8. ¿Es para tostar el pan? (sí) 9. ¿Es el tostador? (sí).** Write possible questions on the board and pair students to play. See the IRK for additional activities: **Veinte preguntas: Los muebles y los aparatos eléctronicos.**

AA 8 (group). Divide the class into two or more teams. Have each team write as many household items (appliances and furniture) as they can in a given amount of time; for example, one minute: **En una casa moderna hay _____ y _____.** or **En un dormitorio hay _____ y _____.**

AA 9 (whole-class). For an enjoyable way to review house vocabulary, create a mural using a large piece of white butcher paper taped to the classroom wall. Have students draw two or more houses with trees, bushes, flower beds, fence, a garage sale with furniture, etc., being as creative as they wish. Give them ten to fifteen minutes on two or three different days to finish the mural. When done, have students add labels in Spanish to everything.

AA 10 (whole-class). Use pictures of houses from your PF to review large numbers: have students estimate the houses' prices.

AA 11 (individual; whole-class). Have students make a floor plan of their house, (as homework) labeling doors, windows, and furniture in Spanish. Divide them into groups of three to four. Each student gives the others a room-by-room tour of his or her house. (You may have them pretend to be giving a tour of a celebrity's home.)

Las actividades en casa

AA 12 (whole-class). Show pictures of people doing common things around the house. Ask: **¿Qué está haciendo?**

AA 13 Optional open dialogue model: E1: **¿Qué tienes que hacer este fin de semana en tu casa?** E2: **Tengo que _____.** E1: **Yo quiero _____, pero debo _____.** E2: **Puedo ayudarte a _____ y despúes podemos _____.**

AA 14 (whole-class). Write a list of household activities on the board: **Recibimos las visitas, reparamos el carro, cenamos, lavamos los platos, estudiamos, nos bañamos, escuchamos la radio, vemos la televisión, dormimos la siesta, cocinamos,** etc. Ask: **¿En qué cuarto cenamos? Y ¿en qué cuarto lavamos los platos?** Review neighborhood places and activities using this same format: **vamos de compras, nadamos, jugamos al básquetbol, compramos libros, compramos papel y lápices, vemos una película, compramos pan, asistimos a misa,** etc. Ask: **¿Dónde compramos la gasolina?,** etc.

¡Cuéntenos usted!

MODELO: El lugar favorito de mi casa es mi patio con jardín. Es un lugar muy tranquilo, pero hay muchos pájaros. Me gusta estar en mi jardín sola o a veces con mis gatos. Me gusta regar las flores y plantas. A veces duermo una siesta en mi jardín o leo una novela.

Lectura   *Las hermosas ciudades hispanas*

Ahora... ¡usted!

1. ¿Le gusta el vecindario donde vive? ¿Le gustaría vivir en otro vecindario? ¿Por qué?
2. ¿Qué le gusta y qué no le gusta de la ciudad donde vive?
3. ¿Conoce alguna ciudad hispana? ¿Le parece muy diferente de una ciudad norteamericana típica? ¿Qué tienen en común? ¿Qué diferencias hay entre las dos?

Optional grammar

6.1 The comparative and superlative with **más/menos** may be practiced easily with your PF: Show two pictures of the same or similar items and ask: **¿Cuál cuesta más? ¿Es más grande la casa o el apartamento?** Review demonstratives: **¿Es más alto este hombre o aquél?**

6.2 Before assigning **Ejercicios 1 y 2** use your PF to ask true/false questions: **Esta señorita no es tan alta como ésta. ¿Están ustedes de acuerdo?** To include **tanto... como** in your input, use play money, distributing various amounts to different students. Ask: **Roberto, ¿cuánto dinero tiene usted? Ajá, tiene $2.300 pesos. Ahora, Ángela, ¿cuánto dinero tiene usted? Clase, Ángela tiene $3.250 pesos. ¿Tiene Roberto tanto (dinero) como Ángela?**

6.5 Use question-and-answer sequences: **¿Adónde fue el sábado? (al cine) ¿Me vio allí? (No, no lo/la vi.)** Use your PF: **¿Cómo se llama este señor? (Spike Lee) ¿Quién lo conoce personalmente? ¿Dónde lo conoció? ¿Dónde lo vio?**

Capítulo 7

Goals

The purpose of **Capítulo 7** is to give students opportunities to interact in situations that deal with past events. However, although students will be able to recognize preterite forms and even produce some, they will not produce them with ease until they have experienced many months of oral and written input. For this reason, the preterite normally occurs in many activities in subsequent chapters. The imperfect will be introduced in the grammar of **Capítulo 9**. (Although differences between preterite and the imperfect are aspectual rather than temporal, simpler terminology is more appropriate for first-year students; we will not discuss aspect [beginning, middle, or end of an action; cyclical or noncyclical; etc.] as it relates to preterite-tense forms.) Indirect object pronouns are reintroduced in this chapter, in combination with **decir.**

Mis experiencias

AA 1 Situación (individual; whole-class). **Usted no hizo la tarea para su clase de español y tiene que darle una buena excusa a su profesor. Invente una excusa original.** Collect excuses and read their excuses. You may vote on **la excusa más imaginativa, la más increíble, la más lógica,** etc.

AA 2 Diálogo original: Las útimas vacaciones. Usted se encuentra con un amigo / una amiga de la universidad. Él / Ella quiere saber qué hizo usted durante las vacaciones. Usted quiere impresionar a su amigo/a, así que invente unas actividades fantásticas. E1: Hola _____. Gusto de verte. ¿Qué hiciste durante las vacaciones? E2: Pues, yo... _____.

Las experiencias de los demás

AA 3 (TPR). Use previous TPR sequences to give commands to individual members of the class. After they have performed a given activity, ask **¿Qué hizo Ted?** and respond for class: **Ted _____.** When you have done single commands several times, students will be able to answer as a group. Then give a sequence of commands. Sample sequence: **Ted, levántense, corra a la pizarra, escriba ahí su nombre, luego vaya al pupitre de Janis y quítele el libro.** Ask the whole class: **¿Qué hizo Ted?** Help the class to form a series of past tense actions: **Ted se levantó, corrió a la pizarra, escribió su nombre ahí, fue al pupitre de Janis y le quitó el libro.** Later, groups of 2–3 students can do the same activity to provide input with third-person plural forms.

AA 4 Game. The instructor leaves the classroom. The class decides on a crime that the instructor committed. The instructor reenters the room and asks questions to determine what crime he or she committed. Class is permitted to answer only **sí** or **no.** After the instructor has played the criminal, student volunteers play the role. You may have to help volunteers ask appropriate questions.

AA 5 Situación (individual; whole-class). **Usted tiene dieciséis años y vive en casa de sus padres. Ellos son muy estrictos y usted siempre tiene que estar en casa antes de las once de la noche. Una noche usted llega a la una de la madrugada. Esplíqueles a sus padres por qué llegó tan tarde.**

AA 6 (TPR). Divide the class into groups of four to five. Give each group (in writing) a TPR sequence with the theme: going out, going to the beach, cooking dinner, and so on. Students read their sequence over as you circulate to answer any questions. Have each group act out its sequence. When each group has finished, have the rest of the class narrate what it did.

¡Cuéntenos usted!

MODELO: El sábado pasado mi novia y yo dimos una fiesta por la noche. Primero limpiamos muy bien la casa y el patio; luego planificamos el menú: preparamos una ensalada, lasaña y pan francés. Compramos flores para la mesa y pusimos nuestra música favorita. Los invitados llegaron a las 7:00 de la noche y todos tomamos un poco de vino antes de cenar. Cenamos y hablamos toda la noche. Nos acostamos cansados pero muy contentos.

Lectura   *Machu Picchu: un viaje por el tiempo*

Ahora ...¡usted!

1. ¿Cuál es su medio de transporte preferido? ¿tren? ¿autobús? ¿carro? ¿Por qué prefiere este medio de transporte?
2. ¿Participó alguna vez en una excursión interesante o divertida? Describa la experiencia. ¿Adónde fue? ¿con quién? ¿Qué hizo?

Optional grammar

7.2 Ejercicio 5 Before assigning the exercise, read the first narrative aloud to students, pausing for comprehension checks. Then reread the narrative in the third person. You may want to write all changes on the board. Have students do the other narrative at home and check the answer key, or in class with a partner and review it with the whole class.

7.4 Ejercicio 8 Precede this exercise with an oral chain exercise. Have one student secretly tell a second student something he or she did the preceding day. For example: **Fui al cine anoche.** Then, have a third student ask the second, **¿Qué te dijo?** The second replies, **Me dijo que fue al cine.**

Capítulo 8

Goals

In this chapter students will interact in situations that involve food and meals in the Hispanic world. They will learn how to order a meal in a restaurant, how to shop for food in a market, and how to follow recipes in Spanish. The grammar section presents the impersonal object pronouns **lo, la, los, las;** more about **gustar;** prepositional pronouns, additional rules for negation; impersonal **se;** and vowel changes in verbs like **pedir** and **servir.**

Las comidas, las bebidas y la nutrición

AA 1 (whole-class). Use pictures, plastic replicas, or actual food items in sentences such as: **Aquí hay una naranja. Le doy la naranja a John. John, aquí tiene usted la naranja. Ahora ¿quién tiene la naranja? (John) Sí, la tiene John.** (or, **La naranja la tiene John.**) Continue until every student has an item. Then have students exchange items: **Y ahora, ¿dónde está la manzana? ¿Quién la tiene?**

AA 2 (individual). Give the class the following instructions and model. **Escoja su bebida favorita según la ocasión. Use me gusta o prefiero. Modelo: en la mañana → Cuando me levanto en la mañana me gusta tomar una taza de café con leche. Posibilidades: agua mineral, batidos de leche, café, cerveza, chocolate, jugos naturales (de naranja, de pera, de tomate, de toronja), leche, limonada, refrescos, té caliente, té helado, vino. Ocasión: 1. el desayuno 2. el almuerzo 3. una fiesta de cumpleaños 4. después de hacer ejercicio 5. para dormir 6. cuando hace frío/calor 7. en un restaurante.**

AA 3 (individual; whole-class). Describe a situation and ask students what they would eat or drink. Possibilities: **1. Es medianoche. Usted está estudiando para un examen de química. Tiene sueño y siente que no tiene energía, pero no quiere beber más café. ¿Qué va a comer/beber? 2. Usted quiere bajar rápidamente de peso. Quisiera bajar seis kilos en tres semanas. ¿Qué dieta piensa seguir?**

La compra y la preparación de la comida

AA 4 (TPR). See the IRK for TPR sequence: **Vamos a preparar un pastel.** Bring ingredients (flour, sugar, butter, milk, eggs, spices, baking soda) and necessary utensils to class for pantomime. Have a cake already prepared, take it out of a bag (the "oven"), and serve pieces to the class. The sequence can be repeated on several days with different foods. See the IRK for other TPR sequences: **Guacamole, una cena especial.**

AA 5 (individual; whole-class). Prepare a tray with pieces of fruit and other food on toothpicks. Blindfold a volunteer and let him or her choose a piece, then ask the volunteer what he or she is eating without saying what it is: **Es dulce, es salado; me gusta, no me gusta; es fruta fresca, es de lata.**

AA 6 (whole-class). Describe how food and drinks are prepared. Have students name favorite foods/drinks. Then solicit from the class how items are prepared: **¿Qué ingredientes necesitamos? ¿Qué hacemos?** Introduce impersonal **se** construction: **¿Qué se hace primero? Y luego, ¿qué se hace?**

AA 7 (whole-class). With the participation of the whole class decide on a menu for a class party. Make a shopping list for the ingredients.

AA 8 (whole-class). Tell the class: **Vamos a hacer un sándwich con nuestros ingredientes favoritos.** Ask the class for ingredients and write them on the board. Then, describe together how to make a sandwich: **Primero se toma el pan y se le pone mayonesa...** Note that you will need to use the impersonal **se** construction to give step-by-step instructions. Variaciones: **Un super taco, una super tostada, una quesadilla,**

una maxitorta mexicana, una ensalada de legumbres. See IRK for sequence: **Vamos a preparar chiles rellenos.**

AA 9 (whole-class). Describe a food and have students try to guess what it is: **Estoy comiendo algo salado, caliente, con pan, mostaza, y cebolla... ¿Qué es? (Es un perro caliente.)**

AA 10 (whole-class). Have students name a common ingredient in each group: **Nombre un ingrediente esencial que tienen en común estas comidas. 1. los panecillos, las «donas», las galletitas 2. el café, el té, la limonada, la cerveza, 3. el helado, la mantequilla, el queso 4. las enchiladas, las tostadas, los tacos.** Add any other foods you wish.

AA 11 (whole-class). Name a word related to food (**taco, pollo frito, zanahorias, mesero/a**) and have the class think of all the words they can associate with that word. Explore associations, developing as much spontaneous conversation as possible.

AA 12 Asociaciones. If students need more practice with low frequency vocabulary, give them these lists orally. Ask: **¿Cuál de éstas no pertenece al grupo? ¿Por qué? 1. el ajo, la cebolla, la sal, las galletitas; 2. la harina, el azúcar, la salchicha, la margarina; 3. la carne molida, el atún, el bistec, las chuletas; 4. el hígado, el ave, el pollo, el pavo; 5. el jamón, el queso, las chuletas, la carne de cerdo; 6. el caldo, el postre, la propina, el cangrejo; 7. el vino, la leche, el batido, la servilleta.**

AA 13 (whole-class). Poll your students about their eating habits. Ask them to raise their hand in response to your questions. If possible, project a transparency so a student can count hands and write the tally by each question. **¿Quién desayunó huevos con tocino esta mañana? ¿Quién desayunó jugo de naranja y cereal esta mañana? ¿Quién hizo la cena y cenó en casa anoche? ¿Quién preparó un platillo exótico el fin de semana pasado? ¿Quién almorzó sándwiches toda la semana pasada? ¿Quién desayuna huevos todos los días? ¿Quién le pone mucha sal/pimienta a la comida? ¿Quién no come fruta nunca? ¿Quién almuerza hamburguesas siempre? ¿Quién cena en restaurantes por lo menos dos veces a la semana? ¿Quién va siempre a restaurantes mexicanos? ¿Quién prefiere restaurantes chinos o japoneses?**

Los restaurantes

AA 14 (TPR). See the IRK for TPR: **Vamos a cenar fuera.** Sample sequence: **Ustedes van a salir a cenar. Pónganse su ropa más elegante y manejen el carro al restaurante. Entren y esperen al mesero. Siéntense a la mesa y lean la carta. Mmm... Ustedes tienen hambre. Ah, ahí viene el mesero. Pidan dos cervezas o refrescos. Tomen un poco, pidan la comida —dos enchiladas suizas y chiles rellenos— esperen y tomen su cerveza, miren a las otras personas en el restaurante. Ah, por fin llegó la comida. Coman y beban. Pidan postre: helado y flan y café. Ah, ¡qué comida tan rica! Pidan la cuenta: «La cuenta por favor». Dejen la propina, levántense y vayan a la caja. Paguen la cuenta y salgan. Den un paseo por la plaza y regresen a casa.**

AA 15 (group). Tell students: **Hable sobre uno de los siguientes temas: 1. Una experiencia chistosa que usted tuvo alguna vez en un restaurante. 2. Una vez que usted comió o tomó demasiado y se enfermó. 3. Una experiencia que usted tuvo mientras comía en un restaurante en un país extranjero. 4. Descríbale un supermercado norteamericano a una persona que no lo conoce. 5. Describa la receta de un platillo especial suyo.**

AA 16 (whole-class). Ask questions such as: **¿Qué pide usted cuando come en... 1. un restaurante mexicano? 2. la cafetería de la universidad? 3. un restaurante de «servicio rápido»? 4. un restaurante italiano? 5. un puesto de comida en la calle? 6. un restaurante chino? 7. su restaurante favorito?**

¡Cuéntenos usted!

MODELO: Una cena ideal es una cena en casa preparada por mi tía. Mi tía es una cocinera fabulosa. Primero hay una sopa de mariscos con limón y después se sirve el arroz con pollo y el plátano frito. Para beber, hay batidos de fruta. Ceno con mis tíos, mis padres, mis primos y mis hermanos. Después de la cena mis hermanos y yo lavamos los platos mientras mis tíos y mis padres conversan en la mesa. De postre mi tía sirve un rico pastel de chocolate.

Lectura   Los deliciosos platos andinos

Ahora... ¡usted!

1. ¿Le gusta a usted el maíz? ¿En qué forma prefiere comerlo? ¿Hay otras legumbres o frutas que le gustan? ¿Cuáles no le agradan y por qué no?
2. De todos los platos mencionados en la lectura, ¿cuáles ha probado usted? ¿Cuáles le gustaría probar y por qué?

Optional grammar

8.1 Bring several food or household items to class. Put each in a particular location and ask **¿Dónde puse el/la/los/las...?** If students need a prompt, ask an either/or question such as: **¿Lo puse debajo o encima de la mesa?** Then let them practice the same question-and-answer sequences with each other, using the **tú** form (**pusiste**).

8.2 Ask students questions like: **¿A quién le gusta la sandía?** Have them respond with short answers: **A mí, A él.** Then make statements such as: **A usted le gusta el helado, ¿verdad?** And have students give short answers: **A mí, no; a mí, sí; A mi hermano también; A mí tampoco.**

Capítulo 9

Goals

The activities in **Capítulo 9** give students the opportunity to understand and talk about habitual activities in the past, including memories of childhood and elementary and secondary school. The grammar section of this chapter introduces imperfect forms with action verbs, stressing the function of habitual, repeated action in the past, i.e., the equivalent of "used to" in English. We also introduce the imperfect with "state-of-being" verbs (**tener, querer, poder,** etc.). The imperfect, to indicate background action or action in progress, is introduced in **Capítulo 11,** as is the contrast between past (preterite) and imperfect. The semantic differences between past (preterite) and imperfect are somewhat complex. It is unrealistic to think that first-year students will acquire them with the language contacts available to them; even acquiring the rudiments of the contrast takes a great deal of language input and effort. We have chosen to simplify presentation and activities as much as possible by keeping the two tenses (in reality, aspects) apart. For now, with the exception of "state-of-being" verbs, we avoid contexts in which students will have to produce the two tenses together or choose between the two.

Use your PF or photos of your own family to review family terms such as **abuelo/a, hijo/a, padres, tío/a, sobrino/a,** etc. Then use the display (or your own family tree on the board) to introduce new terms: **cuñado/a, nuera, suegro/a, yerno/a, padrastro, madrastra,** etc.

La familia y los parientes

AA 1 (whole-class). Make up some simple definitions for family members: for example, **el hermano de mi madre o de mi padre (tío).** Ask the whole class to identify the family member referred to. Then help the class make up simple definitions for family members. You may ask students to make up one or two of their own. Have volunteers read theirs or have pairs read each other their definitions, with the partner supplying the kinship term.

La juventud

AA 2 (whole-class). Tell the class you want to do a survey (**una encuesta**). Type several of the following activities and hand them out to students. Go over the statement orally with the whole class and check for comprehension. Give them a few minutes to complete the survey while you circulate, helping students who do not completely understand. Collect surveys and tally them out loud. Tallying gives you the option to discuss adolescent problems with the class. Possible statements: **Cuando tenía 14 (15, 16, 17) años... 1. No sabía qué carrera quería seguir. 2. Estaba seguro/a que iba a ser rico/a y famoso/a. 3. Creía que mis padres no me comprendían. 4. A veces pensaba que mis padres no sabían nada. 5. No me llevaba bien con mis padres (hermanos, maestros). 6. Tenía muchos amigos. 7. Pasaba muchas horas hablando por teléfono (intercambiando mensajes instantáneos) con mis amigos. 8. No me gustaba asistir a la escuela. 9. En mi opinión, todas las clases eran aburridas.**

AA 3 (whole-class). Ask students to jot down on a small piece of paper one thing they used to do in junior high or high school. Collect the slips of paper, then read each one and have students guess who the writer is. When someone guesses correctly, he or she gets the piece of paper. The student with the highest number wins a small prize.

AA 4 (group; whole-class). Ask students to compare their daily routine in high school with their daily routine in college. Do this activity in groups or with the whole class. Assign the topic for a composition. Ask students to pay particular attention to the use of imperfect and present forms.

AA 5 (whole-class). Topic for discussion. **Describa las modas (de ropa) que se usaban cuando usted era más joven. Compárelas con las modas de hoy día. Incluya dibujos o fotos si quiere.**

¡Cuéntenos usted!

MODELO: Cuando tenía cinco años fui al kínder por primera vez. Mi mamá caminó conmigo el primer día, pero cuando llegamos a la escuela yo tenía miedo. No quería entrar. La escuela era muy vieja, de color gris. Mi salón de clase era muy grande con muchas ventanas y un patio de recreo enfrente. La maestra también era muy vieja, pero muy simpática.

Lectura   *¡Así piensan los niños!*

Ahora... ¡usted!

1. De niño/a, ¿a qué jugaba? ¿Con quién(es) jugaba?
2. De niño/a, ¿qué comía usted con gusto? ¿Qué no comía nunca?
3. ¿Qué hacía cuando su madre le servía algo que a usted no le gustaba? ¿Siempre servían postre en su casa?
4. ¿Comía usted en restaurantes con frecuencia? ¿Cuál era su restaurante favorito y qué pedía allí?

Optional grammar

9.3 There are three verbs in the imperfect that are irregular in the following ways: (1) **ver** uses the stem **ve-** instead of the expected **v-**; (2) **ser** uses a completely different stem and does not take normal endings; (3) **ir** uses **-ar** endings.

9.5 Ejercicio 9 Have students ask you questions like those in the exercise: **¿Por qué no tomó usted café por la noche? ¿Por qué no habló con sus amigos por teléfono? ¿Por qué no hizo usted ejercicio?** Answer each time with **Iba a...** and then explain why you did not do each activity.

Capítulo 10

Goals

The focus of this and the following chapter is travel. **Capítulo 10** emphasizes geography and students' own experiences as well as geography and ecological issues; **Capítulo 11** emphasizes travel by automobile and travel within the Hispanic world. The most important new topic in the grammar section of **Capítulo 10** is the present perfect.

La geografía y el clima

AA 1 (whole-class). Use your PF to relate weather with seasons. Remind students of the reverse seasons north and south of the equator **(en el hemisferio norte/sur).** Then use pictures of various geographic locations to talk about climate: **¿Qué tiempo hace en las montañas? ¿en la playa? ¿en Florida? ¿en Canadá?**

AA 2 Review geographical terms with photos from your PF that include scenes of jungles, beaches, mountains, streams, canyons, etc. As you hold each one up, react to it: **¡Qué cañón más profundo! ¡Qué río más bonito! ¡Qué agua tan cristalina!** Have class help you generate a list of geographical locations and a list of adjectives used to describe places and write these on the board. Pair students and pass out your photos, two to three per group. On the board write: **¡Qué _____ más (tan) _____!** Students react to places in the photos.

Los medios de transporte

AA 3 (TPR). See the IRK for TPR: **Vamos a ir en taxi.** Sample sequence: **Son las diez de la noche y usted acaba de cenar en un restaurante con unos amigos. Van a regresar a casa y necesitan un taxi. Caminen a la plaza central de la ciudad; allí viene un taxi, no está libre, ah, pero ahí viene otro que sí está libre; levanten la mano y háganle una señal al taxista. ¡Ay! ¡Qué lástima! no los vio. Esperen unos minutos. Empieza a llover y ustedes tienen frío. Ahí viene otro taxi. Levanten la mano y háganle una señal al taxista, ¡ay! Por fin, éste sí se detiene, ¡errrk! Pregúntenle: ¿Cuánto nos cobra por llevarnos a _____? Es un buen precio: suban al taxi. Díganle al taxista su dirección. Ya llegaron. Páguenle y denle una propina. Bájense y díganle «Buenas noches».**

AA 4 (whole-class). Use photos from your PF showing travel by plane; recount some of your own experiences traveling by plane. Mention some well-known airlines **(líneas aéreas, compañías de aviación): Iberia (España); Aerolíneas Argentinas; Avianca (Colombia); VIASA (Venezuela).** Introduce vocabulary related to air travel: **abordar, abrocharse los cinturones de seguridad, aeropuerto, asistente de vuelo, aterrizar, despegar, facturar el equipaje, sin escala, sección de (no) fumar, tarjeta de abordaje,** etc.

¡Cuéntenos usted!

MODELO: Hace cuatro años mi familia y yo fuimos al Rincón de la Vieja en Costa Rica. Me impresionó muchísimo ese lugar porque vimos muchos animales como tucanes, perezosos, un tapir y varias serpientes. Pero lo que más me impresionó fueron los grandes cráteres llenos de agua muy caliente de diferentes colores y el volcán activo.

Lectura   Costa Rica, un país ideal

Ahora... ¡usted!

1. ¿Ha estado usted en Costa Rica? Si no ha estado, ¿le gustaría visitar ese país?
2. ¿Le gustaría vivir en un país donde no haya ejército? ¿Cuáles son las ventajas y desventajas de tener una fuerza militar?

3. ¿Le preocupa la cuestión de la repoblación forestal? ¿Qué ideas o planes propone usted para evitar la destrucción de los bosques?

Optional grammar

10.1 Ask students to arrange their desks in a circle. Tell them that they each must think of one activity they have done that they think others in class might not have done: **Piense en una actividad que ha hecho, de la cual está seguro/a que nadie más en clase la ha hecho. Por ejemplo: Yo he ido en barco a la isla de San Miguel por la costa de California.** Ask for a volunteer to begin and write his/her activity on the board: **Jessica ha buceado en las Filipinas.** If someone else has also done this activity then come back to the student later for him/her to come up with another "exclusive" activity.

10.2 In three columns on the board write a list of places, a list of adjectives, and the model: **¡Qué + lugar + tan/más + descripción!** Have students work in pairs to describe these places. Suggestions: **Lugares: el desierto en el sur de España, las autopistas de Alemania, las catedrales del norte de Francia, los campos de flores en Holanda, las playas de la Costa del Sol en España, el bosque en Suiza, el metro en Madrid, los Pirineos, el río Sena en París, los llanos en el centro de España. Descripción: aburrido/a, alto/a, antiguo/a, árido/a, brillante, denso/a, hermoso/a, impresionante, inolvidable, interesante, lento/a, limpio/a, moderno/a, oscuro/a, rápido/a, sucio/a, verde.**

Capítulo 11

Goals

The activities in **Capítulo 11** address common travel situations and topics: making travel plans and reservations, reading maps, travel experiences and information on Hispanic countries, and tourists sites of the Spanish-speaking world. In the grammar section we present rules for formal command forms (students will recognize most of them already from experiences with TPR) and for the present subjunctive after **querer** and **cuando**—the two most common contexts for use of the subjunctive in Spanish. In addition, we introduce the imperfect progressive and imperfect to describe background actions or states that are interrupted by events. (We have included **vosotros/as** forms in all verb paradigms and have footnoted **vos** forms up to now. If you want to give students more practice with both **vosotros** and **vos** pronouns and verb forms, you may want them to read the explanation of these forms in the **Expansión grammatical** section of the **Cuaderno de actividades** and do the accompanying exercises. These forms are also included in some listening materials and in certain readings.)

Los viajes en automóvil

AA 1 (TPR). See the IRK for TPR: **En el carro.** Sample sequence: **Ustedes van a recoger a un amigo suyo para ir al cine. Salgan de casa y suban al carro. Arránquenlo, errr, errr; no quiere arrancar. Bajen del carro y levanten el capó, revisen el radiador, ajá, necesita agua, pónganle agua y suban otra vez al carro. Arránquenlo, brrrrn, brrrrn. Esta vez sí arrancó. Abróchense el cinturón de seguridad y ajusten el espejo. Ya es casi de noche; prendan las luces, manejen, doblen a la derecha, doblen a la izquierda, sigan adelante. Empieza a llover; prendan el limpiaparabrisas, wish/wash/wish/wash. ¡huy! ¡Un perro! Frenen. ¡Errrkkk! ¡Ay, qué susto! Sigan manejando. No están mirando el camino y chocan con un carro estacionado. Apaguen el motor, bajen del carro, sí, sí, ya sé, fue mi culpa,; yo le pago los daños, sí, sí. Denle su nombre y número de teléfono y el número de teléfono y el nombre de su compañía de seguros. Miren los dos carros, miren el guardafango, la puerta y el parachoques; no hay mucho daño. Sigan manejando a la casa de su amigo. Ya se está haciendo muy tarde. Dense prisa. 100, 120 kilómetros por hora, miren su espejo. Ahí está un carro de la policía con las luces prendidas. Deténganse otra vez. El policía les pone una multa por exceso de velocidad. Continúen manejando.**

Por fin llegan a la casa de su amigo; toquen la bocina biip, biip. Ahí está su amigo. Ábranle la puerta del carro y salgan para el cine.

En busca de sitios

AA 2 (whole-class). Have students give directions from one place to another. Suggestions: **1. Usted está en la universidad. Dele instrucciones a una turista para llegar a un lugar de interés en el área. 2. Usted está en casa. Dele instrucciones a un vecino para llegar al hospital más cercano.**

Los planes de viaje

AA 3 (whole-class; individual). Travel itinerary: referring to a large wall map, talk about countries and continents all over the world. Talk about famous tourist sites and geographical characteristics. Write new words on the board. Tell students the places you have traveled to: **He ido/viajado a _____ (dos veces, una vez).** Then tell them about places you would (not) like to travel to: **Quisiera ver/viajar a _____. No tengo ganas de ir a _____.** Ask each student to write a two-week itinerary for you for a wonderful vacation. Remind them to use **va a** + infinitive and have them start the itinerary with **Usted va a salir de _____, el día _____ de...**

Variation: Pair students and have them interview each other, asking **¿Adónde has viajado? ¿Adónde te gustaría viajar? ¿Qué te gusta hacer cuando viajas?** When they gather enough information, have them write an itinerary for their partner.

AA 4 (TPR). See the IRK for TPR. **Llegando al hotel.** Sample sequence: **Ustedes llegan al hotel en taxi. Abran la puerta y bajen de taxi. Recojan su equipaje del maletero (baúl, cajuela) del taxi. Páguenle al chofer y denle una propina. Llega el botones. Muéstrenle su equipaje y síganlo a la recepción. Presenten su tarjeta de crédito y firmen los papeles. Sigan al botones. Tomen el ascensor al séptimo piso. Sigan al botones a la habitación. Tomen la llave que les da el botones y díganle gracias. Denle una propina y pasen a la habitación. Acuéstense en la cama y descansen. ¡Qué viaje tan largo!**

Los sitios turísticos

AA 5 (whole-class; pair). **Situaciones: Problemas en el viaje**

1. **Usted tiene tres hijos; uno tiene ocho años, otro tiene seis, y la más pequeña tiene solamente dos años y medio. Los niños de menos de dos años vuelan gratis. Cuando llega al aeropuerto la señorita que vende los boletos le pregunta a usted la edad de la menor. ¿Qué dice usted?**
2. **Usted tiene reservaciones para volar desde la ciudad de México a Cozumel. Usted llega al aeropuerto un poco tarde, unos quince minutos antes de la salida del vuelo. El señor que asigna los asientos le dice que no puede encontrar su nombre en la lista de pasajeros confirmados y que el avión está lleno. ¿Qué va a hacer usted?**

AA 6 (whole-class). Talk about procedures for using ATMs (**cajero automático**) in Spanish-speaking countries. Remind students that the quantity that they request will be in the **moneda nacional;** if they request $100.00 in Costa Rica they will get 100 **colones** or if they request $100.00 in Spain they will get 100 **euros.** Show sample currencies from Latin America and Spain.

AA 7 (pair). You may also want to role-play a situation at customs: ADUANERO: **¿Tiene usted algo que declarar?** TURISTA: **Traigo varios _____.** ADUANERO: **Déjeme ver. ¿Tiene usted el recibo para esto/a _____?** TURISTA: **Sí, aquí está. Lo/la compré en _____.** ADUANERO: **Está bien, pase usted. (Lo siento, señor[a], pero va a tener que pagar derechos de aduana. Son _____ pesos [euros, colones, etc.].)**

¡Cuéntenos usted!

MODELO: Cuando tenía 12 años viajaba con mis padres y mis hermanitos a San Antonio para visitar a nuestros tíos y primos. Mis hermanos menores y yo íbamos sentados en el asiento trasero del coche. Al principio sólo hablábamos en voz alta, pero luego empezamos a pelearnos un poco y a mi padre no le gustó. Finalmente nos dijo en tono muy severo que no peleáramos más. Entonces tuve una idea excelente. Saqué un marcador negro de mi mochila y empecé a dibujar en las manos, los brazos y en las caras de mis hermanos menores. Cuando por fin paramos para almorzar, ¡Ay, ay, ay! ¡La sorpresa que le dimos a mi pobre papá!

Lectura   *Mérida, ciudad en la montaña*

Ahora... ¡usted!

1. ¿Ha visitado usted la región de Mérida en Venezuela o cualquier otra ciudad en este país? Cuente las experiencias que tuvo durante su visita. Si no ha visitado Venezuela, ¿conoce otro país de América Latina? ¿Cuál? ¿Cuándo viajó usted allí? ¿Qué actividades hizo?
2. Si no conoce la región de Mérida, ¿le gustaría hacerlo? ¿Qué impresión tiene de los lugares mencionados en la lectura? ¿Cuáles le gustaría visitar y por qué?

Capítulo 12

Goals

The goal of **Capítulo 12** is to create opportunities to communicate about good health, illnesses, accidents, and emergencies. In the grammar section we review the tenses of the impersonal **haber** and introduce ways of expressing changes in states (*become, get*). We review direct **usted** command forms, which are used in health-related situations and in emergencies. We describe indirect object pronouns with verbs of volition (**aconsejar, pedir, decir,** etc.) and introduce the use of **se** with unplanned occurrences. There is also a summary of the past tenses presented to date with a more detailed explanation of the functions of past and imperfect in narration.

El cuerpo humano y la salud

AA 1. Entrevista (whole-class; pair). Discuss habits or activities that may affect health. Ask: **¿Cuáles son los hábitos que afectan la salud? ¿Cuáles son los más dañinos** (*harmful*)? Invite students to express their opinions about smoking. Ask students who smoke if they have tried to quit or if they would like to: **¿Han tratado de dejar de fumar? ¿Les gustaría dejar el vicio?** Discuss drug addiction and alcoholism (**la drogadicción y el alcoholismo**): **¿Conocen ustedes a alguien que abuse de las drogas? ¿del alcohol?** Then write these questions on the board and pair students to interview each other: **1. ¿Fumas? ¿Cuántos cigarrillos fumas por día? ¿Quieres dejar de fumar? ¿Por qué? 2. Sí no fumas, ¿tienes otro vicio que quieres dejar? ¿Tomas mucho café? ¿Comes mucha comida chatarra? 3. ¿Puedes nombrar otros hábitos que dañan la salud? 4. ¿Crees que es muy difícil dejar de usar drogas? ¿dejar de beber alcohol? ¿Por qué? Explica.**

Las enfermedades y su tratamiento

AA 2 (TPR). See the IRK for TPR: **Ustedes están enfermos.** Sample sequence: **Ustedes están enfermos. Acuéstense, tomen aspirinas. Ustedes se sienten muy mal. Estornuden, achú, traguen, traguen otra vez, ¡ay, les duele la garganta! Miren la televisión, duerman un poco, despiértense, tosan, caj, caj, caj. Levántense y vayan al baño. Abran el botiquín y saquen el jarabe para la tos; tomen una cucharadita de jarabe y vuelvan a la cama.**

AA 3 (individual; pair). Prepare index cards with situations on each. Example: **Cuando llueve, ¿cómo se siente usted?** Give out one card per student and ask them to think of as many emotions as possible for that

159

situations. Other possibilities: **Cuando nieva... Cuando maneja un carro nuevo... Cuando no puede dormir... Cuando compra ropa nueva... Cuando llega tarde a clase... Cuando come demasiado... Cuando corre más de un kilómetro...**

AA 4 (whole-class). Lead a class discussion about health and nutrition. Possible questions: **1. ¿Qué comidas son buenas para la salud? ¿Y cuáles son malas? 2. ¿Come usted siempre alimentos saludables? ¿Por qué? 3. ¿Come usted comidas con conservadores artificiales? ¿Los considera necesarios? ¿Peligrosos? 4. Si uno quiere adelgazar, ¿qué comidas debe comer? 5. ¿Es importante el desayuno? ¿Desayuna usted generalmente? 6. ¿Es indispensable tomar vitaminas o es suficiente comer comidas nutritivas?**

Las visitas al médico, a la farmacia y al hospital

AA 5 (TPR). See the IRK for TPR: **Una consulta con el médico.** Sample sequence: **Ustedes tienen la gripe. Llamen al médico y hablen con la recepcionista. Ustedes tienen cita en una hora. Acuéstense y descansen por trienta minutos. Manejen su carro al consultorio del médico. Pasen a la oficina y díganle su nombre a la recepcionista. Esperen trienta minutos, lean una revista, y tosan varias veces. La enfermera dice su nombre, levántense y pasen al consultorio del médico. ¡Ay, qué frio! Siéntense en la mesa. Aquí viene el médico. Explíquenle sus síntomas. El médico escucha y entonces les dice: "Quítense la camisa, respiren profundo, tosan tres veces, traguen, otra vez, abran la boca y digan «ah». Tomen la medicina que yo les receto tres veces al día, duerman mucho, tomen muchos líquidos y vuelvan a verme en una semana."**

Los accidentes y las emergencias

AA 6 (individual, whole-class). From your PF select pictures of people doing various activities. Have students pretend they were doing these activities: **¿Qué estaba haciendo? ¿A qué hora? ¿Por qué lo estaba haciendo?**

AA 7 Situaciones adicionales: **1. Usted toma el ascensor para subir al décimo piso de un edificio ultra-moderno. Cuando aprieta el botón número diez, el aparato salta y sube velozmente. Pero al llegar al octavo piso, se detiene. El botón de emergencia no funciona y la puerta no se abre. Usted está atrapado/a. ¿Qué puede hacer? 2. Usted espera su turno para consultar al dentista en el tercer piso de un edificio. De repente usted oye una explosión en el primer piso. Usted está atrapado/a en el consultorio del dentista. Hay dos ventanas pequeñas ¿Qué puede hacer?**

AA 8 Dramas

1. En el consultorio del médico / la doctora

Trabaje con un compañero / una compañera. Una persona va a hacer el papel del médico / de la doctora y la otra, el papel del/de la paciente. Escriban un diálogo para actuar en clase. El/La paciente debe saludar al médico / a la doctora y luego decirle sus síntomas. El médico / La doctora debe escuchar los síntomas, hacerle algunas preguntas pertinentes y luego examinar al / a la paciente. Finalmente, el médico / la doctora debe dar su diagnóstico y recetar las medicinas apropiadas.

2. En el hosptial

Un accidente: Trabaje con otros dos compañeros para representar una escena en el hospital. Una persona es el/la socorrista, otra es el/la paciente y otra es el médico / la doctora. El/La socorrista llega con el/la paciente en una camilla y le da los datos del accidente y la información necesaria sobre el estado del/de la paciente al médico / la doctora. El médico / La doctora recibe al/a la paciente y le hace preguntas sobre el accidente y sobre cómo se siente. El/La paciente contesta. El médico / La doctora dice qué va a hacer para atender al/a la paciente.

AA 9 Imagínese que usted ha descubierto una hierba medicinal muy importante. Describa su descubrimiento: ¿Cómo se llama la hierba? ¿Dónde y cómo la descubrió? ¿Qué padecimientos (*ailments*) puede curar? ¿Cómo se prepara este medicamento? ¿Se toma en forma de pastillas? ¿en forma de bebida? ¿De qué manera piensa usted presentar este nuevo medicamento al mundo?

¡Cuéntenos usted!

MODELO: Cuando tenía siete años tuve la varicela. Me levanté temprano ese día porque era mi cumpleaños y mi madre iba a dar una pequeña fiesta en mi salón de clase. Me vestía y pensaba en el pastel y los globos, cuando de repente vi que tenía una pequeña roncha (*spot*) roja en el brazo. Luego vi que tenía tres ronchas más en el estómago. Cuando se las mostré a mi mamá, ella me explicó que tenía varicela y que no podía asistir a clases ese día. ¡Qué gran desilusión!

Lectura   *El recetario de la abuela*

Ahora... ¡usted!

1. ¿Piensa que es excesivo el uso de las medicinas sintéticas en los Estados Unidos? ¿Dependemos demasiado de las drogas para curarnos en este país? ¿Por qué?
2. ¿Hay problemas de salud que podrían curarse sin medicamentos artificiales? ¿Cuáles, por ejemplo?

Capítulo 13

Goals

Capítulo 13 gives students the opportunity to talk about manufactured products and the materials from which they are made. Students will also talk about their experiences buying and selling. They will use numbers in the thousands and millions through several different types of activities. The chapter also provides information on clothing, fashion, shopping, and commerce in the Hispanic world. The grammar section includes nominalization of adjectives, demonstrative pronouns, additional uses of **por** and **para,** more on indirect object pronouns, and use of direct and indirect object pronouns together.

Los productos y los materiales

AA 1 (whole-class). Use your PF to talk about preferences and styles: **Aquí hay dos faldas. ¿Prefiere usted la roja o la azul?** Clothing, houses, and cars lend themselves well to questions about preferences for items.

Los precios

AA 2 (whole-class). Use the Internet to find out what the current exchange rate is for the money shown in the display. Discuss the monetary status of countries that switched to U. S. currency in the late 1990s (El Salvador and Ecuador). Have students practice converting from dollars to **euros, bolívares, quetzales, colones, pesos mexicanos, pesos argentinos, soles,** etc.

Bring photos of objects and have the class decide on prices for items in **euros** one day, **pesos** another, and so on. If you have samples of these coins or paper bills, bring them in.

La ropa

AA 3 (individual; whole-class). Have students think of special items of clothing they would like to buy for certain people: **Piense en una prenda de vestir muy especial que usted quisiera comprar para las siguientes personas. Explique por qué quiere regalarles lo que ha escogido: su padre, su profesor(a) de español, su hermano/a, su abuelo/a, su novio/a, su esposo/a, su mejor amigo/a.** Ask students to share with the whole class.

AA 4 (whole-class). Bring in a bag of clothing and objects from the vocabulary in this chapter. Arrange students in a circle and distribute items, giving commands: **Russ, quiero que le lleve la chaqueta amarilla a Megan. Ahora, Megan póngasela. Nick, quiero que me traiga el abrelatas que tiene Gayle.** Give as many commands with as many objects as possible, commenting on objects and their use as you go. Some students may be able to give commands to others; some may need a little filling in from you to do so.

Las compras y el regateo

AA 5 (group). Divide students into groups of four to five. Each group must decide on a gift for the instructor, who then guesses what gift each group has selected by asking **sí/no** questions. Alternative: students in pairs guess what gift their partner has selected for them.

AA 6 (individual; whole-class). Have students use formal commands (**compre, disfrute, conozca, tome, pruebe, lleve, viaje, etcétera**) to write ads for various products. You may have them bring a picture of their product to the class and write in class or assign as homework. Follow-up: Have students share their "ads" in groups of three or four.

AA 7 (group). Have students each bring in an object or a picture of an object. In groups of four to six, set up an auction (**subasta**). The auctioneer describes the object, pointing out its qualities and asking for the "public" to bid on the item.

AA 8 (individual; whole-class). Have students think of appropriate birthday gifts for the following people: **Luis Alberto Sánchez, un señor de 60 años de edad, aficionado a la música; María Hinostoza, señora a quien le gusta viajar; Elena Quiroga, señora a quien le gusta esquiar; Juan y Miriam Loredo, recién casados; Julio Espinosa, joven aficionado a los deportes; María Galván, ama de casa a quien le gusta cocinar.** Since by now students know quite a bit about each other, you can also ask: **¿Qué le vamos a regalar a _____?**

AA 9 Entrevista (pair). **1. ¿Has ido de compras en otro país? ¿Qué compraste? ¿Dónde? ¿Cuándo? 2. ¿Pudiste regatear o era una tienda de precios fijos? 3. ¿Qué diferencia hay entre comprar en los Estados Unidos y comprar en el extranjero? 4. ¿Te gusta ir de compras solo/a o prefieres ir acompañado/a? 5. ¿Te gusta ir de compras cuando hay una venta especial o prefieres ir cuando hay menos gente?**

AA 10 (individual; whole-class). Give students two minutes to make a birthday or holiday wish list of clothing and other items they need or want. Have them pick three to four items and write a sentence for each, telling why they need or want the item. Share with the whole class.

AA 11 (individual; whole-class). Give students two minutes to make a holiday wish list of useful items for a homeless shelter (**un albergue para los desamparados**). You could encourage students to bring items into class, reveiw the vocabulary and then donate the items to a local shelter.

¡Cuéntenos usted!

MODELO: Mi tienda favorita es una pequeña librería de libros usados en el centro de mi ciudad. Los dueños son chilenos y muy simpáticos. Cada vez que entro, trato de hablar un poco de español con ellos. Me gusta ese tienda porque hay una gran selección de diversos libros a precios muy módicos. ¡El único problema es que siempre compro muchos libros y no tengo tiempo para leer tantos!

Ahora... ¡usted!

¿Ha tenido usted una experiencia similar a la de don Pedro en este cuento? Es decir, ¿ha tomado una decisión basada en la opinión de los demás y no en lo que le dictaba su propio corazón? ¿Qué pasó? ¿Qué aprendió usted?

Optional grammar

13.1 Emphasize the use of **lo** + adjective for abstract ideas, **lo bueno, lo importante** and the meaning of **lo que: lo que me gusta es..., lo que más le interesa es...** because they are both commonly used and their meaning is not always obvious.

13.5 (whole-class) Bring in a bag of items, many from the vocabulary of **Los productos y los materiales:** nail polish, a ball of wool, jewelery, a small box, thread, scissors, a can opener, a cell phone, a toy hammer, a calculator, etc. Have students sit in a semicircle and distribute items so that most students have an object. Ask: **El martillo, ¿quién lo tiene?** and expand on the students' response by saying: **Sí, Olivia lo tiene.** Write on the board: **Olivia lo/la/los/las tiene.** When you have asked about five to ten items, begin giving commands: **Brandon, llévele (pásele) las tijeras a Lisa.** Write on board: **Llévele las tijeras a Lisa = Lléveselas.** Give a few more commands in this fashion and then use this model: **El abrelatas... Zack, déselo a Gary; Reena... las joyas, lléveselas a Candace,** etc. The goal of this activity is not for students to produce double object pronouns in their own speech, but for them to hear lots of them in your speech and to see the pattern on the board.

Capítulo 14

Goals

Capítulo 14 focuses on persuading others to do things. This includes giving direct commands, giving and following advice, and making dates, suggestions, and invitations. The structures in the grammar section include formal and informal commands, subjunctive forms used in noun phrases preceded by expression of volition, and "let's" commands.

All topics in this and the next chapter are more appropriate for second-year students or advanced first-year students. If you are using this text with second-year students, you will want to follow up each section with more oral work and reading. If you have not done so already, this is a good point to begin a self-selected reading program, using newspapers, magazines, children's stories, or any other interesting printed material for students to read on a daily basis. Reminder: The activities and the grammar are only loosely coordinated, and most of the **Actividades de comunicación** are not designed with obvious grammar focus. The activities in this chapter and the next can be done without emphasizing the grammar in detail. Distinctions between **ser** and **estar** and the command forms may be difficult for students. They should be aware that acquisition of these concepts takes more contact time.

La familia, las amistades y el matrimonio

AA 1 (whole-class). Ask if any students are married. Ask if they had a large or small wedding, if it was very expensive, how many people came, how long it took them to plan it, if anything went wrong, and so on. Or have students describe in detail a wedding they have attended. Ask unmarried students questions such as **¿Van a casarse ustedes? ¿Cómo va a ser la boda? ¿Van a casarse por la iglesia o será una ceremonia civil? ¿Por qué? En su opinión, ¿hoy día hay menos parejas que deciden casarse? ¿Hay más personas solteras hoy? ¿Por qué?**

AA 2 (individual; pair). Give students two minutes to write down as many words for family members as they can think of. Then ask them to write down a name from their family for each family relationship: **tía**-Sharon, **abuela**-Rebecca, **primo**-Kenneth, **suegra**-Betty, etc. (They may have some gaps; they may have written down **cuñado,** without having one.) Have students describe the persons on their list with an adjective, their favorite activity, where they live, and if they get along with this person and why. Write on board: **Tengo un(a) _____ que se llama _____. Es _____ y le gusta _____. Vive en _____. (No) Me llevo bien con el/ella porque _____.** Pair students and have them share information about their families.

AA 3 (pair). Have students work in pairs: **Usted acaba de conocer a un amigo/una amiga y lo/la invitó a una reunión familiar. Ahora tiene que presentarle a todos sus parientes. Explíquele el parentesco entre sus familiares. Mencione por lo menos tres generaciones. Por ejemplo: Quiero presentarte a mi cuñada, _____; es la esposa de mi hermano.** Give one student (the presenter) a card with a description of his or her "family" on it or with a family tree labeled with names. As the first student describes his/her pretend family the other student should try to jot down a description of the family. Then the two can compare notes to see if the family was accurately described and understood.

AA 4 (whole-class). Use these questions to start a discussion about marriage and family: **1. En su opinión, ¿cuál es la edad óptima para casarse? 2. ¿Piensa usted casarse antes o después de los veinticinco años? 3. ¿Cuál es la edad óptima para tener hijos? ¿Cuántos hijos piensa tener? 4. ¿Es mejor tener el primer hijo inmediatamente después de casarse o es mejor esperar un poco? 5. ¿Hay o debe haber una edad límite para tener el primer hijo? 6. ¿Deben quedarse en casa las madres que tienen niños pequeños?** You may want to write these questions on the board in the **tú** form and use them as an **Entrevista.**

Las instrucciones y los mandatos

AA 5 (individual). Show pictures of people doing things. Give a picture to a student and ask him or her to command you to do whatever is being done in the picture.

AA 6 (individual). Review giving directions. Have a volunteer stand up. Command him or her to walk in various directions: **Siga adelante. Doble a la derecha. Doble a la izquierda,** etc. Pair students and have them give each other directional commands.

AA 7 (pair). Have students practice giving commands to each other in pairs, using either **usted** or **tú** commands according to the roles they play: friend-friend, mother-child, teacher-student, etc. Examples: **Explicar cómo llegar a la biblioteca, cómo llegar al restaurante que está cerca, cómo ponerse el maquillaje, cómo vestirse,** etc.

AA 8 (pair; group). Place students in groups of four, then divide each into pairs. Each pair is to make up two commands for the other pair (out-of-the-ordinary commands are fine.) Tell them commands must be performed in class or close by (otherwise you may get statements like (**lávenme el carro**). Give them five minutes or so to work while you circulate to help with vocabulary. Remind them to keep things simple and comprehensible for their group. Then ask for volunteers to give the first commands to the others in their groups.

If the instructor is willing to do the commands of the Pre-Text Oral Activities, students are usually willing to perform, too. Some commands that students have come up with: **canten «De colores», bailen enfrente de la clase, salgan del salón de clase y salúdennos por la ventana, hagan ejercicio enfrente de la clase, bésenle la mano a _____, juegen a la rayuela, limpien el piso.** (Of course, the instructor has veto power.)

Las órdenes, los consejos y las sugerencias

AA 9 Write the following on the board: **Sr. Presidente, Sr. Senador, Sra. Senadora, Sr./Sra. _____ (su jefe/jefa), Profesor/Profesora,** and any other titles or names you consider appropriate. Work with the whole class to formulate advice (using the subjunctive) for these people. You may wish to jot down some ideas such as: **que nos dé más/menos tarea, que (no) suba los impuestos, que me aumente el sueldo, que reduzca el déficit federal,** and so on. Ask students to use phrases like **le aconsejo que, le recomiendo que, le ruego que, espero que, es preferible que, es necesario que.** Give the first one: **Le ruego que (no) nos dé más tarea.**

AA 10 Work with the whole class to formulate advice (using the subjunctive) for some of the students. You may have to jot down such ideas as: **que me prestes tu tarea, que no copies durante el examen, que llegues a clase a tiempo, que le traigas chocolates a la profesora.** Give the first one: **Chicos, les aconsejo que me traigan un refresco mañana antes del examen.** Or: **Clase, espero que mañana lleguen temprano a clase.**

¡Cuéntenos usted!

MODELO: No me llevo muy bien con mi tío Gustavo. Él vive en Florida y es bombero. Es muy hablador, agresivo y tiene opiniones muy fuertes. No nos llevamos muy bien porque siempre me da consejos que no quiero. Él cree que sabe manejar mi vida mucho mejor que yo. Siempre hace comentarios negativos sobre mi ropa, mis amigos, mis notas escolares, en fin, sobre todo. Afortunadamente el tío Gustavo sólo nos visita una vez al año.

Lectura   *Los refranes*

Ahora... ¡usted!

1. ¿Recuerda algún refrán que usted aprendió cuando era niño/a? ¿Cuál es? ¿Quién le enseñó ese refrán? ¿Cree usted que este refrán expresa un aspecto de su cultura?
2. ¿Hay una expresión en particular que su familia usa mucho? ¿Cuál es? ¿Qué significa?
3. ¿Le gusta usar refranes cuando conversa? ¿Por qué?
4. En general, ¿para qué sirven los refranes?

Lectura   *«Lazarillo y el ciego»*

Selección de la novela *Lazarillo de Tormes* (1554)

Ahora... ¡usted!

1. ¿Qué mensaje tiene esta breve historia? Explique.
2. ¿Conoce alguna novela o cuento similar de su país? ¿Cuál es? ¿Qué tiene en común con la historia de Lazarillo?
3. En la novela *Lazarillo de Tormes* hay varios temas importantes e interesantes. Aquí tiene algunos. Escoja el que más le interesa a usted y discuta este tema con su compañero/a.
   * Los niños sin padres (huérfanos) que tienen que ser fuertes y astutos para sobrevivir.
   * Los desamparados (*homeless*).
   * Las personas con desafíos (*challenges*) físicos o mentales y la manera en que los superan.

Optional grammar

14.2 In addition to the two exercises provided, you can use pictures of people doing various things and in various states of being to ask: **¿Cómo está el señor en esta foto? Sí, está enfermo.** Then ask students to describe the person and speculate on his or her personality: **¿Cómo es este señor? Sí, es viejo, de pelo gris. ¿Es rico? Tal vez. Y la señora en esta foto, ¿cómo está? Sí, tienen razón, está muy ocupada. Y, ¿cómo es ella? Sí, es alta y de pelo castaño.**

14.4–14.5 If you go over the exercises on the subjunctive in class, we suggest that you focus on the meaning and use of the matrix expressions (such as **preferir que**) and on the word order of the dependent clause (making sure that the conjunction **que** is used and that the correct pronouns are in proper order). Subjunctive forms themselves are almost always redundant, and students' errors of forms will not cause misunderstanding. On the other hand, leaving out the **que** or misplacing pronouns can lead to confusion.

Capítulo 15

Goals

Discussion topics in **Capítulo 15,** although advanced, are usually quite interesting to students, so participation is not difficult to elicit. Remember, however, that the more comprehensible input you provide at the beginning of the chapter, the easier it will be for students to acquire the vocabulary and a working command of some of these advanced grammar points—especially the future and the conditional. The forms and uses of the subjunctive will still be difficult for students. They should be aware that acquisition of these concepts takes more contact time than that provided by the average length of first-year college courses (100 to 160 contact hours).

El futuro y las metas personales

AA 1 (individual; whole-class). Here are some possibilities for future situations. Have students complete each with a future activity: **Después de graduarse, ¿qué hará? (después de conseguir su primer empleo, después de casarse, después de tener hijos, después de jubilarse)**

AA 2 (individual). Give students two minutes to write down as many future plans and goals as they can think of. Have them look at their list, pick three goals, and write one sentence for each, explaining why they will or will not be able to attain that goal: **Cuando me gradúe, tendré mi propio negocio. No sé si será posible, porque cuesta mucho dinero empezar un negocio.** Do not force students to use the formal future; they may continue to use the periphrastic future (**ir a** + infinitive). The focus here is on their goals, not on correct future forms.

Cuestiones sociales

AA 3 (pair). Pair students and give them three minutes to think of as many urban issues as they can. Combine pairs into groups of four and ask them to brainstorm solutions to each problem. Bring the class back together and ask for one or two problems and solutions from each group. Write these on the board.

AA 4 (group). Have students write a list of the important political and social issues of the last two years. Give them some of these suggestions to get them started: social programs, defense budget, minority participation, nuclear weapons, labor unions, energy, oil consumption, women's liberation, homelessness, child abuse, gays in the military, gangs, etc. Write these on the board and let groups select one or two for discussion.

AA 5 (group; whole-class). Make a list of controversial topics that seem appropriate and of interest to your class. For ideas look at the controversial topics listed in the display art of **Cuestiones sociales. Hay que censurar la violencia y el sexo en los programas de televisión y en las películas. Se debe prohibir que los ciudadanos porten armas de fuego. Hay que ponerle fin a la inmigración ilegal. La ingeniería genética le ofrece grandes beneficios a la humanidad. Los alimentos transgénicos no presentan ningún riesgo a**

nuestra salud. Have each student select two of these statements and write down a few ideas/reactions to each one: **No creo que sea necesario censurar toda violencia en los programas de televisión; Es improbable que le pongan fin a la inmigración ilegal.** Circulate as you help students to express opinions and then ask for volunteers to share their opinions with the class.

El futuro y la tecnología: posibilidades y consecuencias

AA 6 (individual; whole-class). Have students imagine what their life would be like without the following things. **Imagínese su vida sin la electricidad. ¿Cómo cambiaría su estilo de vida? ¿Sería grande el cambio? ¿Se adaptaría usted fácilmente? ¿Es verdaderamente indispensable tener la electricidad? Ahora considere su vida sin las siguientes cosas; un carro propio, las fotocopiadoras, los celulares, el cine, los aviones, el agua corriente, las computadoras.**

AA 7 (individual; whole-class). Have students speculate on what they would do if they had more time or money: **Si usted tuviera más tiempo, ¿qué haría? Si usted tuviera más dinero, ¿qué haría por... sus abuelos? sus hermanos? la sociedad?**

¡Cuéntenos usted!

MODELO: Me preocupa más la sobrepoblación porque no creo que la tierra resista el impacto de tanta gente. Creo que la sobrepoblación es la causa de muchos otros problemas, como las guerras, la escasez de agua y la falta de energía. Espero que la gente deje de tener tantos hijos y que los gobiernos ayuden a establecer más clínicas de planificación familiar.

Lectura   *«El eclipse» por Augusto Monterroso (1921–2003)*

Ahora... ¡usted!

1. ¿Le gusta leer cuentos? ¿Tiene algunos preferidos? ¿Cuáles? ¿Cómo se titulan? ¿De qué temas tratan?
2. Escoja uno de sus cuentos favoritos y describa cinco aspectos de esa obra: 1) el personaje principal o protagonista, 2) el tema, 3) el motivo recurrente, 4) la acción: ¿qué ocurre en el cuento? 5) el final: ¿es sorprendente? ¿feliz? ¿abierto?

Lectura   *«El monopolio de la moda» por Luis Britto García (Venezuela, 1940)*

Ahora... ¡usted!

There are several popular magazines that feature a great deal of fashion and "fashion statements" in the Hispanic communities: *Latina, People en español, Cristina, TV Novela, Vanidades.* Bring copies of one or more of these magazines to class and have students scan for fashion. Help them describe the clothing items in articles and ads, and the ages portrayed. Then have them work on the following questions:

1. ¿Qué imágenes proyectan estas ropas? ¿Hay un estilo que predomina? ¿Cómo es?
2. ¿Hay aspectos en común entre la moda de las mujeres y la de los hombres?
3. ¿Qué ropa les gusta llevar a los jóvenes norteamericanos hoy en día? ¿Es muy diferente de la ropa que llevan los hispanos de estas revistas? ¿Qué diferencias nota usted? ¿Qué cosas tienen en común todos los jóvenes con respecto a su estilo de vestir?

Optional Grammar

15.4 You may wish to point out that some native speakers vary their use of the subjunctive after verb phrases like **¿(No) Cree usted que... ?** to express greater or lesser doubt. We do not practice this point because it will be acquired by advanced students in appropriate contexts.

INSTRUCTOR'S NOTES FOR THE *LECTURAS* AND THE *NOTAS CULTURALES* IN THE *CUADERNO DE ACTIVIDADES*

Capítulo 1

Nota cultural

¡Hola!... ¡Hasta mañana!

Have students do the reading in class. Then enter the classroom and greet your students in a formal manner, shaking hands and saying, **Buenos días, Buenas tardes, ¿Qué tal?**, and so on. Tell them: **Éstos son los saludos.** Then leave the room, saying **Adiós, Nos vemos, Gusto de verlos, Hasta mañana.** Then tell students: **Ésa es la despedida.** Follow up with **Comprensión** and personalized questions: **¿Cómo saluda usted a sus amigos? ¿Y a las personas que no conoce (*know*) muy bien? ¿Piensa usted que hay diferencias entre la manera de saludar y despedirse de los hispanos y la de los norteamericanos? ¿Cuáles son estas diferencias?**

Assign **Un paso más... ¡a escribir!** (UPM) as homework.

Lectura

Los amigos hispanos: Raúl, el superactivo

Have students scan the reading for the general topic of Raúl's favorite activities. Read the passage aloud very slowly, pausing frequently. Use exaggerated intonation and gesture wherever possible to make the meaning clear. Read key words slowly, but quickly pass over function words and phrases not essential to the main ideas. Convey to students that (1) they should not translate and (2) they need not understand every word. Pause and add comments or ask questions that will aid comprehension. For example, after the first sentence you might add: **La Ciudad de México es la capital de México, ¿verdad? Raúl estudia ingeniería. ¿Es difícil la ingeniería?** When you read the second paragraph, ask for the names of the students in Professor Martínez's class.

After you have gone through the passage, have students reread it silently, concentrating on comprehension without translating. Then retell the narration in your own words, stressing the main points. Pause frequently to see if students can finish the sentence you have started. Finally ask the true/false questions and allow volunteers to answer. Stress throughout that reading is not translation. As follow-up, assign UPM as pair work and homework.

Capítulo 2

Nota cultural

Nombres y apellidos

Related topics could be popular names in the United States, and popular names in students' families. Tell students: **En las culturas hispanas, la persona generalmente usa el apellido de la madre también.** Then ask them to give their mother's maiden name, **al estilo hispano: ¿Cuál es el apellido de soltera de su madre?** Ask them how they feel about being named after a relative. Try to find diminutives for the names of some students. Suggested personalized questions: **1. ¿Tienen ustedes dos nombres? ¿Usan los dos? ¿Por qué sí o por qué no? ¿Tienen un sobrenombre o un nombre cariñoso que sólo sus amigos o sus parientes saben? ¿Les gusta ese sobrenombre? 2. ¿Cuáles son sus dos apellidos (paterno y materno)?**

¿Les gustaría usar los dos? ¿Por qué sí o por qué no? Make the corrections in **Comprensión** with the whole class. Then assign UPM as homework.

Lectura

Aquí está Nora Morales

Practice the technique of scanning. Have students focus on scanning for cognates and predicting the gist of the reading. As a variation, have them scan the reading keeping in mind only certain items of information. This limits their focus. For example, ask them to scan in search of the answers to the following two questions: **¿Quién es Nora Morales? ¿Quién es Raúl Saucedo?** When students know what they are looking for in a reading selection, the process of scanning becomes natural. It encourages them not to read word by word.

Preview by reviewing the topic of classes. Ask, **¿Tienen ustedes clases que les gustan mucho? ¿Cuáles son sus favoritas? ¿Les gusta su clase de español? ¿Cuáles son sus actividades favoritas en esta clase?** Then use the "incomplete sentence" technique to check comprehension: **Nora es estudiante en la universidad, ¿no? Sí, en la Universidad de... (Texas, en San Antonio). Nora tiene varias clases, ¿verdad? Sí, pero hay una que le fascina, es la clase de... (la historia de México).** Have students work on **Comprensión** and then correct the answers with the class. Assign UPM as homework.

Capítulo 3

Nota cultural

La variedad musical

Play traditional and contemporary Hispanic music for your students. Many Latin American dances, such as mambo, samba, and salsa, have been popular at one time or another in the United States. Ask students, **Hay varios grupos y cantantes hispanos famosos en los Estados Unidos. ¿Pueden mencionar algunos? ¿Escuchan la música de estos artistas? Descríbanla.** With students' help, make a list on the board of Hispanic celebrities from the world of popular music. Suggestions: Shakira, Christina Aguilera, Gloria Estefan, Carlos Santana, Enrique Iglesias, Ricky Martin, Luis Miguel, Juan Luis Guerra, Rubén Blades. Do a cloze activity with the words to one of these artists' songs: Give students lyrics in which you have replaced every ninth or tenth word with a blank. As students listen to the song, they fill in missing words from the alphabetized list at the top of the page.

Assign **Comprensión** to be done in class, then go over the answers with your students. Have students do UPM individually and then compare their preferences with a partner. At this point they could also interview each other in preparation for the assignment.

Lectura

Los amigos hispanos: Adela Martínez, profe de español

Remind students that as they read they should try to develop the habit of understanding Spanish without translating into English. One way to develop comprehension in Spanish is to try to visualize the meanings of words and phrases. Tell students that when they read a phrase like **conversar con los amigos en algún café,** they should picture a group of friends sitting in a cafe, chatting. Or, when they read **Cuando estoy triste,** they could picture a sad face, maybe with a teardrop on the cheek. You may want to list some phrases from the reading on the board (such as **escucho música; cursos de verano; tengo estudiantes árabes, chinos, japoneses**) and ask students what they visualize as they read the phrase.

Teach students a traditional song in Spanish, such as «**Cielito lindo.**» You could present the song as a cloze activity. Since Adela Martínez teaches **cursos de verano** in Guanajuato, discuss summer language schools: **Hay universidades en países hispanos que ofrecen cursos de verano para las personas que estudian español. En estos programas los estudiantes van a clase por la mañana y por la tarde hacen excursiones y visitan a sus amigos hispanos.**

Have students do **Comprensión** and follow up with personalized questions: **¿Les gustaría viajar a otro país para estudiar? ¿Adónde les gustaría ir? ¿Por qué? Comparen las actividades de Adela Martínez con las actividades de verano que a ustedes les gustan.**

Capítulo 4

Lectura: Poesía

«Cinco de mayo» por Francisco X. Alarcón

Selección de su libro *Jitomates risueños* (1997)

While it is true that Mexican forces succeeded in turning back the French invasion of Puebla in 1862, Mexico was ultimately unable to prevent France from taking power and installing a French emperor in Mexico. The **Cinco de mayo** victory is nevertheless seen as a significant declaration of Mexican sovereignty and rejection of European intervention. Mexican Independence Day is officially September 16, and it commemorates Mexico's liberation from Spanish rule. But **Cinco de mayo** has become a holiday of equal or greater importance in many Mexican-American communities in the United States. Particularly in areas of the U.S. with a substantial Mexican and/or Chicano population, **Cinco de mayo** is celebrated on a grand scale, with neighborhood festivals, traditional foods, music, parades, beauty pageants, and so on.

If students know of local or family **Cinco de mayo** traditions, encourage them to share these with the class. In many places, this festivity has become a somewhat generic "Mexican" fiesta; you could compare it to St. Patrick's Day. Assign **Comprensión** and follow up with personalized questions: **¿Hay un día feriado que ustedes celebran con baile, música y comida? ¿Cuál es? ¿Con quiénes lo celebran normalmente? Mencionen un día feriado de su país como el cinco de mayo. ¿Conocen ustedes el origen de esta celebración? ¿Tiene un significado histórico especial? ¿Cuál es?**

Assign UPM as homework. During the next class period, have volunteers describe their invented holidays to the class. And invent one yourself!

Lectura

Los amigos hispanos: Las distracciones de Pilar

Madrid has been Spain's capital since 1561. This cosmopolitan city is situated on a plateau about 2,150 feet above sea level, making it the highest capital in Europe. The **Parque del Retiro** is the largest park in Madrid, known for its beautiful trees, vast area, and the lake where visitors may canoe. It is most crowded on Sundays with people who enjoy strolling, picnicking, and gathering with the family. Madrid is also well known for its outdoor flea market, the **Rastro.**

Preview with photos and/or slides of the **Retiro,** the **Prado,** and other places of interest in Madrid, such as the **Plaza Mayor.** (See photos in *Dos mundos.*) Ask personalized questions: **¿Es difícil para ustedes estudiar a veces? ¿Por qué? ¿Qué distracciones interrumpen sus estudios? ¿Les gusta el cine? ¿Cuáles son sus películas favoritas? ¿Y a quién le gusta el arte? ¿Va usted a los museos? ¿Cuáles son sus obras o artistas favoritos?**

Follow up with a comprehension check: **¿Qué lugares menciona Pilar? ¿Les gustan a ustedes estos lugares? ¿Por qué? ¿Cuáles son los pasatiempos de Pilar?** Have students describe Pilar's life, asking: **¿Cómo es su vida? ¿Es divertida, aburrida, normal? Pilar dice que su vida es típica. ¿Están de acuerdo?**

(Pilar's life is like that of many young Spanish women today. So, in that sense it is "typical.") Then have students work in pairs to discuss their daily lives, as they compare to Pilar's. Assign **Comprensión** and UPM as homework.

Capítulo 5

Nota cultural

La educación en el mundo hispano

Show pictures or slides to illustrate the countries described. Use the map in the front pages of *Dos mundos* to locate these countries. Encourage students to practice using visual context (art and photographs). Go over the **Vocabulario útil** and follow up with personalized questions: **¿Conoce alguno de los países que se describen en esta Nota cultural? ¿Cuál? ¿Qué impresión tiene de ese país? ¿Le gusta? Si no conoce ninguno, ¿cuál le gustaría visitar y por qué? ¿Le gustaría estudiar en un país hispano? ¿Por qué?** If you are familiar with any study abroad programs in Hispanic universities, share this information with the class. Then prepare students for the written activity. Ask, **¿Qué vemos en la foto? Sí, son estudiantes de secundaria. ¿Piensan ustedes que a ellos les gusta su clase? ¿Por qué? ¿Cómo lo sabemos?**

Lectura

La diversidad económica

Show pictures, slides, souvenirs or travel brochures to illustrate the countries described. Use the map in the front pages of *Dos mundos* to locate these countries. Then relate your travel experiences in the Hispanic world. (Try to keep the use of past tense to a minimum.) Sample input: **Conozco Venezuela. Visité este país en el año 2000. Me gusta mucho Caracas, la capital, porque la gente allí es muy amistosa y hay buenos restaurantes,** and so forth.

Some facts that could be of interest to your students:

- Paraguay produces the beautiful **encaje de ñandutí,** a fine and intricate lace.
- There is an open-air market in Ecuador that attracts many tourists yearly. It is the **mercado de lana de Otavalo,** where the **Otavalo** indigenous group sells its famous wool embroideries.
- Equatorial Guinea received its official name in 1963, and became independent from Spain in 1968. Thus, it is the youngest country in the Hispanic world.

Review **Comprensión** in class, then engage students in a whole-class discussion. Ask, **¿Saben ustedes cuáles son los productos más importantes para la economía de los Estados Unidos? ¿Cuáles son los trabajos que más afectan la economía estadounidense? ¿Trabaja usted? ¿Contribuye su trabajo a la economía de los Estados Unidos? ¿En qué manera?**

Assign UPM as homework. (Students will need to do some research.) You may want to collect and correct the compositions, then select a few to be presented in class as an oral report. Students could also work in groups and compare notes on their respective countries.

Capítulo 6

Lectura

Habla la gata Manchitas

Ask students whether they have pets: **¿Tienen ustedes animales domésticos (mascotas)?** Explore their attitudes, asking why they prefer a cat or a dog, basic differences between the two animals, and so on. Ask: **¿Cómo es su mascota? ¿Hace cosas cómicas a veces? ¿Creen ustedes que los animales tienen** «personalidad»? ¿Cómo es la personalidad de su mascota? ¿Piensan ustedes que los animales reflejan las características de sus amos? ¿Cómo?

Have students do the **Comprensión** in pairs. Then ask personalized questions: **¿Cómo tratan ustedes a sus animales? ¿Les ponen mucha atención? Si no tienen un animal doméstico, ¿por qué no? ¿Les gustaría tener uno? ¿Por qué tienen mascotas las personas? ¿Por qué son tan importantes los animales domésticos en la cultura norteamericana?** For a comical note, have students speak for their pets as suggested in the UPM activity.

Lectura

Los amigos hispanos: ¡Nadie es perfecto!

Peru ranks as the third largest country in South America, with a population of 24 million. Its official name is **República del Perú,** and there are three official languages spoken in the country: Spanish, Quechua and Aimara. Since World War I, a large number of Japanese people have settled in Peru and one of its recent presidents, Alberto Fujimori, was of Japanese origin.

The narrator of this **Lectura** comments, in passing, on gender roles with regard to household activities. Peruvian society is male-dominated, and patriarchal values are reflected in the boy's attitude. We can infer from his comments that his mother is trying to provide a home environment for her children free of machismo. (In **Capítulo 14,** we feature the story **"Los próximos recuerdos,"** narrated by Armando's mother, Susana Yamasaki. She provides further insight into her nontraditional view of society and child rearing.)

Survey your class to find out if students have children, younger brothers and sisters, or friends or relatives with children. Then ask: **¿Qué obligaciones tienen los hermanos menores en su casa? (cortar el césped, lavar el carro, ir de compras con los padres, etcétera). ¿Cuáles son las obligaciones de los otros miembros de la familia?** As a follow-up, have students do the **Comprensión** in pairs. Then ask personalized questions: **¿Piensa usted que Armando es un niño como todos? ¿Piensa usted que los niños deben ayudar en la casa o piensa que trabajan demasiado?** Assign UPM as homework and review part B in class.

Capítulo 7

Lectura: Novela

«Ana Luisa» por José Emilio Pacheco

Selección de su novela *El principio del placer* (1994)

José Emilio Pacheco (1939) is one of Mexico's best-known writers. Famous for his novels and poetry, as well as his journalistic articles, Pacheco writes about Mexican society and culture. He has received several awards, among them the **Premio Octavio Paz** in 2003. Pacheco is the author of numerous collections of poetry, stories, and three novels: *Las batallas en el desierto* (1971), *Morirás lejos* (1978), and *El principio del placer* (1994).

Before assigning this excerpt from *El principio del placer,* have students go over the **Pistas** box and then review the **Vocabulario útil.** You may want to add that Jorge's family has recently moved (**se mudaron**) from Mexico City to Veracruz. As a follow-up, do **Comprensión** with the class to retell the story. Take this opportunity to clarify questions or any passage that may seem unclear to students. Assign UPM as homework. The next class period, have students read their stories to each other in groups. Then ask for volunteers to read their stories to the class.

Lectura: Canción

«Castillos en el aire» por Alberto Cortez

Alberto Cortez (1940) is one of the most esteemed and gifted singer songwriters in the Spanish-speaking world. Composer of classics such as **"En un rincón del alma"** and **"Cuando un amigo se va,"** Cortez left his country, Argentina, in 1961 and made Spain his home. There he launched hundreds of hit songs, such as **"Nanas de la cebolla"** (based on a poem by Spanish poet Miguel Hernández), **"Alfonsina y el mar"** (which tells the story of Argentine poet Alfonsina Storni), and **"Mi árbol y yo."** Cortez has also written four books of songs and memoirs, *Equipaje, Soy un ser humano, Almacén de almas,* and *Desde un rincón del alma.*

Preview **"Castillos en el aire"** with questions about music: **¿Qué tipo de música les gusta? ¿La música popular, rock, clásica, country? ¿Escuchan música en español? ¿Qué cantantes les gustan? ¿Conocen la música de Alberto Cortez?** Have students read the **Pistas** box as an introduction to Cortez. Tell them that many of his songs are **hermosos poemas que cuentan historias humanas.** If time permits, play **"Castillos en el aire"** for your students as they read the lyrics. (You will find all of Cortez's music by visiting his website.) Then read the song to the students, giving them a sense of rhyme and rhythm. Assign **Comprensión** and UPM as homework, then ask volunteers to perform their songs in class. If you assign **"Castillos en el aire"** to be done at home, encourage students to read it aloud first.

Capítulo 8

Lectura

¡Buen provecho!

Ask students to name their favorite foreign foods: **¿Tienen ustedes un plato favorito de otro país? ¿De dónde? ¿Qué ingredientes tiene?** Then ask: **¿Qué platos hispanos han probado?** List their answers on the board, then have students skim the **Lectura** for names and descriptions of dishes. Are there any dishes described in the reading that your students mentioned? If so, point them out. Now have students read for more in-depth information about Hispanic cuisine.

Assign **Comprensión** to be done in pairs. Ask personalized questions: **En algunas ciudades de los Estados Unidos son populares los restaurantes llamados «tapas bar». ¿Conocen alguno de estos lugares? ¿Les gustan las tapas? ¿Cuáles? Cuando ustedes dan una fiesta en su casa, ¿sirven entremeses? ¿Cuáles les gusta servir?**

Assign UPM for homework and tell students that you will choose the best menus and most persuasive letters. You may want to have a party in class at some point and ask volunteers to bring a dish. Or, you could make a class recipe book first and then have the party. Additional UPM activity: Have students write a half-page composition on the following topic: **Si hay un restaurante hispano en su ciudad, vaya a comer allí y pruebe algo nuevo. Luego describa lo que probó. ¿Le gustó ese plato? ¿Qué ingredientes tiene? ¿Lo recomienda? ¿Por qué?**

Nota cultural

Una receta: Los ricos polvorones

Read the recipe with the class, acting out the directions as you go through it (possibly using props). You may also want to do this reading as a TPR activity. If you enjoy baking, prepare the **polvorones** for the class; or perhaps you can find a volunteer among your students to make them. Then have the students read the **receta,** and ask them personalized questions: **¿Les gustaría probar estos polvorones? ¿Por qué? ¿Han probado algún postre similar? ¿Cuál?**

Expand on the **Pistas** questions: **¿Hay algún postre hispano que a ustedes les gusta mucho? ¿Creen que es difícil de cocinar? ¿Cuándo y dónde lo probaron por primera vez? ¿Comen este plato con frecuencia? ¿Cuál es su postre favorito? ¿Por qué les gusta tanto?** Assign UPM as written homework.

Capítulo 9

Lectura

Rubén Blades y su familia musical

Preview with personalized questions: **¿Qué tipo de música le gusta a usted? ¿Quiénes son sus cantantes favoritos?** Play some of Rubén Blades' music for the class. We suggest a song from his breakout album, ***Buscando América.*** Read the first paragraph to your students and have them note the adjective **versátil.** Ask them: **¿Con qué otras palabras podemos describir a Rubén Blades? (talentoso, inteligente, dedicado, estudioso).** Then follow the **Pistas** suggestion. Encourage students to read the **Lectura** twice at least, noting the main idea in each paragraph. (First: **el talento, los estudios y el trabajo de Blades.** Second: **la familia musical de Blades.** Third: **la contribución musical de Blades.** Fourth: **el objetivo artístico de Blades.**)

As an extra assignment, have students watch movies featuring Rubén Blades, such as *The Milagro Bean Field War* (1988) and *Cradle Will Rock* (1999). (Note that he plays convincingly the part of Mexican artist and muralist Diego Rivera in *Cradle Will Rock*). Students will then write a report about the film in Spanish: **Describa al personaje que Rubén Blades representa en la película. ¿Cómo se llama? ¿Dónde vive? ¿Cuál es su profesión? ¿Es un personaje atractivo o negativo? ¿Tiene familia? ¿Cómo contribuye este personaje a la historia que se cuenta?** Show scenes from one of these movies in class and discuss them.

Assign **Comprensión** and UPM as homework. Once you collect their compositions, read to the class some of the more imaginative responses. As a variation, do UPM as a class project. Have students role-play the interview in pairs, with one student playing the journalist and the other student playing Blades. Then ask for volunteers to present the interview to the class.

Nota cultural

Retratos de familia

Preview reading with personal questions about the family: **¿Cómo es su familia? ¿Cómo son sus relaciones con los otros miembros de su familia? ¿Cuántas personas hay generalmente en una familia norte-americana?** Tell students that, after they read these **retratos,** the discussion will focus on how the typical Hispanic family is different from and similar to the non-Hispanic North American family. (You will need to do some generalizing.)

Assign the reading as homework. Then go over the questions in the **Pistas** box during the next class period. Discuss similarities and differences between students' family experiences and those of the Hispanics in the reading. You may want to have students choose one of the people featured and have them tell how their family is similar to or different from that person's family. This idea may also be used as a writing activity, in addition to UPM.

Go over **Comprensión** with your students. Then have them do the first part of UPM (classmates' opinion about family) in class, and assign the composition as homework.

Capítulo 10

Lectura

«La creación del mundo»

Selección del *Popol Vuh,* libro sagrado de los mayas

The ***Popol Vuh*** is based on the oral tradition. Its first written Spanish version, translated from Maya Quiché, is that of the Spanish missionary Francisco Ximénez. This version dates from the eighteenth century. Before assigning the **Lectura,** have students go over the **Vocabulario** and questions in **Comprensión.** And after students read the passage, summarize for them the rest of the ***Popol Vuh*** story, which describes the creation of the first human being. Note that the words in italics may be new: **Después de crear la tierra y los animales, los dioses crearon al ser humano. Primero lo crearon de lodo, pero el lodo era inestable, demasiado blando, y la criatura humana no podía sostenerse. Luego hicieron al ser humano de madera, pero esta figura de madera no tenía alma. Por fin decidieron crear al hombre de maíz, y esta vez sí triunfaron con su creación.** Now you may want to read to your class the concluding paragraph from the *Popol Vuh:* **«Y así encontraron (los dioses) la comida y ésta fue la que entró en la carne del hombre creado, del hombre formado... Así entró el maíz (en la creación del hombre) por obra de los *Progenitores*».**

Prepare students for the written assignment. Point out that numerous cultures of the world have attempted to explain the beginning of life on Earth by inventing a story of creation. Ask, **¿Conocen ustedes los primeros capítulos de Génesis en la Biblia? ¿Conocen otras historias de creación? Vamos a comparar este pasaje de la biblia maya con otras versiones del comienzo del mundo. Comentemos las semejanzas y las diferencias.** Without engaging students in a debate on religion, compare and contrast the *Popol Vuh* story of creation with that of Genesis in the Bible or with other versions. Then encourage students them to narrate their own story of creation, adding interesting, imaginative details.

Lectura

El huracán tropical

Caribbean and Central American countries affected by natural disasters must confront many challenges with fewer resources than more highly developed countries. Hurricanes destroy a major sector of the region's economy, which is agriculture, as well as road networks and supply systems. Economic growth that takes years to develop is wiped out in a matter of hours. The impact of such a catastrophe greatly affects the living standards of the nations involved.

Go over the **Vocabulario útil** with your students and then ask: **¿Qué tema piensan ustedes que va a tratar esta Lectura?** Possible responses: **los efectos de un huracán (daño, derrumbe); la situación de las víctimas (enterradas, esperanza, damnificados, sobrevivir).** Ask, **¿Han sufrido ustedes un huracán? ¿Qué pasó? ¿Qué hicieron?** Continue with the questions in **Pistas.** Discuss natural calamities (**fenómenos naturales**) and then focus on the elements that affect your area. Possibilities: **terremotos, huracanes, tornados, lluvias torrenciales (aguaceros), sequías, nevadas.**

Assign the **Lectura** as homework and review the answers for **Comprensión.** Give students some vocabulary for the UPM assignment. Ask: **¿Qué tipos de ayuda podemos ofrecerle a un campesino que lo perdió todo?** Some possibilities: **ropa, comida, alojamiento (albergue), construcción de una casa, cultivo de la tierra, trabajo en la cosecha, ayuda financiera,** and so on.

Capítulo 11

Lectura

El misterio de las ciudades mayas

Help students expand their base knowledge of cognates. Explain that the more we recognize cognates, the more they work for us. Go over the common endings included in the **Pistas** box. Stress that, once you have a feel for the endings, these can be used with familiar Spanish words to expand vocabulary even further. Have students look for these endings in the reading.

Show pictures and/or slides of Mayan ruins. Briefly describe this pre-Columbian culture. Point out Tikal on the map. Some basic background: Mayan society was organized in a pyramid shape. The ruling class at the top was constituted by the king, his family, and a small group of nobles. The middle class was at the center, with a medium-size population. Below this class were the commoners, who comprised a large group. The lowest and largest group consisted of slaves, criminals, and war captives who were sacrificed at religious ceremonies. The Mayas had many gods, such as the Creator, the Moon Goddess, the God of Rain and Lightning, and the Maize God. They used a complex system of writing called hieroglyphs. The work of deciphering Mayan writing continues today, and major breakthroughs have been made.

Some interesting facts about Tikal: One of its temples, Templo IV, is the tallest pyramid in the Western Hemisphere, at a height of 229 feet. Tikal was one of the most recent pre-Columbian Mayan sites to be discovered. It has been designated a World Heritage Site by UNESCO and is one of two sites in the western hemisphere considered both a Natural and Cultural Heritage Site. The other one is Machu Picchu in Peru.

As a follow-up, ask personalized questions. **¿Conoce usted las ruinas mayas? ¿Ha visitado las ruinas aztecas en México? ¿las ruinas incas en Perú? ¿Cuál fue su impresión?** For students who haven't seen any ruins, ask: **Imagínense que tienen la oportunidad de visitar unas ruinas en cualquier parte del mundo. ¿Cuáles van a visitar? ¿Por qué? ¿Cómo piensan que va a ser su experiencia? Additional questions: ¿Conocen ruinas en los Estados Unidos o en otros países? ¿Dónde están? ¿Cuál fue su reacción al verlas? ¿Les gustaron? ¿Tienen estas ruinas una historia interesante o misteriosa? Cuente algunos detalles de su historia. Si no conoce muchos detalles, aprenda algunos y compártalos con la clase.**

Assign **Comprensión** as homework and go over it the next day. The UPM activity could be done in groups, with one student from each group presenting their theory and discoveries.

Lectura

De visita en México

Tourism is one of Mexico's greatest industries. The cities and places mentioned in the **Lectura** are popular among foreign visitors and Mexicans alike. Show pictures, postcards and souvenirs, and share any personal experiences from your own travels in Mexico.

This is a good reading for students to practice visualizing what they read in conjunction with making intelligent guesses regarding certain vocabulary words. Have them look at the map and ask them to visualize these places as they are described by Paula. For example, when they read about Chapultepec Park in Mexico City, have them picture pens of animals in two different areas of a park. Other personalized questions you could ask: **¿Les gustan estos lugares? ¿Cuál les gusta más? ¿Por qué?**

Remind students that the excitement behind meeting a pen pal is the background of this letter. Ask them if they have ever had a pen pal (**amigos de correspondencia**): **¿Han tenido amigos de correspondencia en otro país o en otra ciudad de su país? ¿Sobre qué temas se escribieron? ¿Visitaron a estos amigos finalmente? ¿Cómo fue su encuentro?**

Have students do **Comprensión** in pairs. Assign UPM as homework. In class the next day allow students to read each other's letters.

Capítulo 12

Lectura

La prevención del SIDA

Encourage students to simplify sentences when they read. Have them focus on the subject and the verb, which are the most important part of a sentence. The verb stem tells us what action is taking place, and the verb ending helps us determine who or what the subject is. Once we know who is doing what, we can see how the other parts of the sentence relate to the main idea. When the verb is a form of **ser** or **estar,** we should determine who or what is being defined or described. In the following sentences from the reading, have students identify the subject of the verb in italics:

- **Hay más de 34 millones de personas en el mundo que están infectadas con VIH.**

- **Los niños pueden contraer el virus al nacer, si la sangre materna está contaminada.**

- **Hoy tenemos avances médicos.**

Introduce the topic of AIDS by asking, **¿Saben ustedes lo que es el SIDA?** Write on the board: **SIDA = síndrome de inmunodeficiencia adquirida.** Tell students: **Es importante estar informado sobre todas las enfermedades letales. Hay que saber cómo prevenirlas, ¿no? ¿Saben ustedes cómo se transmite este virus? ¿Qué podemos hacer para protegernos?**

Assign **Comprensión** as homework and go over answers in class. Then engage students in a discussion based on the personalized questions in the **Pistas** box. You may want to add: **¿Está usted de acuerdo con la opinión de estas personas?**

Lectura: Cuento

«La prueba» por Nancy Alonso

Selección del libro *Cerrado por reparación* (2002)

Go over the **Vocabulario útil,** then have students read Part A of the **Comprensión** activity. By becoming familiar with unknown or difficult words first, the story will be more accessible to them. And the statements in **Comprensión** will give them helpful background for the story.

Preview with these questions: **¿Qué saben ustedes de Cuba? ¿Qué tipo de gobierno tiene este país del Caribe?** In your discussion, underline that Cuba has had a Communist regime for four decades, headed by Fidel Castro. There has been increasing economic hardship on the island since the Revolution of 1959. The story **"La prueba"** depicts a situation that is infused with irony, and it could represent that of many Cubans: the struggles of a woman who is willing to sacrifice her health in order to have a better diet.

Before assigning **"La prueba"** to be read at home, provide some background on the author and her work: **El cuento «La prueba» aparece en el libro *Cerrado por reparación,* que en el año 2002 ganó un premio importante (Narrativa Femenina «Alba de Céspedes»). Los cuentos de Nancy Alonso muestran la vida habitual y diaria en la Habana de hoy: las necesidades y problemas de los cubanos. Sus relatos se enfocan en la naturaleza humana y nos permiten ver el mundo interior de los personajes. Varios de los cuentos de este libro presentan situaciones cotidianas que se vuelven absurdas o humorísticas. En «La excursión», por ejemplo, un hombre trata de encontrar teléfonos públicos que funcionen. Toda la acción de «Motín a bordo» tiene lugar en un autobús —«guagua» en Cuba. Y en «Historia de un bache», una mujer convierte un bache (*pothole*) del camino en un hermoso jardín. Los cuentos de Nancy Alonso son simples pero de una visión profunda.**

Prepare students for the UPM activity by going over the first three questions in class. Before you collect the composition, have students work in groups to discuss questions 4 and 5. Then generate a whole-class discussion based on students' opinion and experience of the story

Capítulo 13

Nota cultural

De compras en el Rastro

Madrid's famous flea market is called **el Rastro.** In other Spanish cities and in other countries the outdoor market might be known by a variety of other terms, such as **el mercado** or **el mercadillo.** This is a good reading to have students practice visualization. Remind them not to translate as they read, but to picture objects, places and scenes described in the text.

Before assigning the **Nota cultural** as homework, ask personalized questions: **¿Han ido ustedes de compras en otro país? ¿Qué compraron? ¿Dónde? ¿Pudieron regatear?** Additional questions: **¿Les gusta ir de compras solos/as o acompañados/as? ¿Por qué? ¿Prefieren ir de compras cuando hay una venta especial o cuando hay menos gente?**

Follow up by talking about **el regateo: En las tiendas de los Estados Unidos, ¿son fijos los precios generalmente o se puede regatear? ¿Donde se regatea en los Estados Unidos? ¿Hay diferencias entre el regateo en este país y el regateo en el extranjero? ¿Les gusta a ustedes regatear? ¿Qué les gusta comprar cuando regatean?**

Assign **Comprensión** and UPM as homework. Then ask volunteers to role-play the reading's dialogue in class. You could vary the situation: Play one of the roles yourself and be a very good or poor bargainer. Bring in objects for students to buy and sell.

Lectura: Cuento

«Un Stradivarius», por Vicente Riva Palacio

Assign the story and then ask students to retell it, following the themes in **Comprensión A.** Then discuss **Comprensión B** with the whole class. Although these questions are personalized, you may want to elicit the following responses (or variations of these): **1. La avaricia de don Samuel lo hace caer en la trampa del músico pobre. Entonces, la moraleja es que no debemos ser avaros. 2. Lo que hizo el músico fue engañar al dueño de la tienda. Aunque el dueño probablemente aprendió una lección valiosa, no podemos justificar la acción del músico, pues se trata de un engaño y un robo. 3. Es posible que don Samuel nunca más se deje afectar por la ambición del dinero. 4. No piense siempre en ganar dinero; No sea tan ambicioso; No se aproveche de** (*take advantage of*) **la gente.**

You may also choose to assign Part I first, then ask students to speculate about the outcome of the story. Here are some questions you can ask to trigger a discussion: **¿Es el violín un objeto muy valioso? ¿es mágico? ¿Piensan ustedes que el dueño de la tienda va a aprender a tocarlo? ¿Qué va a hacer este hombre con el violín? En las Pistas se dice que el músico tiene un plan secreto. ¿Qué quiere conseguir él?** After you assign the entire story, students' responses could be revisited to see how well they predicted the outcome.

Assign UPM as homework. During the following class, have students share their dialogues with a partner. Ask for pairs of volunteers to enact their dialogues for the class.

Capítulo 14

Lectura

Escuche a sus hijos

This piece consists of a series of comments by U.S. Hispanic teenagers about the relationship between parents and adolescents. Topics include single mothers (**madres solteras**), male substitues for fathers (**adultos modelos**), bad grades (**malas notas**), as well as cultural differences between Hispanic countries and the United States regarding gender roles: **la crianza de las niñas en un país hispano comparada con la de las niñas en los Estados Unidos.**

First, help students identify the speakers in this short article. Have them look at the **Comprensión** activity, where all names appear, then look for those names and speakers' age in each paragraph. Once the speakers have been identified, work with students on pinpointing the problem or situation that each youngster brings up. You may want to write these on the board (note that **Rubén** appears twice): **Fernando: problema en la escuela. Rubén: una madre soltera. Angélica: padres de otro país. Rubén: hablar de cosas serias. Julieta: la disciplina y los buenos valores. Eduardo: las críticas de los adolescentes.**

Now preview the reading with personalized questions: **¿Quién en la clase tiene hijos? Los que no tienen hijos, ¿piensan tenerlos? ¿Por qué? Según su experiencia, ¿es fácil o difícil para los adolescentes mantener buenas relaciones con sus padres? ¿Cómo eran las relaciones entre usted y sus padres cuando era más joven? ¿Son mejores estas relaciones ahora? ¿Por qué? ¿A qué atribuye usted el éxito o el fracaso de esas relaciones? ¿Por qué es tan importante el concepto de la familia en una sociedad?**

As follow-up, review the article by going over statements in **Comprensión** with the class. As a variation of UPM, have students write a dialogue between a child or youth and a parent in which there is a dilemma regarding particular rules of the house. In class, set up a forum of discussion: Students present the dilemma and expert psychologists (volunteers and yourself) give advice on the best way to resolve the problems.

Lectura: Cuento

«Ya llega el día», por los autores de *Dos mundos*

Peru ranks as the third largest country in South America. Since World War I , a large number of Japanese people have settled in Peru, and today five percent of Peru's 25 million inhabitants are of Japanese origin. The protagonist of this story is a Japanese Peruvian woman who comments on living within two cultures and laments the traditional expectations for women in what she considers a "macho" society. The development of women's rights has been a slow process in Peru. Peruvian women did not even receive the right to vote until 1956.

Encourage students to visualize Susana's memories as they read. And have them review the **Lectura** "Los deliciosos platillos andinos" in **Capítulo 8** of *Dos mundos,* where there are descriptions of the Peruvian dishes mentioned by Susana. Preview reading by asking questions about family relations and divorce: **¿Hay muchos divorcios en nuestra sociedad? ¿Por qué se divorcia la gente? ¿Es posible resolver los problemas antes de buscar el divorcio? ¿Cuál es el efecto que tiene el divorcio en los niños? ¿Qué problemas podría tener una persona que esté criando a sus hijos sola? ¿Hay aspectos positivos en esta situación?**

Have students in pairs jot down answers to **Comprensión,** then go over answers with the class. Ask, **En su opinión, ¿cambia Susana al final? ¿Qué significa su pensamiento: "Ustedes no serán como su padre"?** Assign UPM for homework. For the second theme, remind students of the two previous readings featuring Armando, in **Capítulo 6** of the **Cuaderno de actividades** and **Capítulo 7** of *Dos mundos.*

Capítulo 15

Lectura: Cuento

«Colores que vuelan», por los autores de *Dos mundos*

Have students go over the **Pistas** box. Then engage the class in a conversation about Mexican-American culture. Talk about the Mexican presence in the United States. A key date to mention is 1848, when the Treaty of Guadalupe Hidalgo was signed following Mexico's surrender to the United States. Under the terms of this treaty, the United States acquired what are now the states of California, Nevada, Utah, Arizona, Colorado, New Mexico, and Texas (nearly 1,000,000 square miles of land for $18 million). As a result of this agreement, the United States border in effect "moved" and tens of thousands of Mexican citizens immediately became U.S. citizens. Mention Chicano writers, actors, political leaders, and musicians or singers. Discuss the movies that depict Mexican-American characters and themes, such as *Stand and Deliver, La Bamba, El Mariachi, Mi Familia,* and *Selena.*

Give students some background for the story: **El protagonista de este cuento es un inmigrante mexicano que reside y trabaja en Kansas. Un día este hombre se pone a pensar en su vida y en su exilio. Descubre entonces que tiene muchas razones para estar feliz. En el cuento se describen algunas de esas razones.**

As follow-up, focus on the modern concept of fame. Ask personalized questions: **¿Les han hecho una entrevista alguna vez? ¿Han salido en el periódico? Describan la experiencia. ¿Conocen ustedes a alguna persona famosa? ¿Cómo la conocieron? ¿Por qué es famosa? ¿Les gustaría a ustedes ser famoso/as? ¿Qué opinan de la fama? ¿Por qué es tan importante la fama en nuestra sociedad? ¿Qué satisfacción o felicidad nos ofrece la fama?**

Help students identify the phrases in **Comprensión.** UPM could be done as a skit in class or as a composition. Encourage students to write longer dialogues than those in the story.

Lectura: Cuento

«Cassette», por Enrique Anderson Imbert

Selección de su libro *Dos mujeres y un Julián* (1982)

A prolific writer and esteemed literary critic, Enrique Anderson Imbert was best known for his books of literary criticism, such as *Historia de la literatura hispanoamericana* (1961), and *Teoría y técnica del cuento* (1979). He taught Latin American literature at the University of Michigan (1947–1965), and at Harvard University (1965–1980), where he was Professor Emeritus. Anderson Imbert published four novels and numerous books of short stories, among them *El gato de Cheshire* (1965) and *Dos mujeres y un Julián* (1982), which featured the fascinating piece "Cassette."

Preview the story with questions about the science fiction genre. Ask, **¿Les gusta a ustedes la literatura de ciencia ficción? ¿Leen libros o miran películas que presentan el futuro?** Ask students to mention sci-fi books, movies or television series they have enjoyed. Cite classics such as *2001: A Space Odyssey* by Arthur C. Clarke. As follow up, use the questions in **Comprensión A** to engage students in a discussion about the story.

You could include some of the following ideas in your discussion: **«Cassette» es un cuento muy interesante. En el mundo que presenta hay aspectos de nuestro mundo de hoy, ¿verdad?, pues la tecnología es accesible y predominante en nuestras vidas. ¡Pero en el futuro del cuento los libros no existen! ¿Creen ustedes que el libro desaparecerá o durará para siempre? ¿Por qué? El cuento tiene un mensaje valioso, ¿cuál es? ¿Y qué visión presenta del futuro? (El gobierno es opresivo, pues decide lo que los ciudadanos deben pensar y ver. Pero tiene una visión de esperanza porque el libro renace —es reinventado— a pesar de tanta tecnología.) La historia se proyecta hacia nuestro tiempo con un artefacto que es como el CD-ROM y el Internet. ¿Cómo se asemeja la «cassette» al Internet? Este cuento fue publicado en 1982, pero parece estar describiendo el mundo de hoy. ¿Creen ustedes que los buenos escritores pueden ver o imaginarse el futuro? ¿Cómo lo hacen?**

Assign **Comprensión B** to be done in small groups in class. Have students explore other aspects of the story, such as: **la imagen de la nube; el paralelo entre el niño protagonista y Blas Pascal, y entre Blas Pascal y Euclides; la descripción detallada del «invento» de Blas.**

USING *DOS MUNDOS* WITH VIDEO

The ***Destinos*** *Video Modules* are available for use with the Sixth Edition of ***Dos mundos.*** The modules contain footage from the popular ***Destinos*** television series, as well as original footage shot on location for the modules in Spain, Mexico, Argentina, and Puerto Rico. Modules are divided into four one-hour segments that focus on vocabulary, situational language, functional language, and culture. They are accompanied by an *Instructor's Manual* that offers suggestions for viewing, in-class activities, and complete scripts of the modules.

The segments of the ***Destinos*** *Video Modules* coordinate with the chapters of ***Dos mundos*** as listed below. Note that these charts offer only the most obvious correlations with the chapters of ***Dos mundos.*** Many segments of the ***Destinos*** *Video Modules* can be used with other chapters of ***Dos mundos*** as well. Instructors may also want to consider using the latter segments in each subsection as review/re-entry of language functions and situations in particular later on in the term, after that material has been introduced.

Segment in Video Modules	Chapter in *Dos mundos*
Module 1: Functional Language	
Greeting Others	A
Meeting Others	A
Saying Good-bye	A
Saying Thank You	A
Formal versus Informal You	B
Asking / Telling the Time	1
Agreeing / Refusing to Do Something	2
Asking for Directions	3, 11
Excusing Oneself / Apologizing	14
Using the Telephone	1
Showing Anger	4
Module 2: Situations	
Ordering a Meal	8
Checking into / out of a Hotel	11
Traveling / Vacations	11
Taking a Taxi	11
Auto Repairs	11
Changing Money	11
Shopping	13
Module 3: Vocabulary	
Los números	A, B, C, 1
Las materias	2, 5
Los colores	A
La ropa	A
El tiempo / Las estaciones	2
La comida	3, 8
La familia	C, 9, 14
Relaciones de la vida social	7, 14

Los deportes y los pasatiempos	1, 2, 3
Las partes del cuerpo	12
La salud	12
Las partes de una casa	6
En una ciudad / las tiendas	3, 13
El dinero	11, 13
Module 4: Culture	
All segments	1–15

Chapter in *Dos mundos*	Segment in Video Modules
A	Module 1: Greeting Others, Meeting Others, Saying Good-bye, Saying Thank You Module 3: **Los números, los colores, la ropa**
B	Module 1: Formal versus Informal *You* Module 3: **Los números**
C	Module 3: **Los números, la familia**
1	Module 1: Asking / Telling the Time, Using the Telephone Module 3: **Los números, los deportes y los pasatiempos** Module 4: Culture (any segment)
2	Module 1: Agreeing / Refusing to Do Something Module 3: **El tiempo / Las estaciones, los deportes y los pasatiempos** Module 4: Culture (any segment)
3	Module 1: Asking for Directions Module 3: **En una ciudad** Module 4: Culture (any segment)
4	Module 1: Showing Anger Module 3: **Los deportes y los pasatiempos** Module 4: Culture (any segment)
5	Module 3: **Las materias** Module 4: Culture (any segment)
6	Module 3: **Las partes de una casa** Module 4: Culture (any segment)
7	Module 3: **Relaciones de la vida social** Module 4: Culture (any segment)
8	Module 2: Ordering a Meal Module 3: **La comida** Module 4: Culture (any segment)
9	Module 3: **La familia** Module 4: Culture (any segment)
10	Module 4: Culture (any segment)

11	Module 1: Asking for Directions
	Module 2: Checking into / out of a Hotel, Traveling / Vacations, Taking a Taxi, Auto Repairs
	Module 3: **En una ciudad / las tiendas, El dinero**
	Module 4: Culture (any segment)
12	Module 3: **Las partes del cuerpo, La salud**
	Module 4: Culture (any segment)
13	Module 2: Shopping
	Module 3: **En una ciudad / las tiendas**
	Module 4: Culture (any segment)
14	Module 1: Excusing Oneself / Apologizing
	Module 3: **La familia; Relaciones de la vida social**
	Module 4: Culture (any segment)
15	Module 4: Culture (any segment)

Video Program to Accompany *Dos mundos*

Videoscripts

Pasos

Escenas culturales: Panamá

Panamá es el istmo que une a América Central con América del Sur. Este país tiene fama internacional por su canal. El canal de Panamá es un canal interoceánico que comunica el mar Caribe con el océano Pacífico. Es una de las vías fluviales más importantes del mundo. El canal de Panamá está rodeado de grandes selvas vírgenes. La ciudad de Panamá es la capital del país. Es una ciudad moderna que está en la costa del Pacífico. En el Casco Viejo, hay edificaciones muy viejas. Pero la atracción principal de Panamá es su gente simpática.

Escenas culturales: Nicaragua

Nicaragua es el país más grande de América Central. Su capital es Managua. En Managua está la antigua Catedral, que resistió el terremoto de 1972. Los mercados son muy populares. En Masaya está el mercado artesanal más grande de Nicaragua. Granada es un pueblo de arquitectura colonial. Caminar por sus calles es como estar en el siglo XVIII. Nicaragua tiene más de 40 volcanes. Son muy conocidos el Masaya y el Momotombo. En el lago de Nicaragua, hay muchas islas habitadas por personas... y animales. Dentro de la literatura nicaragüense, sobresale la poesía de Rubén Darío, y en el arte, la pintura primitivista. Nicaragua es un pueblo sencillo y valiente. La hermosa Nicaragua nos recuerda siempre las raíces y la historia de América Central.

Escenas culturales: Colombia

Colombia está en el extremo norte de América del Sur. Su capital es Bogotá. Colombia tiene ciudades muy importantes, como Medellín, Barranquilla y Cartagena. Algunas de estas ciudades son muy desarrolladas. La economía colombiana es bastante estable. La industria textil es una de las más importantes de Colombia. Colombia tiene bellas playas, valles y montañas. Los colombianos son personas muy alegres. Cada año celebran varios carnavales, desfiles y festivales. La música y los bailes son un elemento muy importante en la cultura de este país. Colombia, un país de grandes atracciones.

Escenas en contexto

MARIELA:	¡Muchas gracias!
RICARDO:	De nada...
MARIELA:	¿Cómo te llamas?
RICARDO:	Me llamo Ricardo. ¿Cómo se llama usted?
MARIELA:	Yo me llamo Mariela Castillo. Mucho gusto, Ricardo.
RICARDO:	Igualmente, Sra. Castillo.
MARIELA:	No soy señora, soy señorita. Por el momento.
MADRE:	Buenos días. Me llamo Margarita Salazar.
RICARDO:	¡Ella es mi mamá! Mamá, ella se llama Mariela. No es señora. ¡Es señorita! ¡Es la señorita Mariela!
MARIELA:	Me llamo Mariela Castillo. Encantada, Señora Salazar.
MADRE:	Igualmente, Señorita Castillo. ¡Y bienvenida!
MARIELA:	Muchas gracias
MADRE:	Vamos, Ricardo.
MARIELA:	¡Adiós, Ricardo!
RICARDO:	¡Hasta luego, Srta. Mariela!

Capítulo 1

Los amigos animados

La música en KSUN, Radio Sol

Mayín Durán habla de la música en KSUN, Radio Sol de California.

MAYÍN:	Hola, amigos. Aquí su amiga Mayín Durán con un saludo muy especial. ¿Cómo están ustedes hoy? Yo estoy muy bien y tengo mucha música para toda la familia. Para los padres, los hijos y los abuelos. En Radio Sol tenemos música rock, y romántica para los adultos... En Radio Sol hay música mexicana, española, argentina, ¡de todos los países de América Latina!

En el parque

Doña Lola Batini y don Anselmo Olivera hablan de las personas en el parque.

DON ANSELMO:	Buenos días, doña Lola. ¿Cómo está usted?
LOLA BATINI:	Muy bien, don Anselmo. Gracias.
DON ANSELMO:	Mire... esa señora que lleva el vestido morado, ¿quién es?
LOLA BATINI:	A ver... el vestido morado... Es doña Rosita Silva.
DON ANSELMO:	Ah, sí. Y el hombre de lentes, ¿es Pedro Ruiz?
LOLA BATINI:	Sí, es Pedro; está con su esposa Andrea y sus hijas.
DON ANSELMO:	Las niñas son gemelas, ¿verdad?
LOLA BATINI:	No. Clarisa es la mayor; tiene seis años.
DON ANSELMO:	¡Caramba! ¡Hay muchas personas en el parque!

Escenas culturales: Cuba

Cuba es la isla mayor de Las Antillas. Su capital es La Habana y fue fundada en 1519 con el nombre de San Cristóbal de la Habana. La Habana Vieja es una joya colonial. Su centro histórico está colmado de construcciones de este estilo. El paseo de Malecón es uno de los sitios más concurridos de la ciudad. Las noches habaneras se llenan de música al caer el sol. Cuba es testigo de gran riqueza cultural. En Santiago de Cuba nacieron el son cubano y el bolero. La alegría del pueblo cubano contagia a quienes recorren sus calles. Cuba, su historia y el sabor de su gente, resultan un paseo inolvidable.

Escenas en contexto

ROBERTO: No entiendo. Ya son las tres. Mi prima Sabina debe estar aquí.

MARTÍN: No, todavía no son las tres. Es temprano. Y tengo las tres menos cinco.

ROBERTO: Ah, bueno.

MARTÍN: ¿Cómo es tu prima?

ROBERTO: Es una chica joven, tiene dieciséis años.

MARTÍN: Mira... la chica allí es joven. ¿Es Sabina?

ROBERTO: No, esa chica es rubia. Sabina es morena.

MARTÍN: Ajá... Mira la chica allí. Es joven y morena. ¿Es tu prima?

ROBERTO: Eh... no. No es ella. Esa chica allí es un poco gorda.

SABINA: ¡Hola!

ROBERTO: ¡Sabina! ¡Aquí estás! ¿Qué onda, chiquita?

SABINA: ¿Cómo estás?

MARTÍN: Hola, yo soy Martín.

Capítulo 2

Los amigos animados

La familia de Esteban

Esteban Brown hace una presentación sobre los miembros de su familia en la clase de español.

ESTEBAN: Hola, amigos. Mi familia no es grande. Somos cuatro: mi madre, mi padre, mi hermano mayor y yo. Mis padres son simpáticos y muy activos. A mi madre le gusta nadar y jugar al tenis. A mi padre le gusta jugar al tenis y al fútbol. ¿Y mi hermano? Pues, se llama Michael y tiene veintinueve años. Él también es simpático, pero no le gusta estudiar. (*Laughing.*) ¡Michael prefiere bailar! A mi hermano también le gustan todos los deportes. ¿Y qué me gusta hacer a mí? Pues, me gusta hablar español y... ¡hacer muchas preguntas!

¡Un momentito, por favor!

Pilar Álvarez está en su trabajo, en la Compañía Telefónica de Madrid.

PILAR: Información, diga.

CLIENTE: Sí, señorita. El número del doctor Manuel Hernández Bartlett.

PILAR: Un momentito, por favor... ¿Cómo se escribe el segundo apellido?

CLIENTE: ¿Bartlett? Se escribe be-a-ere-te-ele-e-doble t.

PILAR: Gracias. Un momentito... sí, aquí está. Es el 5-97-40-03.

CLIENTE: ¿5-97-43?

PILAR: No, no, señor. Es el 5-97-4-0-0-3.

CLIENTE: Ah, claro: cero, cero, tres. Gracias, señorita.

PILAR: De nada, señor, a sus órdenes.

Escenas culturales: Ecuador

En Ecuador está una de las ciudades más hermosas de América del Sur; Quito, su capital. El centro de Quito es famoso por su valor histórico. La arquitectura es colonial. Esto se nota en sus calles, casas, iglesias y palacios. La iglesia de San Francisco es la iglesia más vieja de Ecuador. Fue construida por los españoles en el siglo XVI. Ecuador tiene también lugares de gran belleza natural. Hacia el oeste de Ecuador, en el océano Pacífico, está el archipiélago de Galápagos. En esas islas habitan muchas especies marinas y aves. Las islas Galápagos son un paraíso para los amantes de la naturaleza.

Escenas en contexto

AGENTE: ¿Ya tiene planes este año?

ROBERTO: Quiero hacer un viaje, pero no sé dónde ni cuándo todavía. Quiero bucear.

AGENTE: Bueno, tiene muchas opciones diferentes. ¿A dónde prefiere viajar?

ROBERTO: Prefiero viajar a una isla.

AGENTE: Bien... dicen que bucear en las islas del Caribe es maravilloso.

ROBERTO: ¿Es caro el Caribe?

AGENTE: Depende de la estación. En el invierno, cuesta más. En el verano, cuesta menos.

ROBERTO: Claro. ¿Y qué tiempo hace en el Caribe durante el verano?

AGENTE: Bueno, en julio y agosto, por ejemplo, hace calor. Y llueve mucho también. Llueve casi todos los días.

ROBERTO: ¿Y qué tiempo hace durante el invierno?

AGENTE: Hace más fresco, y no llueve tanto.

ROBERTO: ¿Tiene alguna otra recomendación?

AGENTE: El país de Belice tiene lugares maravillosos para bucear. Pero no es una isla.

ROBERTO: ¡Belice! ¡Qué buena idea!

AGENTE: Desde aquí no es muy caro el viaje.

ROBERTO: Y, ¿qué tiempo hace en Belice?

AGENTE: Es muy húmedo, hace calor, hace mucho sol. Mire, aquí tiene unos folletos. Si quiere viajar a Belice, es más barato en verano, como siempre.

ROBERTO: Muchas gracias. usted puede hacer todas las reservaciones, ¿verdad? ¿Como el avión y el hotel?

AGENTE: Sí, claro.

ROBERTO: ¿Cuándo puedo llamarla para arreglar el viaje?

AGENTE: ¡Cuando quiera!

Capítulo 3

Los amigos animados

El Club Pacífico

Un anuncio del Club Pacífico en KSUN, Radio Sol de California.

MAYÍN: Amigos, ¿les gusta practicar deportes? ¿Les gusta hacer ejercicio en un club moderno y elegante? Ahora, en Los Ángeles, está el Club Pacífico, un lugar para toda la familia.

ANUNCIADOR: ¿Les gusta nadar? ¿Prefieren montar a caballo, correr o simplemente descansar? Tenemos un parque grande y bonito. ¡Y en Los Ángeles siempre hace buen tiempo para estas actividades!

MAYÍN: El Club Pacífico es el lugar ideal para toda la familia. Aquí hay actividades para los niños, los jóvenes y los adultos.

ANUNCIADOR: Ya saben, el Club Pacífico es el lugar favorito de muchas familias hispanas. Para más información, llame al 425-66-35.

AMBOS: ¡Los esperamos!

El tiempo en México y en Buenos Aires

Adriana Bolini es argentina y viaja mucho por su trabajo. Ahora está en la Ciudad de México y conversa con un amigo.

AMIGO: Adriana, ¿qué tiempo hace en Buenos Aires ahora?
ADRIANA: Bueno, en enero estamos en verano. Casi siempre hace muy buen tiempo, calor y mucho sol.
AMIGO: Aquí en México es diferente: en enero estamos en invierno y hace frío.
ADRIANA: Sí, pero no llueve mucho, ¿verdad?
AMIGO: No. Aquí llueve en julio, en el verano.
ADRIANA: ¡Es muy diferente! En Buenos Aires llueve muy poco en el verano. Pero en el invierno llueve muchísimo.
AMIGO: Te refieres a los meses de julio y agosto, ¿no?
ADRIANA: Sí, en julio y agosto en Buenos Aires es invierno. Hay que llevar impermeable y paraguas muchos días. Y hace bastante frío.
AMIGO: ¡Qué interesante! Estamos hablando de los mismos meses, pero de dos estaciones muy diferentes...
ADRIANA: (*Laughing.*) ¡El verano y el invierno!

Escenas culturales: los Estados Unidos

Los Estados Unidos es un país de gran diversidad. Casi la totalidad de su población está compuesta de inmigrantes de distintas partes del mundo. La población hispanoamérica es una de las de mayor crecimiento en los últimos años en los Estados Unidos. Su influencia es cada vez más fuerte. Esto se evidencia en la comida, el arte y las costumbres. Los Estados Unidos es un auténtico mosaico de razas.

Escenas en contexto

JUAN CARLOS: Buenos días... ¿Es la clase de economía?
EDUARDO: Sí, es la clase de economía.
JUAN CARLOS: ¿Qué tal? Soy Juan Carlos Alarcón.
EDUARDO: Buenos días. Me llamo Eduardo Robledo. Mucho gusto.
JUAN CARLOS: Igualmente. ¿Qué hora es?
EDUARDO: Son las once. Oye, tomas también la clase de sociología con el profesor Ramón, ¿verdad?
JUAN CARLOS: Sí, también tomo esa clase.
EDUARDO: ¿A qué hora es la clase de sociología? ¿Es a la una o a la una y media?
JUAN CARLOS: Es a la una y media, creo... Sí, a la una y media.
EDUARDO: Este grupo es excelente.
JUAN CARLOS: Sí, escucho su música con frecuencia. Me gusta mucho el jazz.
EDUARDO: ¿Ah, sí? Yo trabajo en el Café Azul. Allí tocan música jazz todos los fines de semana por la noche.
JUAN CARLOS: ¡Qué bacán! ¿A qué hora?
EDUARDO: A las diez.
JUAN CARLOS: ¡Perfecto! Entonces, este fin de semana escucho jazz en tu café. Oye, ¿qué hora es?
EDUARDO: Son las once y cinco. ¿Dónde está la profesora? La clase es a las once.

Capítulo 4

Los amigos animados

Carla llama a dos profesores

Carla Espinosa necesita hablar de los exámenes finales con dos de sus profesores. Hoy, martes, los está llamando por teléfono.

CARLA:	Buenos días. Quiero hablar con el profesor Rico, por favor.
SECRETARIA:	En este momento no está, señorita. Los martes por la mañana trabaja en su casa. Llame a la una, por favor.
CARLA:	Gracias, pero prefiero ir a su oficina. ¿Va a estar él allí a la una?
SECRETARIA:	Sí, los martes y los jueves el profesor Rico siempre está en la universidad entre la una y las tres menos cuarto. Sale para dar una clase a las tres menos diez.
CARLA:	Muchísimas gracias. Hasta pronto.
	(*Dialing and ringing.*)
SECRETARIO:	Sí, dígame.
CARLA:	Por favor, necesito hablar con la profesora Lecuna.
SECRETARIO:	La profesora Lecuna está conversando con un estudiante.
CARLA:	¿Va a estar ella en su oficina más tarde?
SECRETARIO:	Sí, señorita. La profesora Lecuna trabaja en su oficina los martes por la mañana desde las ocho y media hasta las diez.
CARLA:	(*To herself.*) Martes de ocho y media a diez...
SECRETARIO:	Sí, y también los miércoles en la tarde de las dos a las cuatro.
CARLA:	Gracias. Hasta luego.

Silvia habla con un cliente

Silvia Bustamante está trabajando en la terminal de autobuses.

CLIENTE:	Señorita, ¿a qué hora hay autobús para Tampico?
SILVIA:	El primero sale a las ocho y cuarto, el segundo sale a las once y veinte y el último sale a las cinco y media.
CLIENTE:	(*Confused.*) Un momentito, a ver. El primero sale a las ocho y cuarto.
SILVIA:	Correcto.
CLIENTE:	El segundo a las once...
SILVIA:	No, señor, el segundo sale a las once y veinte.
CLIENTE:	Ah, sí. Y el último sale a las cinco y media, ¿verdad?
SILVIA:	Sí, señor.
CLIENTE:	Muchas gracias, señorita.
SILVIA:	Para servirle.

Escenas culturales: Guatemala

Guatemala está hacia el norte, en América Central. Su capital actual es Ciudad de Guatemala. Antigua, Guatemala fue la capital hasta 1773. Es una de las ciudades más viejas y hermosas de América. Tikal fue el mayor centro ceremonial de la cultura maya durante la época clásica. Estas ruinas incluyen plazas, una acrópolis, pirámides y templos. Las ruinas de Tikal están en medio de la selva tropical. Son un sitio único, bello. Los indios mayas-quichés se visten con trajes coloridos que ellos fabrican. Esta cultura tiene una visión hermosa sobre la creación del hombre y del mundo.

Escenas en contexto

ROBERTO:	Buenos días.
EMPLEADO:	Buenos días. ¿En qué te puedo servir?
ROBERTO:	Quisiera devolver este disco compacto.
EMPLEADO:	Muy bien, un momento... ¿Por qué quieres devolverlo?
ROBERTO:	Ya lo tengo.
EMPLEADO:	¿Tienes tu recibo?
ROBERTO:	No, no tengo recibo. Me regalaron el disco para mi cumpleaños.

EMPLEADO:	Lo siento, pero en ese caso no te puedo reembolsar el dinero. Necesitas el recibo para un reembolso.
ROBERTO:	Qué pena. ¿Puedo cambiar el disco por otro?
EMPLEADO:	Sí, eso está bien.
ROBERTO:	Gracias. Oye, ¿no sabes si ya salió el nuevo disco de Ragazzi?
EMPLEADO:	No, fíjate que no sale hasta el viernes. Todos lo estamos esperando. ¿Te gusta Ragazzi?
ROBERTO:	Me encanta. Es mi grupo favorito.
EMPLEADO:	A mí me encanta también. El guitarrista es increíble, ¿verdad?
ROBERTO:	¡Es buenísimo! ¿Fuiste a su concierto el año pasado?
EMPLEADO:	Sí, ¡qué padre! Fue el mejor concierto del año.
ROBERTO:	Sabes, creo que me voy a esperar hasta el viernes para cambiar este disco.
EMPLEADO:	Está bien.
ROBERTO:	Nos vemos...
EMPLEADO:	¡Hasta luego! ¡Buen día!

Capítulo 5

Los amigos animados

Andrés está aburrido

Hoy es domingo y Susana Yamasaki conversa con Andrés, su hijo menor.

ANDRÉS:	¡Estoy aburrido, mamá!
SUSANA:	¿Por qué no vas a jugar con tus amiguitos?
ANDRÉS:	¡Hoy no quiero jugar!
SUSANA:	Entonces, ¿por qué no vas a andar en patineta?
ANDRÉS:	¿Andar en patineta? No, ¡hoy no!
SUSANA:	Mira, ¿qué tal si leemos tu libro favorito?
ANDRÉS:	Mejor no...
SUSANA:	(*Thinking.*) Bueno, a ver... ¡Ahora sí tengo una idea excelente!
ANDRÉS:	(*Excited.*) ¡¿Una idea?!
SUSANA:	Sí, algo que te va a gustar mucho.
ANDRÉS:	¡¿Qué es?! ¡¿Qué es?!
SUSANA:	Dime qué te parece este plan: te bañas, te vistes muy elegante y sales conmigo al parque...
ANDRÉS:	¡Sí! Pero... ¿solamente al parque? ¿Y no vamos al cine?
SUSANA:	Bueno, está bien, Andresito. ¡También vamos al cine!
ANDRÉS:	¡¡Viva!!

¡Feliz cumpleaños!

Hoy es el cumpleaños de Graciela y hay una fiesta en su casa. Ahora Graciela conversa con su hermano Diego.

(*Party sounds.*)

GRACIELA:	Diego, tengo una amiga que quiero presentarte.
DIEGO:	(*Incredulous.*) ¿Una amiga... ? ¿Y dónde está?
GRACIELA:	Está allí en la sala. ¿La ves? Se llama Rebeca.
DIEGO:	(*Pleased.*) Sí. Es muy bonita.
GRACIELA:	¿Por qué no la invitas a bailar?
DIEGO:	¿A bailar? Es que...
GRACIELA:	Sabes, hoy es su cumpleaños también.

DIEGO:	¡Qué coincidencia!
GRACIELA:	Vamos, te la presento. Mira, Rebeca, éste es mi hermano Diego.
REBECA:	Hola, Diego. ¿Cómo estás?
DIEGO:	(*Nervous.*) Bien, bien. ¡Feliz cumpleaños!
REBECA:	Gracias. ¿Quieres bailar?
DIEGO:	¡Claro que sí!

Escenas culturales: Venezuela

Venezuela está hacia el noreste de América del Sur. Su gente es cálida, al igual que su clima. La capital de Venezuela es Caracas. Es una de las ciudades más grandes y modernas de Sudamérica. Simón Bolívar, «el Libertador» de América del Sur, era nativo de Caracas. El principal recurso económico de Venezuela es el petróleo. Venezuela es uno de los mayores productores de petróleo del mundo. La naturaleza de Venezuela es muy variada: costas, playas, ríos, y los enormes tepuyes. Los tepuyes son unas montañas únicas, que tienen la cima plana. Ciudades hermosas y naturaleza dramática son dos de los grandes atractivos turísticos que tiene Venezuela.

Escenas en contexto

RECEPCIONISTA:	Buenos días, oficina de la consejera Valenzuela. ¿En qué le puedo servir?
MARIELA:	Muy buenos días. ¿Me comunica con la consejera Valenzuela, por favor?
RECEPCIONISTA:	Disculpe, ¿de parte de quién?
MARIELA:	Soy Mariela Castillo.
RECEPCIONISTA:	Un momento, por favor. Lo siento, pero la consejera está con un cliente en este momento. ¿Quiere dejar un recado?
MARIELA:	Bueno, lo que quiero es hacer una cita.
RECEPCIONISTA:	No hay problema. Yo le puedo ayudar con una cita. ¿Qué día de la semana prefiere usted?
MARIELA:	Prefiero el viernes, si es posible.
RECEPCIONISTA:	Tenemos una cita el viernes a las nueve de la mañana. ¿Está bien?
MARIELA:	Sí, está bien. Una pregunta...
RECEPCIONISTA:	¿Sí?
MARIELA:	Quiero hablar con la consejera Valenzuela sobre las posibilidades de empleo para una persona con mi educación y experiencia. ¿Debo traer una copia de mi currículum?
RECEPCIONISTA:	Sí, siempre es recomendable tener una copia de su currículum.
MARIELA:	Muy bien. Muchas gracias.
RECEPCIONISTA:	De nada, Srta. Castillo. La vemos el viernes a las nueve de la mañana. ¡Adiós!
MARIELA:	Gracias a usted. ¡Adiós!

Capítulo 6

Los amigos animados

Experimentos fantásticos

Ramón Gómez está de visita en casa de la familia Saucedo para ver a su novia Amanda. Pero Amanda no está lista, así que Ramón conversa con Ernestito.

ERNESTITO:	Oye, Ramón, ¿te gusta ir a la escuela?
RAMÓN:	Sí, claro; me gusta aprender cosas nuevas. ¿Y a ti te gusta?
ERNESTITO:	Sí, sí. ¡En la escuela puedo jugar con mis amigos! Tengo muchos.
RAMÓN:	¡Qué bueno! Yo también.

ERNESTITO:	Oye, ¿y qué haces en tu escuela?
RAMÓN:	Voy a clases. Tengo historia, biología, matemáticas...
ERNESTITO:	¿Y cuál es tu favorita?
RAMÓN:	La de biología. (*Teasingly.*) En esa clase hacemos experimentos fantásticos...
ERNESTITO:	(*Excited.*) ¡¿Experimentos?! ¡¿Como en la historia de Franquenstén?!
RAMÓN:	Sí, en un laboratorio. (*Laughing.*) ¡Como Franquenstén!
ERNESTITO:	¡Qué divertido!
RAMÓN:	Y otra clase que me gusta mucho es la de educación física. En esa clase corremos, jugamos deportes, hacemos ejercicio.
ERNESTITO:	Mis amigos y yo también corremos y jugamos en mi escuela.
RAMÓN:	Pues ya ves, Ernestito. Tu escuela y mi escuela no son muy diferentes.
ERNESTITO:	(*Disappointed.*) Sí, ¡pero nosotros no hacemos experimentos!

El ingeniero y el profesor

Pablo Cavic y Raúl Saucedo están en la cafetería de la universidad, conversando sobre sus futuras carreras.

PABLO:	Raúl, tú estudias ingeniería, ¿verdad?
RAÚL:	Sí, es una carrera que me gusta mucho.
PABLO:	Pero tus clases son difíciles, ¿no?
RAÚL:	Bastante. Uno tiene que tomar física, cálculo... Y tú, ¿que estudias, Pablo? ¿Cuál va a ser tu carrera?
PABLO:	Yo pienso ser profesor de español.
RAÚL:	¡Qué bueno, hombre!
PABLO:	Me gusta mucho el idioma español y la cultura hispana.
RAÚL:	Pero los profesores necesitan tener mucha paciencia, ¿no?
PABLO:	¿Paciencia? Bueno, sí, para poder enseñar y explicar bien las cosas.
RAÚL:	¿Y tú eres paciente?
PABLO:	Sí, y además, me gusta ayudar a la gente.
RAÚL:	Pues ya veo que vas a ser un profesor excelente. (*Laughing.*) ¡Mejor que la profesora Martínez!
PABLO:	(*Laughing.*) No, ¡eso no es posible!

Escenas culturales: Costa Rica

Costa Rica es conocida por ser una tierra de paz. Su capital es San José. Los «ticos», como se conoce a los costarricenses, son personas amables y alegres. La biodiversidad en los bosques de Costa Rica es una de las mayores del mundo. Su sistema de parques nacionales, refugios y reservas biológicas protege la vida silvestre de Costa Rica. Las playas de Costa Rica son muy famosas. Algunas de ellas son el lugar de desove de la tortuga Baula. El cráter del volcán Poás es uno de los más grandes del mundo. El verdor de sus bosques y montañas durante la estación lluviosa, el atractivo de sus playas doradas en la estación seca, y la calidez de un pueblo hospitalario son los tesoros que tiene Costa Rica.

Escenas en contexto

AGENTE:	¿Juan Carlos Alarcón? Mucho gusto. Yo soy Amanda Villanueva, la agente.
JUAN CARLOS:	Es un placer, señora.
AGENTE:	Igualmente. ¿Así que usted busca apartamento?
JUAN CARLOS:	Sí. Prefiero vivir en un apartamento cerca del centro.
AGENTE:	¿Qué tipo de apartamento prefiere? Tenemos muchísimos...
JUAN CARLOS:	No quiero nada grande. Prefiero un apartamento con un sólo dormitorio.
AGENTE:	Muy bien. ¿Y qué más quiere?

JUAN CARLOS:	Bueno... no necesito mucho. Prefiero un apartamento con sala, una ducha en el baño, una cocina con lavaplatos.
AGENTE:	No hay problema. Tenemos muchísimos apartamentos así. ¿Y cuánto quiere pagar de alquiler?
JUAN CARLOS:	Quiero pagar entre 600 y 700 soles. ¿Le parece posible?
AGENTE:	Sí, es razonable. Mire... este apartamento tiene todo lo que quiere. Sala, un dormitorio, baño con ducha... y lavaplatos en la cocina. ¿Quiere verlo? Está muy cerca de aquí, podemos caminar.
JUAN CARLOS:	Sí, me gustaría verlo. Gracias.
AGENTE:	Bueno, ¿vamos?
JUAN CARLOS:	Vamos.

Capítulo 7

Los amigos animados

La Compañía Reparatodo

Y ahora un anuncio comercial en KSUN, Radio Sol.

ANUNCIADOR:	¡Señor! ¡Señora! Ya no tiene que salir de su casa para llevar a reparar sus aparatos eléctricos. La Compañía Reparatodo hace todo tipo de reparaciones en su casa.
ANUNCIADORA:	Reparamos estufas, refrigeradores, hornos de microondas y otros aparatos. Y le ofrecemos el mejor servicio de reparaciones por el precio más bajo.
ANUNCIADOR:	¡Y eso no es todo! Después de hacer las reparaciones necesarias, sacamos la basura, barremos el piso e incluso pasamos la aspiradora. ¡Siempre le dejamos la casa limpia!
ANUNCIADORA:	Usted ya no tiene que salir de su casa para tener sus aparatos en perfectas condiciones.
ANUNCIADOR:	¡Llame a la Compañía Reparatodo! O visite nuestro sitio Web, en www.reparatodo.com.
AMBOS:	¡Para todo tipo de reparaciones!

El vecindario de Guillermo

Ahora Guillermo Saucedo, el hijo de Ernesto y Estela, lee una composición en su clase de lenguaje y escritura.

GUILLERMO:	¿Qué puedo decir de mi vecindario? Pues, muchas cosas buenas y algunas cosas malas. Una cosa buena es que mi vecindario tiene un parque muy grande donde todos los muchachos jugamos al fútbol. También, cerca de mi casa hay un cine y a veces voy a ver películas cómicas con mis padres, mi hermana y mi hermanito. A todos en mi familia nos gusta mucho el cine, especialmente las películas cómicas. Pero la cosa más fantástica de mi vecindario es que tiene un centro de videojuegos. ¡Ésa es mi tienda favorita! Sé jugar muchos videojuegos y hay uno que me gusta mucho: «¡El mundo atómico!» ¿Y cuáles son las cosas malas de mi vecindario? Pues la verdad es que solamente hay una: cerca de mi casa hay un mercado donde a mi mamá le gusta mucho hacer las compras. Y ustedes probablemente se estén preguntando: ¿Qué tiene de malo un mercado? El problema es que... ¡muchas veces tengo que ir de compras con mi mamá para ayudarla!

Escenas culturales: Argentina

Por la extensión de su territorio, Argentina ocupa el segundo lugar en América del Sur. Buenos Aires, su capital, está junto al Río de la Plata. Este río es considerado el «mar» de los argentinos. Los «porteños», como se les conoce a los bonaerenses, son en su mayoría descendientes de inmigrantes europeos. La influencia europea se nota en el arte y la arquitectura de la capital argentina. La Avenida 9 de julio es una de las avenidas más anchas del mundo. El tango es el baile típico de Argentina. Lugares como el barrio «La Boca» de Buenos Aires inspiraron tangos muy famosos. Este hermoso ritmo que vibra al son del bandoneón nos hace sentir la pasión de una ciudad que no descansa nunca: Buenos Aires.

Escenas en contexto

ROBERTO: ¿Qué te pasa, Martín? Estás muy callado.

MARTÍN: Estoy muy preocupado. Ayer fue un día muy difícil.

ROBERTO: ¿Qué hiciste ayer? No me dijiste nada esta mañana, ¿hmm?

MARTÍN: Fui a la universidad por la mañana. Tuvimos un examen en la clase de historia latinoamericana.

ROBERTO: ¿Saliste bien?

MARTÍN: Eh, creo que sí, pero no estoy seguro. Después almorcé con María y José.

ROBERTO: ¿Dónde almorzaron?

MARTÍN Almorzamos en el nuevo restaurante de comida china en la calle Robledos.

ROBERTO: ¿Es buena la comida?

MARTÍN: Regular. Luego, fui al trabajo. Y a que no sabes qué me pasó en la carretera. ¡Me detuvo un policía por exceso de velocidad!

ROBERTO: ¿Y qué pasó?

MARTÍN: Intenté explicarle que fue sin querer, ¡pero no me creyó! Y me puso una multa.

ROBERTO: ¡Qué pena! Lo siento mucho.

MARTÍN: Claro, luego llegué tarde a mi trabajo ¡y mi jefe se enojó conmigo!

ROBERTO: ¡Qué mala onda! Fue un día terrible, ¿no?

MARTÍN: ¡Sí, terrible! Y, bueno, tú, ¿cómo te la pasaste ayer?

ROBERTO: Pues... fue mi día libre. Así que me levanté tarde, desayuné, miré la televisión, fui al parque y me dormí un poco por la tarde. ¡Fue un día muy ocupado!

MARTÍN: ¡Qué tonto eres, Roberto!

Capítulo 8

Los amigos animados

El secreto

Silvia Bustamante conversa con Alfredo Gil, su amigo uruguayo, en la librería de la universidad.

SILVIA: ¡Hola, Alfredo!

ALFREDO: ¡Silvia! ¿Cómo estás?

SILVIA: Bien, bien. Oye, Nacho y yo te llamamos ayer, pero no contestaste.

ALFREDO: Es que no estuve en casa en todo el día. Salí con una amiga. ¿Y para qué me llamaron?

SILVIA: Para invitarte a ir al cine con nosotros y otros amigos.

ALFREDO: ¿Al cine? ¡Qué divertido! ¿Qué película vieron?

SILVIA: «El parque fantástico.» A todos nos gustó mucho. Pero dime, Alfredo, ¿quién es esa amiga con quien saliste ayer?

ALFREDO: (*Teasingly.*) Ah, es un secreto.

SILVIA: (*Laughing.*) ¡Ay, detesto los secretos! Dime quién es.

ALFREDO: Bueno, sólo te voy a decir que tú conoces a esta muchacha.

SILVIA: Hmmm... yo conozco a varias chicas...

ALFREDO: Hace dos horas ustedes conversaron por teléfono.

SILVIA: ¿Hace dos horas? Ah, sí, estuve conversando con Angélica. (*Surprised.*) ¡No! ¿Saliste con Angélica? ¿Mi mejor amiga?

ALFREDO: Sí. ¿Por qué te sorprende tanto?

SILVIA: Es que ella no me habló de ti.

ALFREDO: (*Surprised.*) ¿No te dijo nada de mí? ¿Ni una palabra?

SILVIA: ¡Nada! Obviamente... ¡a ustedes dos les gustan mucho los secretos!

El periódico La Voz

En este segmento comercial de KSUN, el escritor Pedro Ruiz habla del periódico mexicano *La Voz.*

PEDRO RUIZ: Hola, amigos, les habla Pedro Ruiz. Algunos de ustedes saben que soy escritor y que vivo en México. Pues bien, si lo saben es porque leyeron mis artículos en el periódico *La Voz.* Estoy aquí con ustedes hoy para recomendarles este excelente periódico. Hace más de cincuenta años que *La Voz* comenzó a publicar los artículos más completos sobre México. Durante todos esos años, *La Voz* les trajo a sus lectores las últimas noticias nacionales, además de reportajes sobre los eventos más importantes del mundo. *La Voz* también les ofrece a sus lectores interesantes artículos sobre arte, cultura y literatura. (*Laughing.*) ¡Ésos los escribo yo! Recuerde, si a usted le gusta leer y quiere estar bien informado, lea *La Voz.* ¡Un periódico que es de verdad «la voz» del mundo hispano!

Escenas culturales: Honduras

Honduras. La capital de este país de América Central es Tegucigalpa. Esta ciudad tiene algunos edificios de gran interés cultural. Al oeste de la capital están las ruinas mayas de Copán. Entre sus atracciones están la Plaza Grande y la Acrópolis. Honduras tiene varios parques nacionales. Su fauna incluye, entro otros, jaguares, monos, lagartos y aves. Las islas y playas caribeñas de Honduras son famosas y bellas. El arte, la comida y los bailes son muestras de la cultura popular de los hondureños. Esta gente alegre refleja el carácter amable de los pueblos centroamericanos.

Escenas culturales: El Salvador

El Salvador es un país muy pequeño. San Salvador es su capital y es la ciudad más grande del país. En San Salvador, hay varios mercados populares. Ahí se encuentran mercancías de todo género: comestibles, hierbas medicinales, artesanía. Las pupusas son la comida más popular de El Salvador. Son como tortillas de masa de maíz, rellenas de queso, frijoles fritos o de chicharrón. Las ruinas mayas de Tazumal son las ruinas más importantes y mejor preservadas del país. En El Salvador hay más de veinticinco volcanes inactivos. Esto permite hacer caminatas hasta el cráter de algunos de estos volcanes. Como en otros países de Centroamérica, la belleza de El Salvador está lejos de la ciudad en sus verdes bosques y montañas.

Escenas en contexto

MARIELA: Hola, Sr. Valderrama!

VENDEDOR: Hola, Srta. Castillo. ¿Qué le doy hoy?

MARIELA: Voy a preparar una cena deliciosa. Es la primera vez que los padres de mi novio vienen a cenar. ¡Pienso causar una gran impresión!

VENDEDOR: ¿Qué va a preparar? Tal vez un buen pescado frito con arroz.

MARIELA: No, a mi novio no le gusta el pescado frito.

VENDEDOR: ¿Le gustan los camarones a su novio?

MARIELA: Sí, le gustan muchísimo.

VENDEDOR: Entonces, de primer plato, prepare un ceviche de camarones.

MARIELA: Muy bien consejo. De segundo plato voy a preparar unas chuletas de cerdo. A mí me gustan mucho las chuletas de cerdo.

VENDEDOR: Mire, Srta. Castillo... las zanahorias están buenísimas hoy. Van muy bien con las chuletas de cerdo.

MARIELA:	Tiene toda la razón. Quisiera un cuarto de kilo. Y para el ceviche, necesito tomates y cebollas. ¿Me da medio kilo de cebollas y medio kilo de tomates, por favor?
VENDEDOR:	Muy bien. ¿Y qué más?
MARIELA:	¿A cuánto está el kilo de espárragos?
VENDEDOR:	El kilo de espárragos está a 500 colones.
MARIELA:	Muy bien... un cuarto kilo de espárragos, entonces. ¿Y me da también cuatro limones?
MARIELA:	¡Qué buen tiempo hace hoy! ¿Verdad, Sr. Valderrama?
VENDEDOR:	Ah, Srta. Castillo, donde usted está, siempre hace sol.
MARIELA:	¡Qué flores me echa, Sr. Valderrama!

Capítulo 9

Los amigos animados

El Restaurante Tres Estrellas

Desde Acapulco, un mensaje del Restaurante Tres Estrellas, el restaurante que todos preferimos.

ANUNCIADOR:	En sus viajes a Acapulco, lo invitamos a disfrutar de nuestra deliciosa y variada comida en el Restaurante Tres Estrellas.
ANUNCIADORA:	Tenemos una vista magnífica al mar. Y los viernes, sábados y domingos presentamos al cantante Manuel Rodríguez y su conjunto.
ANUNCIADOR:	Usted puede escuchar los éxitos musicales del momento mientras saborea nuestros ricos platillos.
ANUNCIADORA:	Abrimos a las seis de la tarde y cerramos a las dos de la mañana.
AMBOS:	¡Restaurante Tres Estrellas!
ANUNCIADOR:	Para hacer de sus vacaciones en Acapulco las mejores vacaciones de su vida. ¡Disfrute de una noche inolvidable!
ANUNCIADORA:	Haga sus reservaciones con tiempo. Llámenos al 3-17-21-14 o visite nuestro sitio Web en www.tresestrellas.com.
AMBOS:	¡Restaurante Tres Estrellas!

Algo diferente

Andrea Saucedo y su esposo, Pedro Ruiz, van a salir a cenar con sus hijas Marisa y Clarisa. Ahora están decidiendo qué tipo de comida prefieren comer.

ANDREA:	¿Vamos a comer comida mexicana? Un platillo de carne asada o pollo con mole...
PEDRO:	(*Thinking it over.*) Eh... Arroz, frijoles, unas enchiladas... No, hoy no quiero comida mexicana. Quiero algo diferente.
ANDREA:	Entonces, ¿qué tal si vamos a un restaurante de comida italiana?
PEDRO:	Pizza, espaguetis... No, no tengo ganas de comer pastas.
ANDREA:	Bueno, Pedro, podemos ir a un restaurante chino. A ti te gusta mucho la comida china.
PEDRO:	No, mejor no... ¿Qué tal comida francesa?
ANDREA:	¡Qué buena idea! Sí, vamos.
PEDRO:	Eh... No. Pensándolo bien, la comida francesa es muy cara.
ANDREA:	Pedro, no podemos esperar más. ¡Hay que tomar una decisión!
PEDRO:	Sí, sí. Es que quiero algo diferente.
ANDREA:	Pues mientras tú decides, las niñas y yo vamos a comer algo...
PEDRO:	¡Ya está! ¿Por qué no comemos tortas aquí en casa?
ANDREA:	¿Tortas? ¿Y eso es «algo diferente»?
PEDRO:	(*Laughing.*) Bueno, sí, ¡porque *yo* voy a prepararlas!

Escenas culturales: Bolivia

Hacia el centro de América del Sur está Bolivia. Este país del altiplano tiene una cultura muy rica. Esta cultura mantiene las mismas tradiciones, valores y creencias de las antiguas civilizaciones. En Bolivia, muchas personas son de ascendencia amerindia. La lengua oficial es el español. También se hablan el quechua y el aymará, dos lenguas indígenas. La Paz es la capital de Bolivia y la ciudad más alta del mundo. El lago Titicaca es un lugar sagrado para los incas. Su belleza geográfica, desde Los Andes hasta los bosques amazónicos, y el misterio de su pasado hacen de Bolivia un enigmático y llamativo país.

Escenas en contexto

LUPE: Y después de un año, regresaron a México. Mi padre encontró un trabajo en el D.F. y aquí estamos todavía. ¿Cuál es la historia de tus padres, Diego?

DIEGO: Pues, mi padre llegó a California cuando tenía diez años. Sus padres vinieron para trabajar en la fábrica de su tío. La familia de mi madre ya vivía en California. Mis padres se conocieron en la universidad. ¿Y tú, Antonio? Cuéntanos la historia de tu familia.

ANTONIO: Huy. Mi familia tiene una larga historia. Según mi abuelita, mis antepasados llegaron en el siglo XVII.

DIEGO: ¿Sí? ¿Cómo vivían en esa época? ¿Qué hacían?

ANTONIO: Bueno, vengo de una familia de campesinos. Mis antepasados trabajaban la tierra. Cultivaban el maíz y otras cosechas. Y siempre vivieron en el campo. Mis padres son los primeros de la familia que viven en la ciudad. Vivimos en una finca hasta que yo tenía trece años. Ese año mis padres vendieron la finca y nos mudamos a la ciudad.

LUPE: Así que, ¿te criaste en una finca? ¿Dónde estaba?

ANTONIO: Estaba cerca de Guadalajara. Mi tío le compró la tierra a mi padre. Pero de vez en cuando vuelvo para visitar a mi tío y recordar el lugar.

LUPE: ¿Te gustaba vivir en el campo?

ANTONIO: Sí, me gustaba. Pero, también me gusta vivir en la ciudad.

DIEGO: ¿Cómo fue tu niñez?

ANTONIO: Pues, supongo como la de cualquier niño que crece en una finca. Una prima y un primo vivían con nosotros. Y nos divertíamos como todos los niños. Recuerdo que jugábamos al escondite o al gato. Y por lo general, nos llevábamos bien. De vez en cuando nos peleábamos. Y claro, todos ayudábamos en la finca también.

LUPE: ¿Cómo fue tu niñez, Diego? ¿Es diferente en los Estados Unidos?

DIEGO: Supongo que hay ciertas diferencias. En general allá las familias no son tan grandes como aquí en México. Además, aquí es común vivir rodeado de parientes, ¿no?

LUPE: Sí. Aunque eso está cambiando poco a poco. Hoy en día la gente se muda más y así las familias se separan.

DIEGO: Pues, mi familia está por todas partes. Nos vemos nada más los días festivos. Yo me crié en Los Ángeles. No sabía nada de las fincas ni del campo. En mi barrio jugábamos en la calle, en los parques, también en los patios de recreo.

ANTONIO: ¿Qué hacías? ¿Practicabas deportes?

DIEGO: Sí, de niño practicaba muchos deportes. Jugaba al fútbol, también me encantaban el básquetbol y el fútbol americano. Hacíamos otras cosas también. A veces, volaba papalotes o jugaba la bebeleche con mi hermana, aunque sólo cuando mis amiguitos no me veían. Jugar a la bebeleche no era para muchachos. Por lo menos, en esos días.

LUPE: Bueno, no es muy diferente de la vida de los niños aquí.

DIEGO: Hmm, no. De veras no es muy diferente. Oigan. Nuestra clase comienza en diez minutos. ¿Vamos?

LUPE: Sí, vamos.

Capítulo 10

Los amigos animados

La familia de Carla

Carla y Rogelio conversan sobre la familia de Carla.

ROGELIO:	Bueno, Carla, tú ya sabes mucho de mi familia. Pero yo de la tuya no sé nada. ¡Cuéntame!
CARLA:	Bueno, somos seis hermanos. Tengo tres hermanos y dos hermanas.
ROGELIO:	¿Y todos son solteros?
CARLA:	No, dos ya están casados.
ROGELIO:	¿Cuándo se casaron?
CARLA:	Roberto, mi hermano mayor, se casó hace tres años. Y Gabriela, mi hermana mayor, se casó el año pasado.
ROGELIO:	¿Tienes sobrinos?
CARLA:	Sí, un sobrinito de dos años, hijo de Roberto y mi cuñada, Alicia. Y también tengo una sobrinita de un mes, hija de Gabriela y mi cuñado, Jorge.
ROGELIO:	Oye, ¿y te gusta ser tía?
CARLA:	¡Me encanta ser tía!
ROGELIO:	Me imagino que tus padres son muy felices con sus nietos.
CARLA:	Sí, chico. ¡Y son los mejores abuelos del mundo!

Los recuerdos de doña María

Cuando Esteban y Raúl visitaron a doña María en Guanajuato, la abuela de Raúl le contó un poco de su vida a Esteban. Ésta es su historia.

DOÑA MARÍA:	Bueno, Esteban, usted ya sabe que me llamo María. Mi nombre completo es María Eulalia González de Saucedo. Tengo setenta y nueve años. Mis dos hijos ya están casados y ahora tengo muchos nietos. Mi hijo Javier tiene cuatro hijos, que son Ernesto, las gemelas Paula y Andrea, y Raulito, ¡Caray! Quise decir *Raúl*. (*Laughing*.) Ya no le gusta que le llame Raulito porque... ¡dice que está muy grande! Pues bien, mi otra hija, Leticia, tiene cinco hijos y vive aquí en Guanajuato con su esposo y sus hijos. ¡Me gusta mucho tenerlos tan cerca! Javier y su familia viven en el D.F. y vienen a visitarme los días de fiesta. ¡Siempre en Navidad y a veces para mi cumpleaños! Antes, cuando Javier y sus hijos vivían aquí en Guanajuato, me visitaban casi todos los sábados. Yo les preparaba una gran comida y, después de comer, los adultos nos sentábamos a conversar mientras los niños jugaban afuera. Pero esos niños ahora son todos grandes, como Raulito. (*Laughing*.) ¡Caray! Quise decir *Raúl*...

Escenas culturales: La República Dominicana

La República Dominicana está en el corazón del Caribe. Santo Domingo, su capital, fue la primera ciudad que se fundó en el Nuevo Mundo. Esta ciudad tiene una historia muy rica. En ella se fundaron la primera catedral, el primer monasterio y la primera universidad del Nuevo Mundo. Por todo esto, es considerada patrimonio cultural de la humanida. La mayoría de su gente lleva sangre taína en sus venas. Los dominicanos son personas hospitalarias. La riqueza natural de la República Dominicana hace de esta isla un lugar único y privilegiado. La República Dominicana es, sin duda, un auténtico paraíso tropical.

Escenas culturales: Puerto Rico

Esta hermosa isla fue descubierta por Cristóbal Colón en 1493. Su capital es San Juan. Puerto Rico se conoce también como Borinquen; a los puertorriqueños se les llama boricuas. Algunas edificaciones, como los fuertes San Felipe del Morro, el castillo de San Cristóbal y el palacio de la Fortaleza, son un legado de la arquitectura militar española. Puerto Rico es uno de los lugares más bellos de América. Con toda razón, en su canto a Puerto Rico, el gran poeta Gautier la llamó la Perla de los Mares. Sus playas, bosques y montañas son algunas de las maravillas que encantan a todo el que visita esta joya del Caribe.

Escenas en contexto

JUAN CARLOS:	Buenas tardes. Un billete de ida y vuelta para Tarma, por favor. Sale a las dos y media, ¿verdad?
VENDEDORA DE BILLETES:	Lo siento, pero ese tren está atrasado hoy. No sale hasta las seis y cuarto.
JUAN CARLOS:	¿Por qué? ¿Qué pasa?
VENDEDORA DE BILLETES:	No estoy segura, pero parece que hay un problema mecánico.
JUAN CARLOS:	¡Pero sólo son las dos y cuarto! ¡Faltan todavía cuatro horas!
VENDEDORA DE BILLETES:	De veras, lo siento. Pero no hay remedio.
JUAN CARLOS:	Pero, los trenes en las otras líneas no están atrasados, ¿verdad?
VENDEDORA DE BILLETES:	No, los otros trenes deben salir a la hora en punto.
JUAN CARLOS:	¿A qué hora sale el próximo tren para Chincheros?
VENDEDORA DE BILLETES:	Sale... cinco para las tres.
JUAN CARLOS:	Bien. Un billete de ida y vuelta para Chincheros, por favor. Es que quiero escribir una guía turística sobre los pequeños pueblos peruanos, y no importa qué pueblo visito hoy.
VENDEDORA DE BILLETES:	Ajá, ya veo. ¡Qué buena idea! Una guía sobre los pequeños pueblos. Muy interesante.
VENDEDORA DE BILLETES:	¿Prefiere usted un asiento de ventanilla o de pasillo?
JUAN CARLOS:	Prefiero un asiento de ventanilla, por favor.
VENDEDORA DE BILLETES:	¿Y tiene equipaje para facturar?
JUAN CARLOS:	No, sólo tengo esta mochila.
VENDEDORA DE BILLETES:	Muy bien. El tren sale del andén número cinco.
JUAN CARLOS:	Muchas gracias.
VENDEDORA DE BILLETES:	De nada.

Capítulo 11

Los amigos animados

Anuncio comercial: AMTRAINS

Ahora en KSUN, Radio Sol, escuchemos un mensaje comercial de AMTRAINS, la compañía de trenes.

ANUNCIADORA 1:	¿Está pensando hacer un viaje por los Estados Unidos? ¿Quiere usted conocer muchas ciudades norteamericanas? Entonces, ¡le invitamos a viajar por AMTRAINS!
ANUNCIADORA 2:	Nuestros trenes van a más de 500 ciudades a bajo costo y con la mayor comodidad.
ANUNCIADORA 1:	¡Sí! En los modernos vagones de AMTRAINS usted puede viajar cómodamente, descansando en asientos amplios y reclinables.
ANUNCIADORA 2:	Puede disfrutar del paisaje gracias a nuestras grandes ventanas panorámicas. ¡Y siempre llega rápidamente!
ANUNCIADORA 1:	¡Descubra los Estados Unidos!
AMBAS:	¡Viaje por todo el país con AMTRAINS!

El viaje de Pilar

Pilar Álvarez está conversando con Ricardo Sícora sobre el viaje que ella hizo a Venezuela.

RICARDO: Entonces, ¿te gustó mi país, Pilar?

PILAR: Claro que me gustó. ¡Y mucho!

RICARDO: ¿Estuviste solamente en Caracas?

PILAR: ¡No! Estuve en Caracas sólo unos días. Es una ciudad muy moderna, con tantos coches y tantas autopistas...

RICARDO: ¡Y con tanta contaminación!

PILAR: Bueno, sí, el aire está un poco contaminado. Pero el clima es fabuloso.

RICARDO: ¿Y adónde más fuiste?

PILAR: Me quedé con unos amigos que tienen una casa de campo en Cumaná.

RICARDO: ¡Qué coincidencia! Cuando era más joven yo pasaba todos los veranos en Cumaná.

PILAR: Ya lo sé; tú me contaste. Por eso me dio tanto gusto ir a ese bello lugar.

RICARDO: ¿Fuiste a la playa cumaná?

PILAR: Sí, sí. Esa playa está a sólo unos pocos kilómetros de la casa de campo.

RICARDO: ¡Ah, Cumaná! El agua es de un azul intenso, la arena es fina y hace un sol brillante todo el día...

PILAR: (*Laughing.*) ¡Chico! ¡Pareces un anuncio comercial!

Escenas culturales: Uruguay

Uruguay es uno de los países más pequeños de Hispanoamérica. La capital es Montevideo. Esta ciudad está junto al estuario del río de la Plata. Es una ciudad muy pintoresca. Su arquitectura es un mosaico de estilos colonial español, italiano y Art-Deco. En la Ciudad Vieja hay varios edificios y monumentos de interés histórico. Montevideo tiene también edificios modernos. Los centros comerciales son muy grandes y muy visitados por los jóvenes uruguayos. Lejos de la ciudad, en las pampas uruguayas, viven los gauchos. Los gauchos viven de la ganadería y la agricultura. Pequeño en tamaño pero grande en colorido y sorpresas... así es Uruguay.

Escenas culturales: Paraguay

Muy al sur del continente está Paraguay. Su capital es Asunción. Es la ciudad más grande de Paraguay. Presencia una mezcla de arquitectura antigua y edificios modernos. El río Paraguay separa la región este del país de la región del Chaco. Otro río importante es el Paraná. Es la única salida que tiene Paraguay al mar. En río Paraná se construyó la represa de Itaipú. Ésta es la represa hidroeléctrica más grande del mundo. Hacia el sur de Paraguay están las ruinas de las antiguas misiones jesuitas. Las cataratas del Iguazú están entre Paraguay, Brasil y Argentina... La belleza de Paraguay llega hasta ese majestuoso lugar.

Escenas en contexto

ROBERTO: Esto es imposible... estoy totalmente perdido. Ésta es la calle Milagros. Acabo de venir de la calle Ibáñez. ¡El bar debe estar cerca! No lo entiendo. Disculpe, señor...

SEÑOR: ¿Sí?

ROBERTO: Perdone la molestia... pero estoy perdido. Busco el bar «La copa alegre». ¿Lo conoce usted?

SEÑOR: No estoy seguro. ¿Me puede decir en qué calle queda?

ROBERTO: Queda en la calle Santiago de Chile.

SEÑOR: Ah, sí. Conozco el bar. Mire, es muy fácil llegar. No queda lejos. ¿Ve usted el teléfono?

ROBERTO: Sí.

SEÑOR: Ésa es la calle Martín Gómez. Doble a la derecha en esa calle. Luego camine dos cuadras y doble a la izquierda en la avenida Flores. ¿Me entiende?

ROBERTO: Sí... doblo a la derecha en la calle Martín Gómez, y luego a la izquierda en la avenida Flores.

SEÑOR:	Así es. Luego camine una cuadra y doble a la derecha en la calle Santiago de Chile. Siga derecho y a unos cien metros va a ver el bar a la izquierda.
ROBERTO:	Bien... a ver si entiendo. A la derecha en Martín Gómez, a la izquierda en Flores, a la derecha en la calle Santiago de Chile y el bar está a la izquierda.
SEÑOR:	Exactamente.
ROBERTO:	Muchísimas gracias, señor.
SEÑOR:	No hay de qué, joven.
ROBERTO:	Es usted muy amable.
SEÑOR:	Qué la vaya bien.
ROBERTO:	Igualmente, señor.

Capítulo 12

Los amigos animados

Una llamada al gerente

Adriana Bolini está pasando unos días en Bariloche, Argentina, con sus padres. Ahora su mamá llama a la recepción del hotel donde se hospedan.

SRA. BOLINI:	Necesito hablar con el gerente, por favor.
GERENTE:	Yo soy el gerente, señora. ¿En qué puedo servirle?
SRA. BOLINI:	Mire, le habla la señora Bolini del cuarto 322.
GERENTE:	Ah, sí. Usted y su familia van a hospedarse con nosotros por tres días, ¿verdad?
SRA. BOLINI:	Sí. Y lo llamo para informarle de varios problemas...
GERENTE:	Dígame.
SRA. BOLINI:	Para empezar, la habitación de mi hija está muy sucia. Parece que la camarera no la limpió. Además, en su cama no hay almohadas. ¡Y en el baño tampoco hay toallas!
GERENTE:	Lo siento mucho, señora.
SRA. BOLINI:	Pero eso no es todo. Mire, yo reservé una habitación con cama matrimonial para mi esposo y para mí, pero este cuarto tiene dos camas pequeñas.
GERENTE:	¡Perdone el error! Resolveremos esos problemas inmediatamente. Un cuarto limpio para su hija y un cuarto con cama matrimonial para usted y su esposo. ¿Está bien?
SRA. BOLINI:	Sí, está bien. ¡Muchas gracias!

Las discotecas madrileñas

Esta noche hay una fiesta en casa de las hermanas Pilar y Gloria Álvarez. Clara Martín conversa con Felipe Álvarez, el hermano menor de Gloria y Pilar.

FELIPE:	Clara, ¿te gusta Madrid?
CLARA:	Sí, mucho. Hay tantos lugares interesantes en esta ciudad. ¡Madrid está llena de sitios turísticos!
FELIPE:	A mí también me gusta Madrid. Yo vivo en Sevilla con mis padres, pero visito mucho a mis hermanas. A veces vengo durante las vacaciones. Oye, si quieres, puedo llevarte a algunos lugares de Madrid que conozco bien.
CLARA:	¿Lugares turísticos?
FELIPE:	No, Clara. La Plaza Mayor y el Museo del Prado los puedes ver tú sola. Yo voy a llevarte a discotecas, adonde van los jóvenes madrileños.
CLARA:	¿Discotecas? Eh... sí, ¡me encanta bailar!
FELIPE:	¿Quieres ir esta noche?
CLARA:	Es un poco tarde para ir esta noche, ¿no?

FELIPE:	No, Clara, sólo son las 11:30. Para nosotros, los madrileños, es temprano. Mira, hay una discoteca que a mí me gusta mucho donde la gente no empieza a llegar hasta medianoche.
CLARA:	¡Pues vamos!

Escenas culturales: Chile

Chile es un país famoso por su geografía única. Tiene al oeste la costa del océano Pacífico; al este, la Cordillera de los Andes. Hacia el sur tiene tierras heladas. Al norte de Chile está el desierto de Atacama, el lugar más seco del planeta Tierra. Santiago, la capital de Chile, es una ciudad inmensa de amplias calles y plazas, iglesias, parques y edificios modernos. La cultura chilena es una mezcla de las influencias europeo e indígena. Esto se ve en su música, arquitectura, arte y literatura. Chile, un hermoso país, de contrastes culturales y naturales.

Escenas en contexto

DRA. MÉNDEZ:	¿Así que no te sientes bien, Marta? Dime lo que te pasa.
MARTA:	Anoche me dolió mucho el estómago. Y también la garganta.
LOLA:	Sí, y ayer por la tarde estaba muy congestionada.
DRA. MÉNDEZ:	¿Sí? ¿Y cuándo comenzó a sentir estos síntomas?
LOLA:	Fue unos días después de que se reunió con su amiga Carolina, quien ya estaba enferma.
DRA. MÉNDEZ:	Ajá. Marta, saca la lengua, por favor. Di «ahhh».
MARTA:	Ahhh...
DRA. MÉNDEZ:	Ahhh...
MARTA:	Ahhh...
DRA. MÉNDEZ:	Ahhh...
MARTA:	Ahhh...
DRA. MÉNDEZ:	A ver... Respira. Más fuerte. Otra vez.
LOLA:	¿Qué pasa, doctora? ¿Es grave?
DRA. MÉNDEZ:	No, no se preocupe. No es nada grave. Lo que tiene es un resfriado. Marta, debes guardar cama durante unos días y tomar muchos líquidos. Sra. Durán, voy a darle dos recetas. Las pastillas son para quitarle la congestión. Y el jarabe se lo puede dar cuando ella tosa.
LOLA:	Muy bien, doctora.
DRA. MÉNDEZ:	Y debes quedarte en casa algunos días.
MARTA:	¡Estupendo!
LOLA:	Marta, por favor...
DRA. MÉNDEZ:	Vamos.
LOLA:	¿Dra. Méndez? Está mañana me sentí muy mareada, y no pude comer. Sospecho que etoy embarazada.
DRA. MÉNDEZ:	Ah, ¿sí? Muy bien, pues, hagamos el análisis. Eh... Marta, ¿por qué no vas a la sala de espera? Hay allí varios libros que te van a interesar.
MARTA:	Vale.
DRA. MÉNDEZ:	Vamos.
MANOLO:	Bueno, ¿qué te dijo la doctora?
LOLA:	Me dijo que Marta no tenía nada grave, lo cual es un alivio. Yo estaba algo preocupada. Y, claro, Marta se puso muy contenta cuando la doctora le dijo que no podía asistir a la escuela por varios días.
MANOLO:	Pues, es natural... Recuerdo cuando yo era niño, eso era lo mejor de estar enfermo.
LOLA:	Manolo, ¿te acuerdas de nuestra Marta cuando era pequeña? ¡Qué preciosa era!
MANOLO:	Sí... Todas las noches nos levantábamos dos o tres veces a cambiarle los pañales y a darle de comer... ¡uf!

LOLA:	Manolo... ¿Te acuerdas de, del día en que nació Marta? Estaba tan pequeña y roja... ¿Y cuando regresamos del hospital?
MANOLO:	Me acuerdo que te dabas miedo de cada estornudo, te preocupabas cada vez que tosía...
LOLA:	Bueno, sí me... me preocupaba un poco... Pero eso es natural, ¿no?
MANOLO:	Bueno, claro.
LOLA:	Ah... Perfecto.
MANOLO:	¿Qué es lo «perfecto»?
LOLA:	¿Entramos un ratito, Manolo?
MANOLO:	¿Aquí? ¿Pero por qué? Ésta es una tienda para señoras embarazadas.
LOLA:	Sí, ya lo sé. Por eso...
MANOLO:	Pero... pero... ¿¡Vamos a tener otro hijo?! ¡Lola, espera! ¡Lola!

Capítulo 13

Los amigos animados

Vitaminas Vida

Y ahora escuchemos un mensaje comercial de vitaminas Vida.

ANUNCIADOR:	Viva su vida con buena salud. ¡Tome vitaminas Vida!
ANUNCIADORA:	¿Se siente cansado todos los días? Tome nuestra fórmula especial de las vitaminas B y C.
ANUNCIADOR:	Nuestra fórmula tiene además muchas otras vitaminas importantes. Este excelente producto le da la energía que su cuerpo necesita.
ANUNCIADORA:	Si quiere mejorar su salud y sentirse más fuerte, pida vitaminas Vida, una combinación perfecta de las vitaminas B y C.
ANUNCIADOR:	Nuestra marca, Vida, es símbolo de buena salud y mejor vida. Búsquela en su farmacia o supermercado favorito.
AMBOS:	¡Tome vitaminas Vida!

Más preguntas sobre la salud

En KSUN, la doctora Virginia Béjar contesta preguntas de los radioyentes.

MAYÍN:	Bien, ya tenemos la primera llamada.
OYENTE 1:	Doctora Béjar, ¿es verdad que hay que beber mucha agua todos los días?
BÉJAR:	Sí, señor. Lo ideal es beber ocho vasos al día. Los líquidos, y especialmente el agua, son muy importantes para la salud.
MAYÍN:	Y ahora otra pregunta. Sí, hable usted, por favor.
OYENTE 2:	Doctora, yo juego mucho al tenis y, a veces, me duelen muchísimo el brazo y el codo.
BÉJAR:	Bueno, probablemente esté jugando demasiado.
OYENTE 2:	Pues... yo juego todos los días.
BÉJAR:	¡¿Todos los días?! ¡Pobre cuerpo! Mire, usted debe tomar un descanso de vez en cuando. Juegue solamente tres o cuatro días a la semana, y se va a mejorar muy pronto.
OYENTE 2:	Buen consejo. Gracias, doctora.
BÉJAR:	Ah, y otra cosa. Si el dolor continúa, consulte a su médico.
MAYÍN:	Bien, doctora Béjar y amigos radioyentes, ahora vamos a escuchar unos anuncios comerciales. ¡Gracias a todos!

Escenas culturales: Perú

Perú limita con el océano Pacífico, en América del Sur. Lima es la capital de Perú. La cuenca del Amazonas ocupa gran parte de Perú. La vida silvestre de esta zona es espectacular. Los Andes peruanos son uno de los lugares más bellos del continente. Ahí viven muchos indígenas. Ellos hablan quechua. En los Andes se encuentra el cóndor y también la llama. Cuzco fue la capital de imperio incaico. Es un pueblo colonial hermoso. Al oeste de Cuzco están las ruinas de Machu Picchu, la ciudad perdida de los Incas. Perú: su gente y cultura están llenas de magia.

Escenas en contexto

MARIELA:	Buenos días, señora.
VENDEDORA:	Buenos días.
MARIELA:	¿De qué son las chaquetas?
VENDEDORA:	Las chaquetas son de pura lana. Son muy bonitas, ¿verdad?
MARIELA:	Sí, son bonitas. ¿Cuánto cuestan?
VENDEDORA:	Cuestan 5.000 colones. Son muy buenas chaquetas.
MARIELA:	No estoy segura... Es mucho.
VENDEDORA:	¡Pero el precio es una ganga! Son realmente buenas.
MARIELA:	Sí, usted tiene razón, son chaquetas muy bonitas, pero de todos modos son un poco caras.
VENDEDORA:	Vamos, señorita...
MARIELA:	Bueno, voy a ver las chaquetas que tienen en el otro mercado. Muchas gracias. Adiós.
VENDEDORA:	¡Señorita! Puedo vender las chaquetas en 4.500 colones. ¿Está bien?
MARIELA:	Sí, está bien. Muchas gracias, muy amable. Busco un regalo para mi hermana.
VENDEDORA:	¿Qué medidas usa? ¿Qué colores prefiere?
MARIELA:	Mediano. Prefiere amarillo o blanco. Usted es de Argentina, ¿verdad?
VENDEDORA:	Ah, sí, soy argentina.
MARIELA:	Buenos Aires es una ciudad tan linda.
VENDEDORA:	¡Ah, sí! Es lindísima. ¿Usted estuvo una vez allá?

Capítulo 14

Los amigos animados

El nuevo vestido de Amanda

Amanda conversa con su madre sobre una compra que la joven hizo hoy.

AMANDA:	Mamá, mira, me compré este vestido. ¿Te gusta?
ESTELA:	Sí, es muy bonito. ¡Pero te queda muy grande!
AMANDA:	Es verdad; me queda grande. ¡Qué pena!
ESTELA:	¿No te lo probaste en la tienda?
AMANDA:	Sí, mamá, me lo probé y me gustó. Y la vendedora me dijo que me quedaba perfecto.
ESTELA:	¡Claro! La vendedora te dijo eso porque quería vendértelo.
AMANDA:	¿Y ahora qué hago?
ESTELA:	Pues, debes devolverlo o cambiarlo por otro más pequeño.
AMANDA:	¡Ay! Es que no tenían una talla más pequeña.
ESTELA:	Bueno, a ver, quizás yo pueda arreglarlo.
AMANDA:	¿De verdad, mamá? ¿Puedes arreglármelo?
ESTELA:	Sí, sí. Ya sabes que me gusta coser un poco de vez en cuando.
AMANDA:	¡Qué mamá tan buena tengo!
ESTELA:	Pero, hija, la próxima vez que compres ropa, ¡busca bien tu talla!
AMANDA:	Sí, mamá. ¡Y ya no escucho más la opinión de las vendedoras!

¡Qué rápido aprendes!

Clara conversa con Gloria Álvarez, la hermana de Pilar, sobre una compra reciente que hizo.

GLORIA:	Clara, ¿por fin conseguiste el suéter que buscabas?
CLARA:	Sí, finalmente lo conseguí. ¡Pero no fue fácil!
GLORIA:	¿Por qué no?
CLARA:	Bueno, porque tenía poco dinero y quería un suéter grueso y de buena calidad. Tuve que ir a varios almacenes y tiendas de ropa...
GLORIA:	¿Y dónde lo encontraste por fin?
CLARA:	¿Dónde crees? ¡En el Rastro!
GLORIA:	¿En el Rastro? Chica, pero, ¿tú sabes regatear?
CLARA:	(*Laughing.*) Sí, sí. ¡Soy experta!
GLORIA:	¿Y quién te enseñó a regatear?
CLARA:	José me enseñó a hacerlo.
GLORIA:	Y dime, ¿conseguiste un buen precio?
CLARA:	Conseguí una ganga.
GLORIA:	¡Qué rápido aprendes, chica!
CLARA:	Sí. Pronto voy a saber regatear mejor que mi maestro.
GLORIA:	¿Mejor que José? (*Laughing.*) ¡Eso no es posible!

Escenas culturales: España

España está en la Península Ibérica, en Europa meridional. Su capital es Madrid. España cuenta con verdaderas joyas arquitectónicas. En el Escorial, municipio de Madrid, está el monasterio famoso de San Lorenzo. Éste fue construido por Felipe II para conmemorar el triunfo de los españoles en la batalla de San Quintín. La Giralda de Sevilla, construida en la época almohade en el siglo XII. La Alhambra de Granada, una exquisita muestra del arte islámico, la bella Toledo con su arquitectura medieval. Todos estos lugares hermosos son los que hablan de la historia de España.

Escenas en contexto

JOSÉ MIGUEL:	Paloma, tengo un problema.
PALOMA:	¿Qué te pasa, José Miguel? Cuéntame.
JOSÉ MIGUEL:	Pues, muy bien, pero antes tienes que prometerme algo. No quiero que le menciones esto a nadie.
PALOMA:	Te lo prometo. Mira, ¿por qué no entramos, nos sentamos y me cuentas qué te pasa? ¿Y bien?
JOSÉ MIGUEL:	Pues, no sé qué hacer. Hace un mes conocí a una chica. Se llama Teresa. Es una compañera de clase.
PALOMA:	¿Y entonces?
JOSÉ MIGUEL:	Ah, bueno, Teresa me cae muy bien. Es muy bonita, muy inteligente. Me gusta mucho. Me gustaría pasar más tiempo con ella. Es una buena persona.
PALOMA:	Sí, José Miguel. Quiero saber qué es lo que pasa.
JOSÉ MIGUEL:	Perdona. Hace unos días, Teresa y yo fuimos al cine. La pasamos muy bien. Pero luego sucedió algo que me preocupa mucho. Paloma, de veras te pido que no le cuentes a nadie lo que te voy a decir.
PALOMA:	No te preocupes. Te doy mi palabra de honor.
JOSÉ MIGUEL:	Cuando Teresa subió al auto, se le cayó la mochila. Todo lo que tenía dentro se le cayó al suelo y vi que tenía una pequeña bolsa de plástico con algo blanco adentro. Sospecho que eran drogas.

PALOMA:	¿Y tú? ¿Qué hiciste? ¿Le dijiste algo?
JOSÉ MIGUEL:	En ese momento no supe qué hacer y no le dije nada. Tampoco sé si ella se dio cuenta que yo vi la bolsa de plástico.
PALOMA:	Y ella, ¿qué hizo?
JOSÉ MIGUEL:	La puso dentro de su mochila sin decir nada y luego me pidió que la llevara a su casa. Y cuando llegamos, se bajó sin despedirse.
PALOMA:	Ay, José Miguel. Estás entre la espada y la pared, ¿no?
JOSÉ MIGUEL:	Así es. Si no le digo nada, nunca voy a saber la verdad. Y voy a seguir sospechando. Pero si le pregunto y ella me dice que sí eran drogas las que estaban en su mochila, ¿qué hago?
PALOMA:	¿Quieres que te dé un consejo?
JOSÉ MIGUEL:	Sí, claro. Por eso te digo todo esto.
PALOMA:	Bueno, yo te aconsejo que hables con ella y le digas lo que viste. Puede que no sean drogas, José Miguel. Pudo haber sido otra cosa.
JOSÉ MIGUEL:	Lo dudo mucho, Paloma, pero tienes razón. Es mejor que hable con ella.
PALOMA:	Si ella no acepta la ayuda que tú le ofreces, no hay nada que tú puedas hacer pero si la acepta, te sugiero que la lleves a hablar con el consejero de la universidad. Pero te voy a decir una verdad.
JOSÉ MIGUEL:	Habla, Paloma. Tú siempre llamas al pan, pan y al vino, vino.
PALOMA:	Bueno, si ella acepta la ayuda que tú le ofreces, no se la puedes quitar después. Es importante que la apoyes. Tienes que hacer un compromiso y no va a ser nada fácil. ¿Es ella tan importante para ti?
JOSÉ MIGUEL:	Sí, es una persona muy especial. Si tiene un problema, le quiero ayudar.
PALOMA:	Entonces, no tienes opción. Pregúntale y si en algo te puedo ayudar, no tienes más que pedírmelo.
JOSÉ MIGUEL:	Gracias, Paloma. Eres una verdadera amiga.

Capítulo 15

Los amigos animados

Los consejos de un amigo

Ernesto Saucedo está en casa de Pedro Ruiz, hablando de sus preocupaciones.

ERNESTO:	¿Sabes, Pedro? Creo que el problema es que trabajo demasiado.
PEDRO:	Te entiendo, Ernesto.
ERNESTO:	Tengo muy poco tiempo para estar con la familia.
PEDRO:	Oye, te aconsejo que tomes unas vacaciones. A mí me ayuda mucho tomar vacaciones de vez en cuando.
ERNESTO:	Es que ahora no es posible. Hay mucho trabajo en la compañía.
PEDRO:	Comprendo. Bueno, de todos modos, trata de pasar más tiempo con Estela y tus hijos.
ERNESTO:	Sí, trato de estar con ellos los domingos. Pero a veces también tengo que trabajar los fines de semana.
PEDRO:	Ernesto, habla con tu jefe. Explícale la situación. Mira, dile que necesitas un poco de tiempo libre. Sólo unos días...
ERNESTO:	¿Y crees que unos días va a resolver el problema?
PEDRO:	Sí, a veces un breve descanso puede ayudar mucho.
ERNESTO:	Está bien. Voy a hablar con mi jefe. Gracias por escucharme, Pedro.
PEDRO:	¡No tienes que darme las gracias, hombre! ¡Para eso son los amigos!

El concierto de guitarra

Nora, Esteban y Carmen están en una fiesta en casa de un compañero de clase.

NORA:	Esta fiesta está un poco aburrida, ¿no creen ustedes?
ESTEBAN:	Sí, es que toda la gente está sentada, sin hablar, sin bailar.
CARMEN:	Nadie baila porque no hay música. ¡Pongamos un disco!
NORA:	No. Tengo una mejor idea. ¡Escuchemos a Esteban!
CARMEN:	(*Teasingly.*) ¿Qué dices? ¿Estás sugiriendo que escuchemos a Esteban?
NORA:	¡Sí! El toca la guitarra muy bien.
ESTEBAN:	No, no, yo no toco bien...
NORA:	Esteban, trajiste tu guitarra española, ¿verdad?
ESTEBAN:	Sí, la puse en un cuarto de la casa. Pero, ¿cómo sabes que la traje?
NORA:	¡Porque siempre la llevas a todas las fiestas!
CARMEN:	(*Laughing.*) ¡Claro! Para darles conciertos a sus amigos...
NORA:	Esteban, por favor, anda al cuarto y busca tu guitarra. ¡Y toca tus canciones mexicanas!
CARMEN:	Sí, las canciones que aprendimos en la clase de español... «Cielito lindo». ¡Vamos!
ESTEBAN:	¿De verdad que ustedes quieren que cante y toque música?
NORA:	Sí, Esteban. ¡Esta fiesta te necesita!
ESTEBAN:	Bueno, pero acompáñenme a cantar. ¿Está bien?
CARMEN:	¡Con mucho gusto!
	(*Accompanied by Esteban on guitar, they sing "Cielito lindo."*)

Escenas culturales: México

México. Su capital es México, Distrito Federal. El D.F., como se conoce, es la ciudad más grande y poblada de México. Los mexicanos aman sus raíces. Ellos conservan hermosas tradiciones que muestran al mundo el orgullo que sienten por su pasado. El arte en México es muy variado: va desde las antiguas edificaciones y arte prehispánico hasta el colorido muralismo mexicano. Ciudades prehispánicas como Teotihuacán... coloniales como Oaxaca... o como Guadalajara con todo el sabor de las costumbres mexicanas... y las playas soleadas como Acapulco y Cancún... son sólo una muestra de la diversidad y la belleza de México.

Escenas en contexto

ESTUDIANTE:	Disculpe, Srta. Castillo. ¿Me puede ayudar?
MARIELA:	Claro que sí.
ESTUDIANTE:	Gracias, muy amable. Es que no sé manejar bien este programa.
MARIELA:	A ver... ¿qué es lo que intenta hacer?
ESTUDIANTE:	Quiero mandar este documento por correo electrónico a mi profesor, pero no funciona.
MARIELA:	Vamos a ver. Con permiso...
ESTUDIANTE:	¿Quiere usted hacerlo?
MARIELA:	No. Prefiero que usted lo haga. Así aprende mejor. Bien. Primero, abra su cuenta de correo electrónico. No, es mejor que no abra el documento. Bien. Ahora, sugiero que ponga primero la dirección electrónica del profesor en ese espacio. Cuidado, un error tipográfico y no funciona.
ESTUDIANTE:	Ya está.
MARIELA:	Ahora, con el ratón, escoja «adjuntar documento» del menú... y es necesario que elija el documento que quiere mandar.
ESTUDIANTE:	Es éste. Ya. Listo, ¿no?
MARIELA:	Sí. Haga «clic» para mandarlo, y...
ESTUDIANTE:	¿Qué es eso?
MARIELA:	¡Es mi teléfono celular! ¿Aló? Momentito...